NATIONAL GEOGRAPHIC

Compact
Atlas OF THE World

NATIONAL
GEOGRAPHIC

Compact

Atlas OF THE World

NATIONAL GEOGRAPHIC, WASHINGTON, D.C.

CONTENTS

Continued on next page

AUSTRALIA & OCEANIA 146–161

POLAR REGIONS 162–167

WORLD FLAGS 168–175

APPENDIX 176–179

PLACE-NAME INDEX 180–253

ACKNOWLEDGMENTS 254–255

NORTH AMERICA
26–53

GREATER
OCEANIA
160–161

SOUTH AMERICA
54–73

44

40–41

88–8

42–43

50–51

52–53

138–139

68–69

70–71

72–73

45

48–49

110–111 Page(s) on
which map appears

8

KEY TO ATLAS MAPS

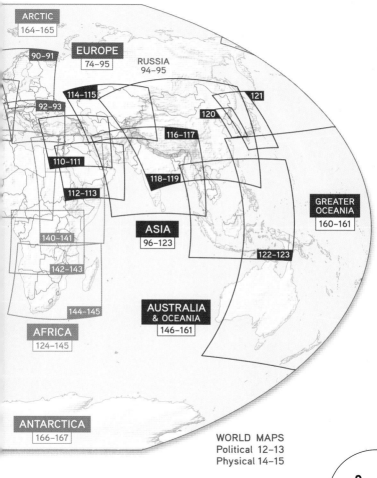

ARCTIC
164–165

EUROPE
74–95

RUSSIA
94–95

90–91

114–115

92–93

121

120

116–117

110–111

118–119

112–113

GREATER
OCEANIA
160–161

140–141

142–143

ASIA
96–123

122–123

144–145

AUSTRALIA
& OCEANIA
146–161

AFRICA
124–145

ANTARCTICA
166–167

WORLD MAPS
Political 12–13
Physical 14–15

WORLD

WORLD POLITICAL DATA

TOTAL NUMBER OF COUNTRIES: 195

LARGEST COUNTRY BY AREA: Russia
17,075,400 sq km (6,592,850 sq mi)

SMALLEST COUNTRY BY AREA:
Vatican City   0.4 sq km (0.2 sq mi)

MOST POPULOUS COUNTRY: China
1,336,720,000

LEAST POPULOUS COUNTRY: Vatican City
830

LARGEST CITIES BY POPULATION:
Tokyo, Japan   36,669,000
Delhi, India   22,157,000
Mumbai (Bombay), India   20,041,000
Shanghai, China   16,575,000
Kolkata (Calcutta), India   15,552,000

WORLD PHYSICAL DATA

TOTAL AREA: 510,066,000 sq km
(196,938,000 sq mi)

LAND AREA: 148,647,000 sq km
(57,393,000 sq mi), 29.1% of total

WATER AREA: 361,419,000 sq km
(139,545,000 sq mi), 70.9% of total

EQUATORIAL CIRCUMFERENCE: 40,075 km
(24,902 mi)

POLAR CIRCUMFERENCE: 40,008 km
(24,860 mi)

EQUATORIAL RADIUS: 6,378 km (3,963 mi)

POLAR RADIUS: 6,357 km (3,950 mi)

HIGHEST POINT: Mount Everest,
China-Nepal   8,850 m (29,035 ft)

DEEPEST POINT: Challenger Deep,
Pacific Ocean   -10,994 m
(-36,070 ft)

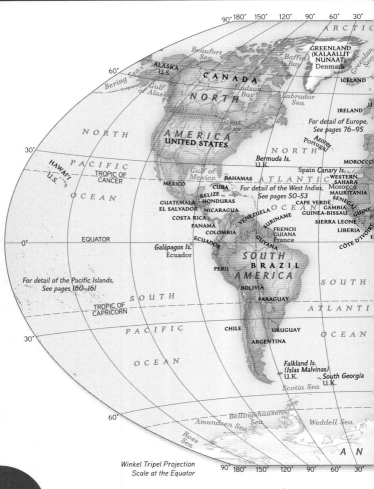

90° 180° 150° 120° 90° 60° 30°

ARCTIC

Beaufort Sea

GREENLAND (KALAALLIT NUNAAT) Denmark

60° ALASKA U.S. **CANADA** *Baffin Bay*

Bering Sea *Gulf of Alaska* **NORTH** *Hudson Bay* *Labrador Sea*

ICELAND

IRELAND

For detail of Europe,
See pages 76–95

AMERICA *Great Lakes*
UNITED STATES

30° *NORTH* **NORTH** *Azores* Portugal

HAWAI'I U.S. *PACIFIC* Bermuda Is. U.K. Spain Canary Is. MOROCCO

TROPIC OF CANCER *Gulf of Mexico* MEXICO BAHAMAS *ATLANTIC* WESTERN SAHARA Morocco

OCEAN CUBA *For detail of the West Indies,* MAURITANIA

GUATEMALA BELIZE HONDURAS *See pages 50–53* *OCEAN* SENEGAL CAPE VERDE

EL SALVADOR NICARAGUA GAMBIA GUINEA-BISSAU GUINE

COSTA RICA PANAMA VENEZUELA SURINAME SIERRA LEONE LIBERIA

0° EQUATOR COLOMBIA FRENCH GUIANA France CÔTE D'IVOIRE

Galápagos Is. Ecuador ECUADOR GUYANA

PERU **SOUTH** *SOUTH*

For detail of the Pacific Islands, **B R A Z I L**

See pages 160–161 **AMERICA**

BOLIVIA

SOUTH PARAGUAY

TROPIC OF CAPRICORN *ATLANTI*

30° *PACIFIC* CHILE URUGUAY *OCEAN*

ARGENTINA

OCEAN Falkland Is. (Islas Malvinas) U.K. South Georgia U.K.

Scotia Sea

60° *Bellingshausen Sea* *Weddell Sea*

Amundsen Sea

A N

Ross Sea

Winkel Tripel Projection
Scale at the Equator

90° 180° 150° 120° 90° 60° 30°

12

OCEAN

30° 60° 90° 120° 150° 180° 90°

Barents Sea
NORWAY

Kara Sea

Laptev Sea

East Siberian Sea

ARCTIC CIRCLE

Bering Sea

60°

SWEDEN FINLAND

R U S S I A

EUROPE

Sea of Okhotsk

KAZAKHSTAN

MONGOLIA

N. KOREA

JAPAN

NORTH

GEORGIA AZERB.
ARM.
TURKEY UZB.
TURKM.
KYRG.
TAJ.
CHINA
S. KOREA
30°

SYRIA
IRAQ
IRAN
AFGHAN.
PAKISTAN
NEPAL
BHUTAN
East China Sea
PACIFIC

Mediterranean Sea
JORDAN

RIA LIBYA EGYPT
SAUDI ARABIA
U.A.E.
OMAN
BANGLADESH
INDIA
MYANMAR (BURMA)
LAOS
VIETNAM
Taiwan

Philippine Sea

OCEAN

NIGER CHAD ERITREA
YEMEN
DJIBOUTI
Arabian Sea
THAILAND
Bay of Bengal
CAMBODIA
South China Sea
PHILIPPINES
MARSHALL IS.

AFRICA
CAMEROON
CEN. AF. REP.
S. SUDAN
ETHIOPIA
SOMALIA
SRI LANKA
MALAYSIA
BRUNEI
PALAU
FEDERATED STATES OF MICRONESIA

INEA DEM. REP. OF THE CONGO
UGANDA
KENYA
MALDIVES
NAURU

ABON CONGO
TANZANIA
SEYCHELLES
INDONESIA
PAPUA NEW GUINEA
SOLOMON ISLANDS
TUVALU

ANGOLA
ZAMBIA
MALAWI
COMOROS
INDIAN
TIMOR-LESTE (EAST TIMOR)
VANUATU
FIJI

NAMIBIA
ZIMBABWE
MOZAMBIQUE
MADAGASCAR
MAURITIUS
OCEAN
Coral Sea
New Caledonia Fr.

BOTSWANA
SWAZILAND
LESOTHO
Réunion Fr.
AUSTRALIA

SOUTH AFRICA
Cape of Good Hope
Great Australian Bight
North I.
30°

Kerguelen Is. Fr.
Tasmania
Tasman Sea
NEW ZEALAND

South I.

ANTARCTIC CIRCLE
60°

ARCTICA

30° 60° 90° 120° 150° 180° 90°

0   2000   4000 MILES
0   2000   4000 KILOMETERS

13

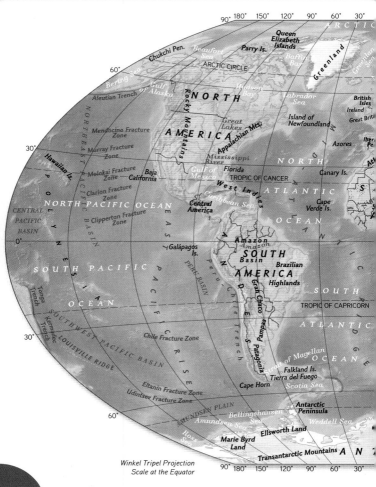

Winkel Tripel Projection
Scale at the Equator

90° 180° 150° 120° 90° 60° 30°

90° 180° 150° 120° 90° 60° 30°

Queen Elizabeth Islands
Parry Is.
Baffin Bay
Greenland
Chukchi Pen.
Beaufort Sea
ARCTIC CIRCLE
ARCTIC

Bering Sea
Gulf of Alaska
Aleutian Trench
Rocky Mountains
Hudson Bay
Labrador Sea
British Isles
Ireland
Great Brita

N O R T H
A M E R I C A

Great Lakes
Appalachian Mts.
Island of Newfoundland

NORTHEAST PACIFIC BASIN
Hawaiian Is.
Mendocino Fracture Zone
Murray Fracture Zone
Molokai Fracture Zone
Clarion Fracture Zone
Baja California
Mississippi River
Florida
TROPIC OF CANCER
Gulf of Mexico
West Indies
Azores
Canary Is.
Iber

N O R T H   A T L A N T I C

NORTH PACIFIC OCEAN
CENTRAL PACIFIC BASIN
P O L Y N E S I A N

Clipperton Fracture Zone
Central America
Caribbean Sea
Galápagos Is.
O C E A N
Cape Verde Is.

EAST PACIFIC BASIN
PERU BASIN
Amazon
Amazon Basin
S O U T H
A M E R I C A
Brazilian Highlands

SOUTH PACIFIC
OCEAN
Tonga Trench
Kermadec Trench
SOUTHWEST PACIFIC BASIN
PACIFIC RISE
Peru-Chile Trench
Gran Chaco

S O U T H
A T L A N T I C
TROPIC OF CAPRICORN

LOUISVILLE RIDGE
Chile Fracture Zone
Eltanin Fracture Zone
Udintsev Fracture Zone
AMUNDSEN PLAIN
Cordillera
Patagonia
Strait of Magellan
Falkland Is.
Tierra del Fuego
Cape Horn
Scotia Sea
O C E A N

Bellingshausen Sea
Antarctic Peninsula
Amundsen Sea
Ellsworth Land
Weddell Sea
Ross Sea
Marie Byrd Land
Transantarctic Mountains A N

14

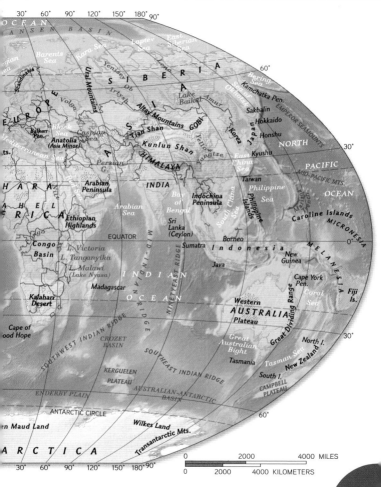

30° 60° 90° 120° 150° 180° 90°

OCEAN

NANSEN BASIN

Barents Sea

Laptev Sea

East Siberian Sea

Kara Sea

Scandinavia

Ural Mountains

Yenisey

Ob

Lena

S I B E R I A

60°

Bering Sea

Kamchatka Pen.

EUROPE

Volga

Irtysh

Lake Baikal

Amur

Okhotsk

Sakhalin

EMPEROR SEAMOUNTS

Balkan Pen.

Black Sea

Caspian Sea

Altay Mountains

GOBI

Korea

Hokkaido

NORTH

Mediterranean (Sea)

ts.

Anatolia (Asia Minor)

Tian Shan

Kunlun Shan

Yellow Sea

Japan

Honshu

30°

HIMALAYA

Yangtze

Kyushu

East China Sea

PACIFIC

Persian G.

Taiwan

MID-PACIFIC MTS.

H A R A

Arabian Peninsula

INDIA

Philippine Sea

OCEAN

A H E L

ago

Red Sea

Arabian Sea

Bay of Bengal

Indochina Peninsula

South China Sea

Philippine Islands

Caroline Islands

MICRONESIA

RICA

Ethiopian Highlands

Sri Lanka (Ceylon)

EQUATOR

Sumatra

Borneo

I n d o n e s i a

0°

Congo Basin

L. Victoria

L. Tanganyika

MID-INDIAN RIDGE

Java

New Guinea

M E L A N E S I A

L. Malawi (Lake Nyasa)

I N D I A N

NINETYEAST RIDGE

Madagascar

OCEAN

Cape York Pen.

Coral Sea

Fiji Is.

Kalahari Desert

Western Plateau

AUSTRALIA

Great Dividing Range

30°

Cape of Good Hope

SOUTHWEST INDIAN RIDGE

CROZET BASIN

Great Australian Bight

North I.

Tasmania

Tasman Sea

New Zealand

KERGUELEN PLATEAU

SOUTHEAST INDIAN RIDGE

South I.

CAMPBELL PLATEAU

ENDERBY PLAIN

AUSTRALIAN-ANTARCTIC BASIN

60°

ANTARCTIC CIRCLE

en Maud Land

Wilkes Land

ARCTICA

Transantarctic Mts.

30° 60° 90° 120° 150° 180° 90°

| 0 | 2000 | 4000 MILES |
| 0 | 2000 | 4000 KILOMETERS |

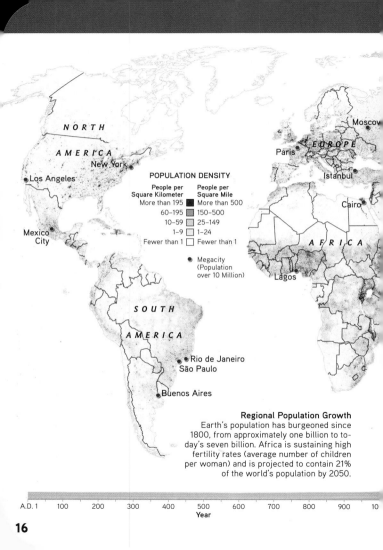

NORTH

AMERICA

New York

Los Angeles

POPULATION DENSITY

People per Square Kilometer	People per Square Mile
More than 195	More than 500
60–195	150–500
10–59	25–149
1–9	1–24
Fewer than 1	Fewer than 1

Mexico City

● Megacity (Population over 10 Million)

SOUTH

AMERICA

● Rio de Janeiro
São Paulo

●Buenos Aires

Moscow

EUROPE

Paris

Istanbul

Cairo

AFRICA

Lagos

Regional Population Growth

Earth's population has burgeoned since 1800, from approximately one billion to today's seven billion. Africa is sustaining high fertility rates (average number of children per woman) and is projected to contain 21% of the world's population by 2050.

A.D. 1	100	200	300	400	500	600	700	800	900	10

Year

Geographers approach the study of human populations, or demography, from a spatial perspective, asking why density, distribution, resources, births, deaths, and migrations vary from place to place. Earth's population, now at 7 billion, grows by about 78 million a year, or 1.1% annually. The bulk of the increase occurs in developing countries in Asia, Africa, and Latin America. Worldwide, people are also moving into ever growing cities. There are currently 21 "megacities" in the world, each with over 10 million people.

Population Density
can be measured as the average number of people per square unit in a given area. Populations, however, are not evenly distributed. Often, they're gathered around arable land.

Asia
Africa
Latin America
Europe
North America
Australia & Oceania

ASIA

Beijing
Tokyo
Osaka-Kobe
Delhi
Karachi
Shanghai
Dhaka
Kolkata (Calcutta)
Mumbai (Bombay)
Manila

AUSTRALIA

Number of people (in billions)

Projected growth

9
8
7
6
5
4
3
2
1
0

1100 1200 1300 1400 1500 1600 1700 1800 1900 2000 2050
Year

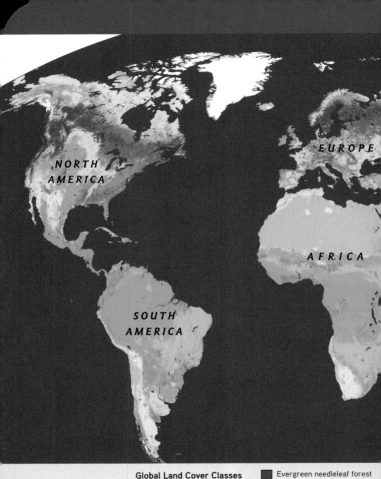

NORTH
AMERICA

EUROPE

AFRICA

SOUTH
AMERICA

Global Land Cover Classes
Three characteristics underlie these categories: life-form (woody, herbaceous, or bare); leaf type (needle or broad); and leaf duration (evergreen or deciduous).

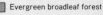

Evergreen needleleaf forest

Evergreen broadleaf forest

Deciduous needleleaf forest

Deciduous broadleaf forest

Satellite data provide the most reliable picture of global vegetative cover over time. Few natural communities of plants and animals have remained the same; most have been altered by humans. The "natural" vegetation reflects what would grow there, given ideal conditions. By recording the data at different wavelengths of the electromagnetic spectrum, scientists can derive land cover type through spectral variation. Changes in vegetation are captured, contributing to studies in conservation, biodiversity assessments, and land resource management.

ASIA

This map is based on global satellite imagery from the Moderate Resolution Imaging Spectroradiometer (MODIS), at a spatial resolution of 500 meters (1,640 feet).

AUSTRALIA

Mixed forest	Open shrubland	Urban or built up	
Woody savanna	Grassland	Snow and ice	
Savanna	Cropland	Cropland / natural vegetation mosaic	
Closed shrubland	Barren or sparsely vegetated	Wetland	

19

GEOLOGIC FORCES

Six processes are responsible for the geologic landforms that shape our world. ① **Seafloor Spreading**–Where plates diverge and new crust is formed. ② **Subduction**–One plate dives beneath another. ③ **Accretion**–Seamounts are skimmed off and piled up. ④ **Collision**–Continental plates meet and mountains are pushed up. ⑤ **Faulting**–Boundaries where plates meet and move against each other. ⑥ **Hot Spots**– Where thermal plumes push up, burning through Earth's crust.

ARCTIC

GREENLAND

RING OF

Kodiak-
Bowie

Cobb

NORTH
AMERICA

Yellowstone

Iceland

NORTH
ATLANTIC
OCEAN

NORTH
PACIFIC
OCEAN

San Andreas Fault

ROCKY MTS.

NORTH
AMERICAN

Raton

Azores

Bermuda

New England

Hawai'i

Hawai'i-
Emperor

Edge of diffuse
plate boundary

Nubi

Cape
Verde

Plat

EQUATOR

Galapagos

SOUTH
AMERICA

St. Helena

Samoa

Tahiti-
Society

RING OF FIRE

Gambier

Easter

Juan
Fernández

SOUTH
AMERICA

Trindade

RING OF FIRE

A N D E S

Austral-
Cooks

SOUTH
PACIFIC
OCEAN

Louisville

Walvis Ridge

Plate Boundary
⚏ Divergent
▲▲ Convergent
— Transform zone

Volcanic Eruption
▲ Notable
▲ Known during the
past 10,000 years

E arth's crust may appear stable and fixed, but, as earthquakes and volcanoes remind us, Earth's crust is in motion, propelled by the heat and pressure of a 2,900-kilometer (1,800-mile)-thick zone of molten rock surrounding a metallic core.

Major Tectonic Event, Last 100 Years

Earthquake
○ Ten deadliest
△ Ten costliest
◼ Other

OCEAN

EURASIAN PLATE

URAL MTS.

ASIA

EUROPE

ALPS

HIMALAYA

NORTH PACIFIC OCEAN

RING OF FIRE

Location uncertain

besti plift ○

ARABIAN PLATE

Afar

INDIA

AFRICA

AFRICAN PLATE

East Africa ○

Comoros

INDIAN OCEAN

Edge of diffuse plate boundary

EQUATOR

Caroline ○

RING OF FIRE

Réunion

AUSTRALIAN AUSTRALIA PLATE

RING OF FIRE

Location uncertain

Location uncertain

SOUTH ATLANTIC OCEAN

Bouvet

Crozet

Kerguelen

East Australia ○

Tasmantid ○

Earth's brittle surface—the lithosphere—is cracked into great rafts of rock, called plates, averaging 97 kilometers (60 miles) thick and thousands of kilometers wide.

ANTARCTIC PLATE ANTARCTICA

Plate Motion
⬌ Divergent (arrow length proportional to plate motion speed)
→ Convergent
○ Hot spot

21

CLIMATIC ZONES
(based on modified Köppen system)

Humid equatorial climate (A)
- No dry season (Af)
- Short dry season (Am)
- Dry winter (Aw)

Dry climate (B)
- Semiarid (BS) } h = hot
- Arid (BW) } k = cold

Humid temperate climate (C)
- No dry season (Cf)
- Dry winter (Cw)
- Dry summer (Cs)

a = hot summer
b = cool summer
c = short, cool summer
d = very cold winter

Cold polar climate (E)
- Tundra and ice

Highland climate (H)
- Unclassified highlands

Ocean current
- Cold
- Warm

Humid cold climate (D)
- No dry season (Df)
- Dry winter (Dw)

Spring Equinox
Northern Hemisphere

Winter Solstice
Northern Hemisphere

Summer Solstice
Northern Hemisphere

North Pole

Fall Equinox
Northern Hemisphere

Tropic of Cancer

Equator

Tropic of Capricorn

South Pole

The Köppen system,
used here, classifies Earth's
climatic zones based on
precipitation, temperature,
and vegetation. These zones
can shift over time.

Beaufort Gyre

Greenland Current

Alaska Current

Labrador Current

Subarctic Current

Gulf Stream

North Pacific Drift

North Atlantic Drift

California Current

Canary Current

North Equatorial Current

PACIFIC OCEAN

ATLANTIC OCEAN

Equatorial Countercurrent

Equatorial Countercurrent

South Equatorial Current

South Equatorial Current

South Subtropical Current

Peru Current

Brazil Current

Falkland Current

Weddell Gyre

ARCTI

Seasons and Rotation of the Earth

The tilt of the Earth on its axis causes seasonal change. Summer arrives when the rays become more direct and their heat is more concentrated. Winter's cold comes as the sun's rays slant at a steeper angle and cover a larger area.

Climate is the average of the elements of weather over time. Climatic patterns are established primarily by the energy of the sun and the distribution of solar radiation, which is greatest at the Equator and least at the Poles, and is modified by altitude and distance from the sea.

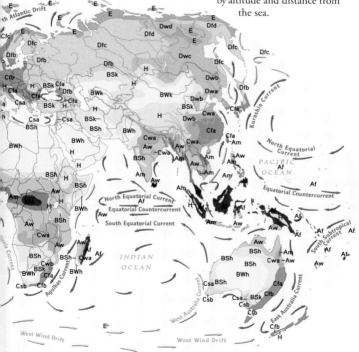

Greatest Tidal Range ■
Bay of Fundy, Nova Scotia,
Canada: 16 m (52 ft)

Most Crowded Country
Monaco: 15,270 per sq km
(38,173 per sq mi)

Least Populous Country
Vatican City: 830 people
Smallest Country
Vatican City: 0.4 sq km (0.2 sq.mi)

Largest Canyon
Grand Canyon,
Arizona, U.S.:
446 km (277 mi)
long along river,
180 m (600 ft) to
29 km (18 mi) wide,
about 1.8 km (1.1 mi) deep

**Hottest Recorded
Temperature**
Al Aziziyah, Libya:
58°C (136.4°F),
September 13, 1922

Highest Waterfall
Angel Falls, Venezuela:
979 m (3,212 ft)

**Longest Mountain Range
(submarine)**
Mid-Atlantic Ridge,
Atlantic Ocean:
approximately
19,700 km (12,240 mi)

Largest Drainage Basin
Amazon, South America:
7,050,000 sq km (2,722,000 sq mi)

Driest Place ■
Arica, Atacama Desert, Chile:
rainfall barely measurable

**Longest Mountain Range
(continental)**
Andes, South America:
approximately 7,200 km (4,500 mi)

GEOGRAPHIC EXTREMES

Largest Country
Russia: 17,075,400 sq km (6,592,850 sq mi)

Least Crowded Country
Mongolia: 2.0 per sq km
(5.2 per sq mi)

Most Populous Country
China: 1,336,720,000 people

**Most Populous
Metropolitan Area**
Tokyo, Japan:
36,669,000 people

Lowest Point
Dead Sea: -422 m (-1,385 ft)

Highest Point
Mount Everest:
8,850 m (29,035 ft)

**Longest Suspension
Bridge**
Akashi-Kaikyo Bridge,
Japan: total length
3,911 m (12,831 ft),
longest span
1,991 m (6,532 ft)

**Longest
River**
ile, Africa:
6,695 km
(4,160 mi)

**Tallest Manmade
Structure**
Burj Khalifa, Dubai,
United Arab Emirates:
828 m (2,716 ft)

Wettest Place
Mawsynram, Meghalaya, India:
annual average rainfall
1,187 cm (467 in)

**Deepest Point
in Ocean**
Challenger Deep:
-10,994 m (-36,070 ft)

Hottest Place
Dalol, Danakil
Desert, Ethiopia:
annual average
temperature
34°C (93°F)

Longest Reef
Great Barrier Reef, Australia:
2,300 km (1,429 mi)

Map Key

- Physical Extreme
- Human Extreme

Coldest Place
Ridge A, Antarctica:
annual average temperature
-74°C (-94°F)

Coldest Recorded Temperature
Vostok Research Station, Antarctica:
-89.2°C (-128.6°F), July 21, 1983

25

Yukon

Mackenzie

Mount McKinley
(Denali)
6,194 m
(20,320 ft)

Peace

C A N A D A

Lake
Superior

Missouri

Mississippi

Death Valley
(-282 ft) -86 m

Los Angeles

U N I T E D   S T A T E S

Lake
Michig

Mexico
City

NORTH AMERICA

GEOGRAPHIC EXTREMES

CONTINENTAL POLITICAL FACTS

TOTAL NUMBER OF COUNTRIES: 23

LARGEST COUNTRY BY AREA: Canada
9,984,670 sq km (3,855,103 sq mi)

SMALLEST COUNTRY BY AREA:
St. Kitts and Nevis 261 sq km (101 sq mi)

MOST POPULOUS COUNTRY: United States
313,232,000

LEAST POPULOUS COUNTRY: St. Kitts and
Nevis 50,000

LARGEST CITIES BY POPULATION:
Mexico City, Mexico 19,460,000
New York, United States 19,425,000
Los Angeles, United States 12,762,000
Chicago, Untied States 9,204,000
Miami, United States 5,750,000

CONTINENTAL PHYSICAL FACTS

AREA: 24,474,000 sq km (9,449,000 sq mi)

HIGHEST POINT: Mount McKinley (Denali),
Alaska, United States 6,194 m
(20,320 ft)

LOWEST POINT: Death Valley, California,
United States -86 m (-282 ft)

LONGEST RIVERS:
Mississippi-Missouri 5,970 km
(3,710 mi)
Mackenzie-Peace 4,241 km (2,635 mi)
Yukon 3,220 km (2,000 mi)

LARGEST NATURAL LAKES:
Lake Superior 82,100 sq km
(31,700 sq mi)
Lake Huron 59,600 sq km
(23,000 sq mi)
Lake Michigan 57,800 sq km
(22,300 sq mi)

Lake Huron

New York

Chicago

Miami

**ST. KITTS
AND NEVIS**

800 MILES

800 KILOMETERS

400

Azimuthal Equidistant Projection

NEW YORK
PHILADELPHIA
Washington
Bermuda Is.
U.K.
Richmond
Raleigh
Columbia
APPALACHIAN MTS.
Atlanta
Nashville
Montgomery
Detroit
Indianapolis
Jacksonville
Tallahassee
Orlando
MIAMI
Tampa
Okeechobee
Florida
BAHAMAS
Nassau
PUERTO RICO
U.S.

LESSER ANTILLES
DOM. REP.
San Juan
HAITI
Santo Domingo
Port-au-Prince
Kingston
JAMAICA
CUBA
La Habana (Havana)
Cancún
WEST INDIES
See pages 52–53 for the Lesser Antilles.
Port of Spain

Caracas
VENEZUELA
Barranquilla
Maracaibo
Medellín
BOGOTÁ
COLOMBIA
Cali
Panama
City
PANAMA CANAL
Golfo de Panamá
Quito
ECUADOR
PERU
Galápagos
Islands
Ecuador
I. del Coco
Costa Rica

CARIBBEAN SEA
Belmopán
BELIZE
GUATEMALA
Guatemala City
HONDURAS
Tegucigalpa
EL SALVADOR
San Salvador
NICARAGUA
Managua
San José
COSTA RICA

Memphis
Dallas
HOUSTON
Austin
San Antonio
Oklahoma City
Denver
Ft. Worth
Monterrey
Chihuahua
MEXICO CITY
Guadalajara
Mazatlán
Tampico
Puebla
Veracruz
Mérida
Acapulco
GULF OF MEXICO
TROPIC OF CANCER
MEXICO
Gulf of Honduras

Salt Lake City
Las Vegas
PHOENIX
Tucson
LOS ANGELES
San Francisco
San Diego
Tijuana
Channel Is.
Golfo de California
Cabo Falso
PACIFIC OCEAN
Is. Revillagigedo
Mexico
I. Guadalupe, Mexico
Punta Eugenia

ALASKA
Anchorage
Nome
Bethel
Cold Bay
Fox Is.
ALEUTIAN ISLANDS
Same scale as main map
Long. 165°W Greenwich

BERING SEA AND THE ALEUTIAN ISLANDS
ARCTIC CIRCLE
RUSSIA
Chukotsky
Poluostrov
Anadyr
St. Lawrence Island
Nunivak I.
St. Matthew Is.
Pribilof Is.
Nuniwak I.
Bristol Bay
Alaska Pen.

Enmelen
Beringovskiy
BERING SEA
Andreanof Islands
Rat Is.
Near Is.
Komandorskie O.
(Commander Is.)
Russia
Poluostrov
Kamchatka
Kyuchi
Long., East of Greenwich
Long. 165°E Greenwich
Sunday
Monday
Long., East

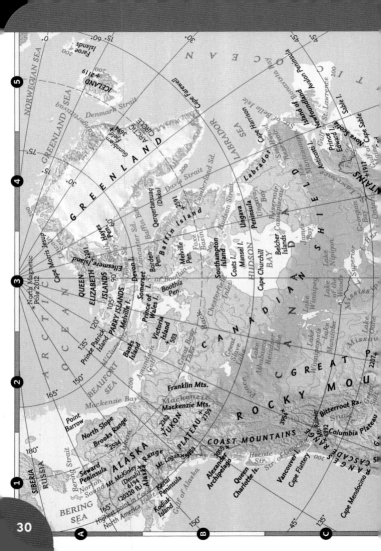

NORWEGIAN SEA
Faroe Islands
GREENLAND SEA
ICELAND +2119
Denmark Strait
ARCTIC CIRCLE
Cape Morris Jesup
Gunnbjorn 3694
Cape Brewell
GREENLAND
ATLANTIC OCEAN
Qeqertarsuaq (Disko)
+2591
Davis Strait
LABRADOR SEA
Cumberland Sd.
Cape Harrison
Island of Newfoundland
Gulf of St. Lawrence
Cape St. Lawrence
Sable I.
Ungava Peninsula
Labrador
Hudson Strait
Resolution I.
Belle Isle
Prince Edward I.
Gulf of Cape Sable
Nova Scotia
Avalon Peninsula
Grates Pt.
Anticosti I.
1917

North Magnetic Pole 2012
Hayes Pen.
Ellesmere Island
Lincoln Sea
+2201
QUEEN ELIZABETH ISLANDS
Devon I.
Lancaster Sd.
Baffin Bay
Baffin Island
Foxe Basin
Ungava Bay
Lake Mistassini
Belcher Islands
Mansel I.
Coats I.
Southampton Island
HUDSON BAY
Cape Churchill
Lake Nipigon
Lake Superior

PARRY ISLANDS
Prince Patrick Island
Melville I.
Melville Pen.
Borden Pen.
Somerset I.
Prince of I. Wales I.
Boothia Pen.
Chesterfield Inlet
CANADIAN SHIELD
Lake Winnipeg
Lake of the Woods
Lake Nipigon
Mississippi

Banks Island
McClure Str.
Victoria Island
+503
Gulf of Boothia
Great Bear Lake
Great Slave Lake
Lake Athabasca
Reindeer Lake
Lake Manitoba
Lake Winnipegosis

BEAUFORT SEA
Amundsen Gulf
Franklin Mts.
Mackenzie Bay
Mackenzie Mts.
Mackenzie
ROCKY MOUNTAINS
+2759
YUKON
GREAT PLAINS
Lake of the Woods
Missouri
220+

Point Barrow
North Slope
Brooks Range
+2594
ALASKA
Alaska Range
Mt. McKinley (Denali) 6194
(20320 ft) Highest point in North America
PLATEAU
COAST MOUNTAINS
+2759
Mt. Rainier 4392
Bitterroot Ra.
Columbia Plateau
Snake
CASCADE RANGE

SIBERIA
RUSSIA
Bering Strait
Seward Peninsula
Norton Sound
BERING SEA
Kenai Peninsula
Cook Inlet
Kodiak Island
Gulf of Alaska
Mt. Logan 5959
Alexander Archipelago
Queen Charlotte Is.
Hecate Str.
Vancouver I.
Str. of Georgia
Cape Flattery
Cape Mendocino

A   B   C

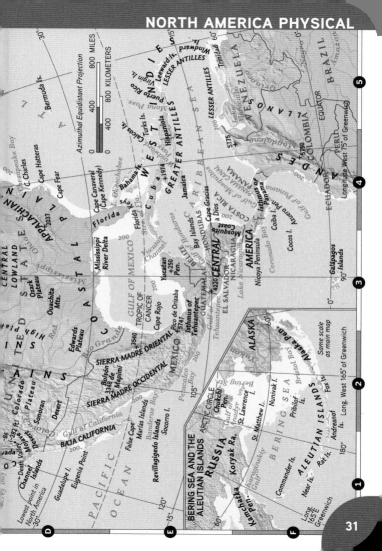

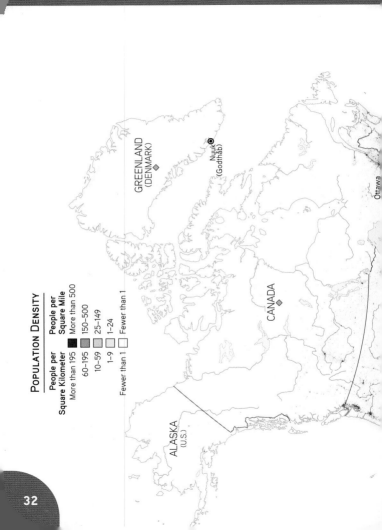

POPULATION DENSITY

People per Square Kilometer	People per Square Mile
More than 195	More than 500
60–195	150–500
10–59	25–149
1–9	1–24
Fewer than 1	Fewer than 1

GREENLAND (DENMARK)

Nuuk (Godthåb)

CANADA

ALASKA (U.S.)

Ottawa

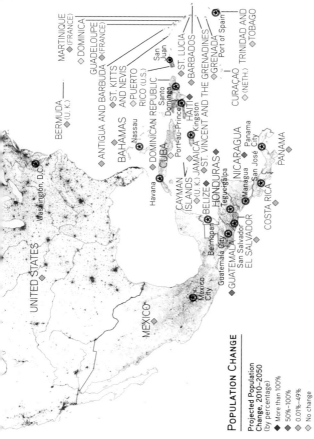

MARTINIQUE (FRANCE)
DOMINICA
GUADELOUPE (FRANCE)
ST. KITTS AND NEVIS
ANTIGUA AND BARBUDA
PUERTO RICO (U.S.)
San Juan
ST. LUCIA
BARBADOS
ST. VINCENT AND THE GRENADINES
GRENADA
Port of Spain
TRINIDAD AND TOBAGO
CURAÇAO (NETH.)
BERMUDA (U.K.)
BAHAMAS
Nassau
DOMINICAN REPUBLIC
Santo Domingo
HAITI
Port-au-Prince
CUBA
Havana
Kingston
JAMAICA (U.K.)
CAYMAN ISLANDS
BELIZE
Belmopan
NICARAGUA
Managua
Panama
Panama City
PANAMA
San José
COSTA RICA
HONDURAS
Tegucigalpa
GUATEMALA
Guatemala City
San Salvador
EL SALVADOR
Washington, D.C.
UNITED STATES
MEXICO
Mexico City

POPULATION CHANGE

Projected Population
Change, 2010–2050
(by percentage)

- ◆ More than 100%
- ◆ 50%–100%
- ◆ 0.01%–49%
- ◇ No change
- ◇ Population loss

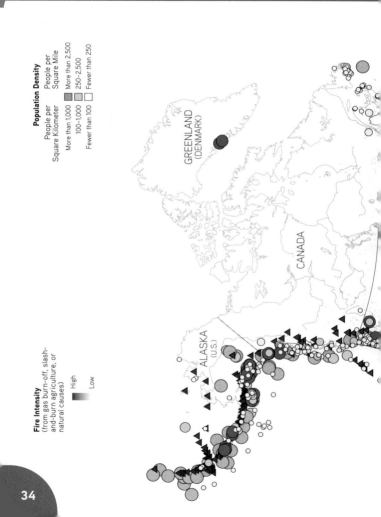

Fire Intensity
(from gas burn-off, slash-and-burn agriculture, or natural causes)

High

Low

Population Density

People per
Square Kilometer

People per
Square Mile

More than 1,000 — More than 2,500

100–1,000 — 250–2,500

Fewer than 100 — Fewer than 250

GREENLAND
(DENMARK)

CANADA

ALASKA
(U.S.)

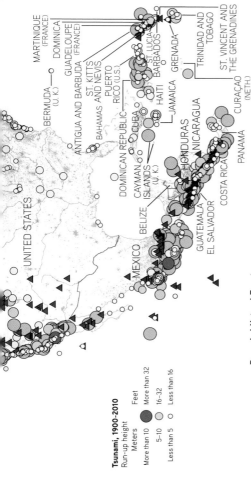

MARTINIQUE (FRANCE)
DOMINICA
GUADELOUPE (FRANCE)
ST. KITTS AND NEVIS
ANTIGUA AND BARBUDA
ST. LUCIA
BARBADOS
GRENADA
TRINIDAD AND TOBAGO
ST. VINCENT AND THE GRENADINES

BERMUDA (U. K.)
BAHAMAS
PUERTO RICO (U.S.)
HAITI
CUBA
DOMINICAN REPUBLIC
JAMAICA
CURAÇAO (NETH.)

UNITED STATES

CAYMAN ISLANDS (U. K.)
HONDURAS
NICARAGUA
PANAMA

BELIZE
MEXICO
GUATEMALA
EL SALVADOR
COSTA RICA

Tsunami, 1900-2010
Run-up height
Meters — Feet
More than 10 — More than 32
5–10 — 16–32
Less than 5 — Less than 16

Recorded Natural Event

Major Earthquake, 1900-2010
Moment magnitude
More than 7.0
6.0–7.0
Less than 6.0

Volcano

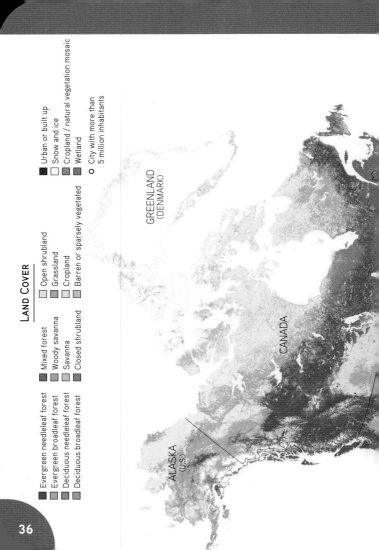

LAND COVER

- Evergreen needleleaf forest
- Evergreen broadleaf forest
- Deciduous needleleaf forest
- Deciduous broadleaf forest
- Mixed forest
- Woody savanna
- Savanna
- Closed shrubland
- Open shrubland
- Grassland
- Cropland
- Barren or sparsely vegetated
- Urban or built up
- Snow and ice
- Cropland / natural vegetation mosaic
- Wetland
- ○ City with more than 5 million inhabitants

ALASKA
(U.S.)

CANADA

GREENLAND
(DENMARK)

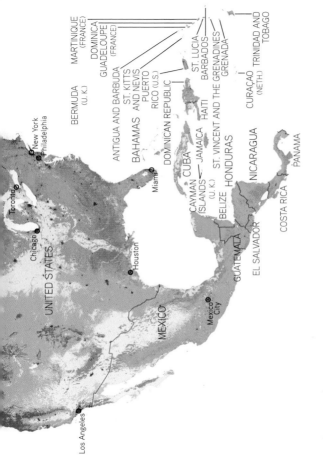

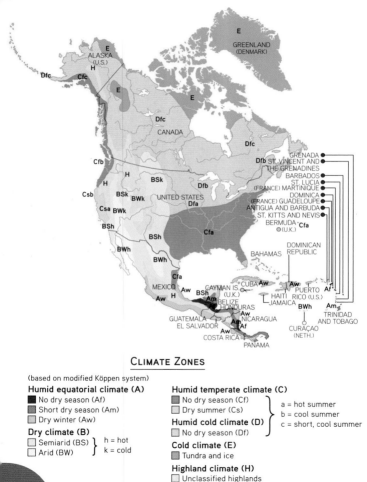

CLIMATE ZONES

(based on modified Köppen system)

Humid equatorial climate (A)
- No dry season (Af)
- Short dry season (Am)
- Dry winter (Aw)

Dry climate (B)
- Semiarid (BS) } h = hot
- Arid (BW) } k = cold

Humid temperate climate (C)
- No dry season (Cf)
- Dry summer (Cs)

Humid cold climate (D)
- No dry season (Df)

a = hot summer
b = cool summer
c = short, cool summer

Cold climate (E)
- Tundra and ice

Highland climate (H)
- Unclassified highlands

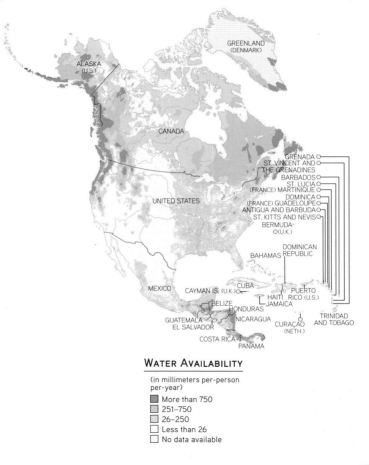

GREENLAND
(DENMARK)

ALASKA
(U.S.)

CANADA

GRENADA
ST. VINCENT AND
THE GRENADINES
BARBADOS
ST. LUCIA
(FRANCE) MARTINIQUE
DOMINICA
(FRANCE) GUADELOUPE
ANTIGUA AND BARBUDA
ST. KITTS AND NEVIS
BERMUDA
(U.K.)

UNITED STATES

DOMINICAN
REPUBLIC
BAHAMAS

MEXICO   CAYMAN IS. (U.K.)   CUBA   PUERTO
                                    HAITI   RICO (U.S.)
                            JAMAICA
                    BELIZE
            HONDURAS   TRINIDAD
GUATEMALA   NICARAGUA   AND TOBAGO
EL SALVADOR   CURAÇAO
        COSTA RICA   (NETH.)
                PANAMA

WATER AVAILABILITY

(in millimeters per-person
per-year)

- More than 750
- 251–750
- 26–250
- Less than 26
- No data available

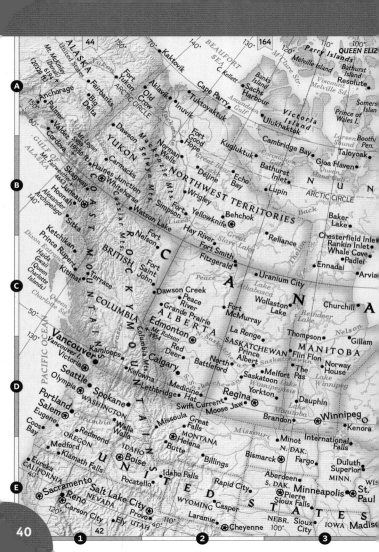

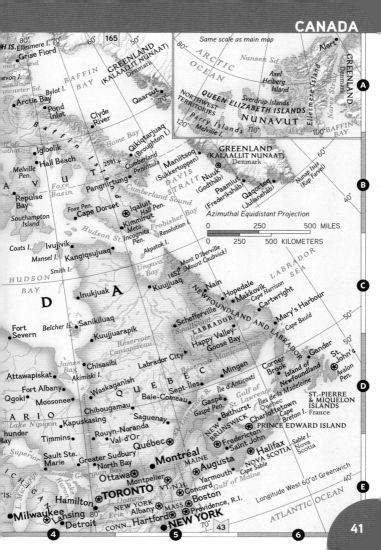

BRITISH COLUMBIA
Red Deer
ALBERTA
Prince Albert
SASKATCHEWAN
MANITOBA

Vancouver
Vancouver I.
Victoria
Cape Flattery
Kamloops
Kelowna
Calgary
Medicine Hat
Lethbridge
Saskatoon
Regina
Moose Jaw
Weyburn
Brandon
C A N
Lake Manitoba
Winnipeg

A

Olympia
Seattle
Tacoma
WASH.
Spokane
Walla Walla
Havre
Great Falls
MONTANA
Missouri
Minot

Portland
Salem
Eugene
Coos Bay
Redmond
OREGON
CASCADE RANGE
COAST RANGES
Columbia
Missoula
Bitterroot Range
Helena
Butte
Bozeman
Billings
Miles City
NORTH DAKOTA
Bismarck
Fargo

Medford
Klamath Falls
IDAHO
Boise
Absaroka Range
Bighorn Mts.
Worland
Aberdeen
SOUTH DAKOTA
Pierre

B

Eureka
Alturas
Snake
Idaho Falls
Pocatello
WYOMING
Black Hills
Rapid City
Sioux Falls

40°
Sacramento
Reno
Carson City
NEVADA
GREAT
Salt Lake City
Provo
Casper
Laramie
Cheyenne
NEBRASKA
Sioux City
Omaha
Lincoln
Platte

San Francisco
Oakland
San Jose
Fresno
BASIN
Ely
UTAH
U N I T E D
Boulder
Denver

C
CALIFORNIA
Bakersfield
Santa Barbara
Channel Is.
LOS ANGELES
SIERRA NEVADA
Death Valley -282 ft
Mojave Desert
Las Vegas
COLORADO PLATEAU
Grand Canyon
San Juan Mts.
COLORADO
Colorado Springs
KANSAS
Wichita

Riverside
Long Beach
San Diego
Tijuana
Ensenada
Mexicali
Yuma
ARIZONA
Flagstaff
PHOENIX
NEW MEXICO
Santa Fe
Albuquerque
Amarillo
OKLAHOMA
Oklahoma City
OKLAHOM
Wich Falls

Tucson
Douglas
Nogales
Llano Estacado
Lubbock
Hobbs
Dallas
Fort Worth
Waco

D
30°
BAJA CALIFORNIA
Ciudad Juárez
Carlsbad
El Paso
Odessa
TEXAS

Hermosillo
Chihuahua
Rio Bravo del Norte
Edwards Plateau
San Antonio
Austin

PACIFIC OCEAN
45
120°
GULF OF CALIFORNIA
Guaymas
La Purísima
Delicias
M E X I C O
Nuevo Laredo
Monclova
Corpus Christi
Laredo
Brownsville

E
TROPIC OF CANCER
Los Mochis
Torreón
Saltillo
Monterrey
Matamoros

La Paz
Culiacán
Durango
Mazatlán
Ciudad Victoria
100°

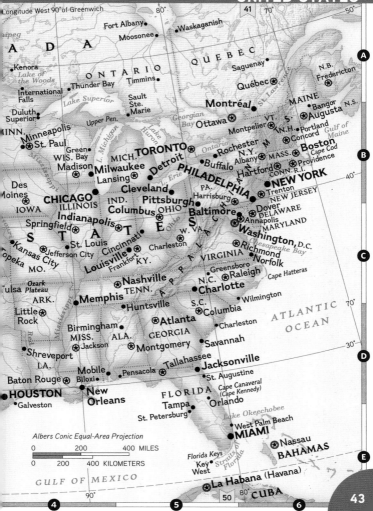

Longitude West 90° of Greenwich

Fort Albany
Waskaganish
Moosonee

A

CANADA
ONTARIO
QUEBEC

Kenora
Lake of the Woods
Saguenay
N.B.
Fredericton

Thunder Bay
Timmins
Québec
St. Lawrence

International Falls
Sault Ste. Marie
Montréal
MAINE
Bangor
N.S.

Duluth
Superior
Upper Pen.
Georgian Bay
Ottawa
Montpelier
VT.
Augusta
Gulf of Maine

MINN.
Lake Superior
Lake Michigan
Lake Huron
N.H.
Portland
Concord

Minneapolis
St. Paul
Green Bay
MICH.
TORONTO
Ontario
Rochester
N.Y.
Albany
MASS.
BOSTON
Cape Cod

B

WIS.
Madison
Milwaukee
Lansing
Detroit
Buffalo
Erie
Hartford
CONN.
Providence
R.I.

Des Moines
IOWA
CHICAGO
ILLINOIS
IND.
Cleveland
PHILADELPHIA
NEW YORK
40°

Springfield
STATES
Columbus
OHIO
Pittsburgh
PA.
Harrisburg
Trenton
NEW JERSEY
Dover
DELAWARE

Indianapolis
Baltimore
Annapolis
MARYLAND

Kansas City
Jefferson City
MO.
St. Louis
Cincinnati
Charleston
W. VA.
Washington, D.C.

C

Topeka
Louisville
Frankfort
KY.
Richmond
VIRGINIA
Norfolk
Chesapeake Bay

Ozark Plateau
Nashville
TENN.
Greensboro
Raleigh
N.C.
Cape Hatteras

Tulsa
ARK.
Memphis
Huntsville
Charlotte
70°

Little Rock
Birmingham
S.C.
Columbia
Wilmington

MISS.
ALA.
Jackson
Atlanta
GEORGIA
Montgomery
Charleston
Savannah
ATLANTIC OCEAN

D

Shreveport
LA.
Mobile
Biloxi
Pensacola
Tallahassee
Jacksonville
30°

Baton Rouge
HOUSTON
New Orleans
St. Augustine

Galveston
FLORIDA
Cape Canaveral (Cape Kennedy)
Tampa
Orlando

St. Petersburg
Lake Okeechobee

West Palm Beach
MIAMI

Albers Conic Equal-Area Projection

0   200   400 MILES

0   200   400 KILOMETERS

Nassau
BAHAMAS

E

Florida Keys
Key West
Straits of Florida

GULF OF MEXICO

La Habana (Havana)
CUBA

4   5   6

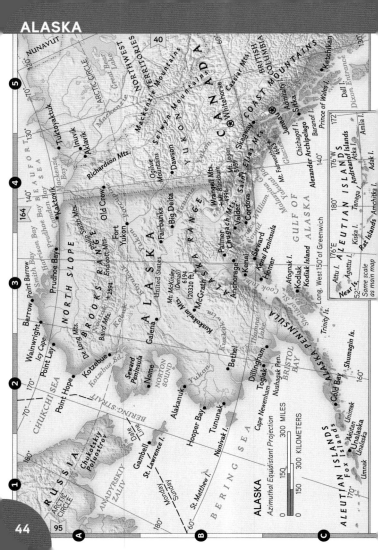

ALASKA

NUNAVUT

40

5

NORTHWEST TERRITORIES

ARCTIC CIRCLE

Great Bear Lake

CANADA

BRITISH COLUMBIA

Cassiar Mts.

Ketchikan

Dixon Entrance

Dall I.

Prince of Wales I.

Whitehorse

Skagway

Juneau

Sitka

Admiralty I.

Baranof I.

Chichagof I.

Alexander Archipelago

COAST MOUNTAINS

Mackenzie Mts.

Selwyn Mountains

YUKON

Mackenzie

Tuktoyaktuk

Inuvik

Aklavik

Richardson Mts.

Ogilvie Mountains

Dawson

Old Crow

BEAUFORT SEA

Camden Bay

Kaktovik

4

164

Mt. Fairweather 4663

Glacier Bay

Mt. Logan 5959

St. Elias Mts.

Mt. St. Elias

Mt. Blackburn 4996

Wrangell Mts.

Valdez

Cordova

Yakutat

GULF OF ALASKA

Yukon

Porcupine

Fort Yukon

Fairbanks

Big Delta

Phillip Smith Mts.

Smith Bay

Harrison Bay

Prudhoe Bay

Point Barrow

Barrow

Wainwright

Icy Cape

Point Lay

NORTH SLOPE

BROOKS RANGE

Endicott Mts.

Baird Mts.

De Long Mts.

Noatak

Kobuk

United States

Mt. McKinley (Denali) 6194 (20320 ft.)

McGrath

ALASKA

ALASKA RANGE

Palmer

Chugach Mts.

Anchorage

Kenai

Seward

Homer

Kenai Peninsula

Cook Inlet

Prince William Sound

Kodiak

Kodiak Island

Afognak

Shelikof Str.

Trinity Is.

3

Point Hope

Kotzebue

Kotzebue Sd.

Seward Peninsula

Nome

NORTON SOUND

Galena

Kuskokwim Mts.

Kuskokwim

Tanana

Bethel

Dillingham

Togiak

Nushagak Pen.

BRISTOL BAY

ALASKA PENINSULA

Cape Newenham

Iliamna Lake

Yukon

CHUKCHI SEA

Point Hope

BERING STRAIT

Alakanuk

Hooper Bay

Tununak

Nunivak I.

St. Matthew I.

BERING SEA

Date Line

Monday

Sunday

2

170°

70°

60°

RUSSIA

Chukotskiy Poluostrov

ANADYRSKIY ZALIV

Gambell

St. Lawrence I.

ARCTIC CIRCLE

180°

1

A

B

C

44

95

Long. West 150° of Greenwich

172°

Inset: ALEUTIAN ISLANDS

176°E

176°W

180°

172°

Near Is.

Attu I.

Agattu I.

ANDREANOF ISLANDS

Adak I.

Amlia I.

Atka I.

Tanaga I.

Amchitka I.

Kiska I.

Rat Islands

52°15′

Some islands as main map

Shumagin Is.

Cold Bay

Unimak

ALEUTIAN ISLANDS

Fox Islands

Akutan

Unalaska

Umnak

ALASKA

Azimuthal Equidistant Projection

0 150 300 MILES

0 150 300 KILOMETERS

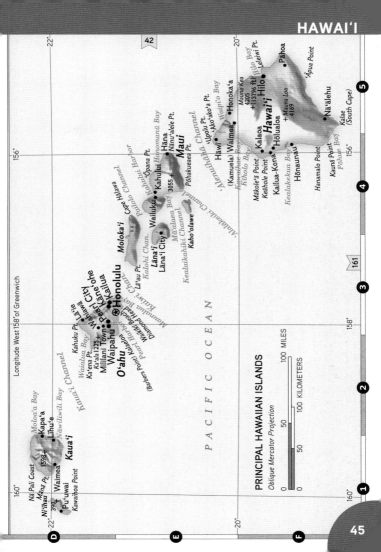

42

Longitude West 158° of Greenwich

160°   158°   156°

Kaua‘i

Nā Pali Coast
Moloa‘a Bay
Mina Pk. 1598+ • Kapa‘a
Ni‘ihau • Līhu‘e
39+ • Waimea   Nāwiliwili Bay
Pu‘uwai
Kawaihoa Point

22°

O‘ahu

Kaua‘i Channel
Kahuku Pt. • La‘ie
Waialua Bay
Ka‘ena Pt. • Wahiawā • Kāne‘ohe
Ka‘ala 1225 • Wai Pahu • Kailua
Mililani Town • Pearl City
Waipahu • ⊛ **Honolulu**
(Barbers Point) Kalaeloa • Pearl Harbor
Makaha • Diamond Head
Mamala Bay

Moloka‘i
Cape Hālawa
Kalaupapa Pt.
Pailolo Channel
Kaunakakai
Kalohi Chan.
La‘au Pt.

Lāna‘i
Lāna‘i City
Kaho‘olawe
Kohohi Chan.

Kalaupapa Pt.
Kaumalapa‘u

Honomanū Bay
Wailuku • Kahului   Opana Pt.
Wailuku • Kahului • Hāna
3055 + • Nānu‘alele Pt.
Maui
Pōhakueaea Pt.
Mā‘alaea Bay
Kealaikahiki Channel
‘Alalākeiki Channel
‘Au‘au Channel

‘Upolu Pt.
‘Alenuihāhā Channel
‘Āko‘ako‘a Pt.
Waipi‘o Bay
Honoka‘a
Hāwī • Honoka‘a   Mauna Kea   Hilo Bay
(Kamuela) Waimea •   4205 +(13796 ft) • Leleiwi Pt.
Kawaihae Bay   Mauna Kea • Hilo • Pāhoa
Kalaoa   + Mauna Loa
Kiholo Bay   **Hawai‘i**   4169   ‘Āpua Point
Makole‘a Point   Hōlualoa
Keāhole Point   Hōlualoa
Kailua-Kona
Kealakekua Bay   Kaunā Point
Hōnaunau   Pōhue Bay
Hanamalo Point   Kaunā Point   Nā‘ālehu
Kalae (South Cape)

P A C I F I C   O C E A N

20°

PRINCIPAL HAWAIIAN ISLANDS

Oblique Mercator Projection

```
0        50       100 MILES
0    50   100 KILOMETERS
```

160°

D

E

F

1   2   3   161   4   156°   5

20°

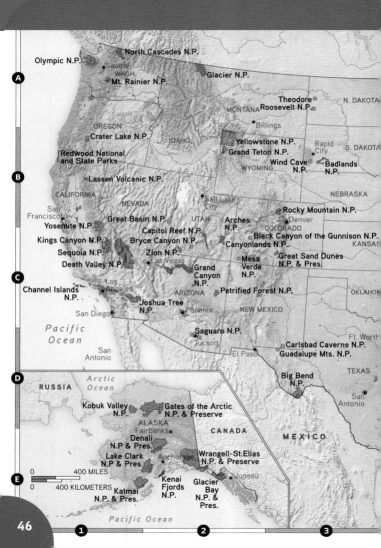

North Cascades N.P.
Olympic N.P.
Seattle
WASH.
Mt. Rainier N.P.
Glacier N.P.
Theodore
Roosevelt N.P.
N. DAKOTA
MONTANA
Billings
OREGON
Crater Lake N.P.
IDAHO
Yellowstone N.P.
Grand Teton N.P.
Rapid
City
S. DAKOTA
Redwood National
and State Parks
WYOMING
Wind Cave
N.P.
Badlands
N.P.
Lassen Volcanic N.P.
NEBRASKA
CALIFORNIA
NEVADA
Salt Lake
City
San
Francisco
Rocky Mountain N.P.
Great Basin N.P.
Yosemite N.P.
UTAH
Arches
N.P.
Denver
COLORADO
Capitol Reef N.P.
Kings Canyon N.P.
Bryce Canyon N.P.
Black Canyon of the Gunnison N.P.
KANSAS
Canyonlands N.P.
Sequoia N.P.
Zion N.P.
Death Valley N.P.
Las Vegas
Mesa
Verde
N.P.
Great Sand Dunes
N.P. & Pres.
Grand
Canyon
N.P.
Channel Islands
N.P.
Los
Angeles
ARIZONA
Petrified Forest N.P.
OKLAHOMA
Joshua Tree
N.P.
NEW MEXICO
San Diego
Phoenix
Pacific
Ocean
Ft. Worth
Saguaro N.P.
San
Antonio
Tucson
Carlsbad Caverns N.P.
El Paso
Guadalupe Mts. N.P.
TEXAS
Big Bend
N.P.
San
Antonio
RUSSIA
Arctic
Ocean
Kobuk Valley
N.P.
Gates of the Arctic
N.P. & Preserve
ALASKA
Fairbanks
CANADA
MEXICO
Denali
N.P. & Pres.
Lake Clark
N.P. & Pres.
Anchorage
Wrangell-St. Elias
N.P. & Preserve
Kenai
Fjords
N.P.
Glacier
Bay
N.P. &
Pres.
Juneau
0   400 MILES
0   400 KILOMETERS
Katmai
N.P. & Pres.
Pacific Ocean

A
B
C
D
E
1   2   3

CANADA

Voyageurs N.P.

Isle Royale N.P.

MINN.

MICHIGAN

CANADA
U.S.

ME.

Acadia
National
Park

VT.

N.H.

St. Paul

WIS.

N.Y.

MASS.

Boston

inneapolis

CONN. R.I.

Detroit

Cleveland

PA.

New York

IOWA

Chicago

Cuyahoga
Valley N.P.

N.J.

Philadelphia

ILL.

IND.

OHIO

MD.

DEL.

Washington, D.C.

Kansas City

St. Louis

W. VA.

Shenandoah
National Park

MO.

KY.

VA.

Atlantic
Ocean

Mammoth Cave
N.P.

Great Smoky Mts. N.P.

N.C.

ARK.

Little
Rock

Memphis

Columbia

S.C.

Hot Springs
N.P.

Atlanta

Congaree N.P.

MISS.

ALA.

GA.

allas

LA.

FLA.

Houston

New Orleans

Map Key

National Park

Urban area

Albers Conic Equal-Area Projection

0   200   400 MILES

0   200   400 KILOMETERS

Tampa

Miami

Everglades N.P.

Biscayne N.P.

BAHAMAS

Dry Tortugas N.P.

Pacific Ocean

Honolulu

HAWAI'I

0   100 MILES

Haleakalā N.P.

0   100 KILOMETERS

CUBA

Hilo

Hawai'i Volcanoes N.P.

A

B

C

D

E

4   5   6

47

Map of Mexico and Southwestern United States

UNITED STATES (region labels)

San Diego
Tijuana
Mexicali
San Luis
Río Colorado
PHOENIX
Tucson
Roswell
Lubbock
Alamogordo
Carlsbad
Abilene
Fort Worth
Dallas
Nogales
Nogales
Douglas
El Paso
Ciudad Juárez
Odessa
Waco
Austin
Cananea
Agua Prieta
Punta Prieta
Hermosillo
BAJA
Nuevo Casas Grandes
San Antonio
Ciudad Acuña
Punta Eugenia
CALIFORNIA
Ciudad Obregón
Guaymas
Chihuahua
Delicias
Piedras Negras
Corpus Christi
Nuevo Laredo
Laredo
Navojoa
Hidalgo del Parral
Loreto
El Fuerte
Monclova
Brownsville
McAllen
Reynosa
Rocas Alijos
Cabo San Lázaro
Los Mochis
Gómez Palacio
Torreón
Saltillo
Monterrey
Guasave
Matamor
TROPIC OF CANCER
La Paz
Culiacán
M E X I C O
Cabo San Lucas
Durango
Ciudad Victoria
Mazatlán
Fresnillo
Zacatecas
Tampico
Ciudad Madero
Escuinapa
Tecuala
Tuxpan
San Luis Potosí
Aguascalientes
Ciudad Valles
Islas Marías
Tepic
León
Puerto Vallarta
Irapuato
Islas Revillagigedo
Mexico
Guadalajara
Salamanca
Querétaro
Pachuca
Poza Rica
Colima
Uruapan
MEXICO CITY
Xalapa
Manzanillo
Apatzingán
Netzahualcóyotl
Veracruz
Iguala
Ixtapa
Chilpancingo
Acapulco
Oaxaca
Sierra Madre del Sur
Ometepec
Puerto Ángel

P A C I F I C   O C E A N

Golfo de California

Sierra Madre Occidental

Sierra Madre Oriental

Río Grande

Clipperton
France

Azimuthal Equidistant Projection

0	200	400 MILES
0	200	400 KILOMETERS

30°
20°
10°

110°
100°

A
B
C
D
E

1
2
3

STATES

Shreveport • Jackson • Montgomery • Birmingham • Atlanta • Augusta • Columbus • Charleston • Savannah

90° | 43 | 80°

eaumont • Baton Rouge • Mobile • Biloxi • Pensacola • Tallahassee • Jacksonville • St. Augustine

30°

HOUSTON • New Orleans

ATLANTIC OCEAN

Orlando • Cape Canaveral (Cape Kennedy)

St. Petersburg • Tampa • Lake Okeechobee • West Palm Beach

Sarasota • Fort Myers • Fort Lauderdale

MIAMI • Nassau

GULF OF MEXICO

Florida Keys

BAHAMAS

Key West • Straits of Florida

La Habana (Havana) • Matanzas • TROPIC OF CANCER

Pinar del Río • **CUBA** • Santa Clara

Ciego de Ávila • Camagüey

CUBA • Holguín

Motul • Tizimín • Yucatan Channel

Mérida • Cancún

Valladolid • Manzanillo

Yucatán • Isla Cozumel • **CAYMAN ISLANDS** U.K.

Peninsula • Santiago de Cuba

Campeche • Ciudad del Carmen

Istmo de Tehuantepec

Coatzacoalcos • Villahermosa • Chetumal

Orange Walk • Belize City

Montego Bay • Kingston

JAMAICA

Spanish Town • Jamaica

Minatitlán • Belmopan

Tuxtla Gutiérrez • San Cristóbal de Las Casas • **BELIZE** • Islas de la Bahía

Juchitán • Tonalá • **GUATEMALA** • San Pedro Sula • La Ceiba

Tapachula • Guatemala City • **HONDURAS** • Cabo Gracias a Dios

Quetzaltenango • Escuintla • **Tegucigalpa** • Cayos Miskitos • Coco

Santa Ana • Estelí • Puerto Cabezas

San Salvador • **EL SALVADOR** • San Miguel • León • **NICARAGUA**

Managua • Granada • Islas del Maíz • Bluefields

Lago de Nicaragua

Liberia • San Juan del Norte

Alajuela • Heredia • Limón

Puntarenas • Colón • **Panama City** • Panama Canal

San José • Cartago • **PANAMA** • La Palma

COSTA RICA • David • Chitré • Penonomé

Punta Burica • Las Tablas

Península de Azuero

Tampa
St. Petersburg
Tampa Bay
Sarasota
UNITED
STATES
Fort Myers
Charlotte Harbor
Cape Romano
Homestead
Cape Sable
Ponce de Leon Bay

FLORIDA
Kissimmee
Orlando
Cape Canaveral
(Cape Kennedy)
Fort Pierce
West Palm Beach
Lake Okeechobee
Fort
Lauderdale
MIAMI
Miami Beach
Florida Keys
Key
West
Dry
Tortugas

Little Abaco I.
Cooper's Town
Grand Bahama I.
Freeport
Northwest Providence Channel
Abaco
Island
Southwest Point

B A H

41

GULF
OF
MEXICO

Bimini
Islands
Joulter
Cays
Williams I. +15
New Providence ⊛ **Nassau**
Berry
Islands
Eleuthera
Island
Rock Sou

Big Wood Cay

Andros
Island
Kemps Bay

Cape Santa Maria
*Great
Exuma*
*Little
Exuma*
Deadmans C

Tongue of the Ocean

Cistern Pt.

25°

STRAITS OF FLORIDA

Península de Hicacos
Matanzas
Archipiélago de Sabana
Nichotas Channel
Old Bahama Channel

Exuma
Sound
*Flami
Ca*

LA HABANA
(HAVANA) ⊛
+692
Los Palacios
Pinar del Río
Golfo de Batabanó
Artemisa Güines
Península
de Zapata
CUBA
Santa Clara
Cienfuegos
Morón
Archipiélago de Camagüey

Guane
Bahía Guadiana
Cabo
Francés
Pta. Frances
+310
Nueva Gerona
Isla de la Juventud
(Isle of Youth)
Punta del Guanal
Archipiélago de los Canarreos
Sancti
Spíritus
Ciego de
Ávila
Golfo de Ana María
San
Pedro
Camagüey

Las Tunas
Holguín
Bah

Cabo de San Antonio

Yucatan Channel

Jardines de la Reina

Pta. Macuriges
Guayabal
Cauto
Bayamo
J:

Golfo de Guacanayabo
Manzanillo
Cabo
Cruz
Sierra Maestra
Pico +2005
Turquino
Santiago de Cuba
Guantána
U
NAV.
BA
GUANTANAM
B:

20°

85°

G
R
E
A
T

Little
Cayman
Cayman
Brac
CAYMAN ISLANDS
U.K.

George Town ⊛
*Grand
Cayman*

C
A
Y
M
A
N

*Montego
Bay* **Montego Bay**
Saint Ann's Bay
Port Antonio
Northeast
Point
North Negril Point
South Negril Point
Blue Mt. Pk.
+2256
Morant Po
Savanna-la-Mar
JAMAICA ⊛
May Pen
Kingston
Spanish Town
Great Pedro Bluff
Portland Point

T
R
E
N
C
H

Islas Santanilla
(Swan Islands)
Honduras

Pedro Cays
Jamaica

B

A

N

HONDURAS
Laguna de Caratasca
Cabo Falso

1   2   3

49

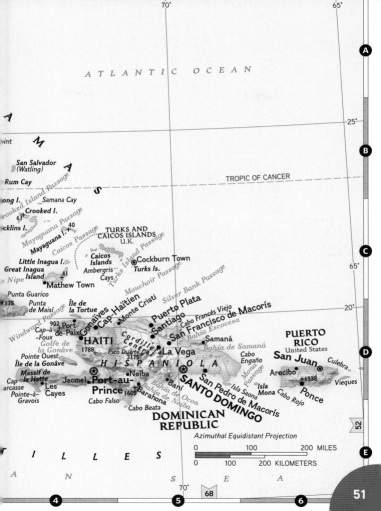

ATLANTIC OCEAN

25°

B

TROPIC OF CANCER

San Salvador
(Watling)

Rum Cay

ong I.   Samana Cay
61   Crooked I.
cklins I.

Mayaguana Passage   40
Mayaguana I.

TURKS AND
CAICOS ISLANDS
U.K.

Little Inagua I.   Caicos
Great Inagua   Islands
Island   Ambergris   ●Cockburn Town
Nipe   Cays   ●Turks Is.

65°

Mouchoir Passage

C

Silver Bank Passage

Punta Guarico
175   Punta   Île de
de Maisí   la Tortue   ●Monte Cristi   Puerto Plata   Cabo Francés Viejo
902 Port-   Gonaïves Cap-Haïtien   ●Santiago   ●San Francisco de Macorís
Cap-à-Paix   ●   Cordillera   Bahía Escocesa
-Foux   HAITI   Central   ●Samaná   PUERTO
Golfe de   1788,   Pico Duarte   Bahía de Samaná   RICO
la Gonâve   3175   ▲+   ●La Vega   United States
Pointe Ouest   HISPANIOLA   Cabo   San Juan ◎
Île de la Gonâve   Engaño
Cap   Massif de   Isla Saona   Mona   Arecibo
arcasse   la Hotte   ●Jacmel ✪Port-au- ●Neiba ●   ●San Pedro de Macorís Passage +1338
Pointe-à-   Les   Prince Bahía de Ocoa Barahona SANTO DOMINGO ●Ponce
Gravois   Cayes   1605+ Baní   Isla   Culebra
                Bahía de Neiba   ●   Mona Cabo Rojo   Vieques
            Cabo Falso   DOMINICAN
                Cabo Beata   REPUBLIC

20°

D

52

Azimuthal Equidistant Projection

0   100   200 MILES
0   100   200 KILOMETERS

E

TILLES

A   N   S   E   A

70°   68

51

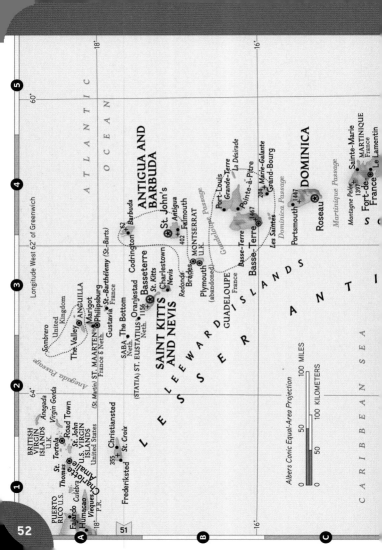

18°

60°

64°

16°

Longitude West 62° of Greenwich

A **1** **2** **3** **4** **5** **B** **C**

A T L A N T I C

O C E A N

C A R I B B E A N   S E A

L E S S E R   A N T I

L E E W A R D   I S L A N D S

PUERTO
RICO U.S.
Fajardo • Culebra
Humacao • Vieques
P.R.

St. Thomas
Charlotte Amalie
BRITISH
VIRGIN
ISLANDS
U.K.
Tortola
St. John
Road Town
Virgin Gorda
Anegada

U.S. VIRGIN
ISLANDS
United States

Christiansted •
St. Croix
355 •
Frederiksted •

Anegada Passage

Sombrero •
Sombrero
ANGUILLA
The Valley ◉
United
Kingdom

SABA • The Bottom
(STATIA) ST. EUSTATIUS
Neth.
Neth.

SAINT KITTS
AND NEVIS

Oranjestad •
1156 ▲
St. Kitts
Basseterre ◉
Charlestown ◉
Nevis

St.-Barthélemy (St-Barts)
Gustavia • France
ST. MAARTEN-
Marigot •
ST. MARTIN
France & Neth.
(St. Martin)
Philipsburg •
Neth.

Redonda •
St. Kitts

52 •
Codrington •
Barbuda

ANTIGUA AND
BARBUDA

St. John's ◉
402 ▲
Antigua
Falmouth •

MONTSERRAT
U.K.
Brades ◉
Plymouth ◉
(abandoned)

Guadeloupe Passage

Port-Louis •
Grande-Terre
La Désirade

GUADELOUPE
France
Basse-Terre
Basse-Terre ◉
1467 ▲
Pointe-à-Pitre ◉
204 ▲ Marie-Galante
Grand-Bourg •
Les Saintes •

Dominica Passage

DOMINICA

Portsmouth •
441 ▲
Roseau ◉

Martinique Passage

Sainte-Marie •
MARTINIQUE
France
Montagne Pelée
1397 ▲
Fort-de-
France ◉
Le Lamentin •

S

Albers Conic Equal-Area Projection

0   50   100 MILES

0   50   100 KILOMETERS

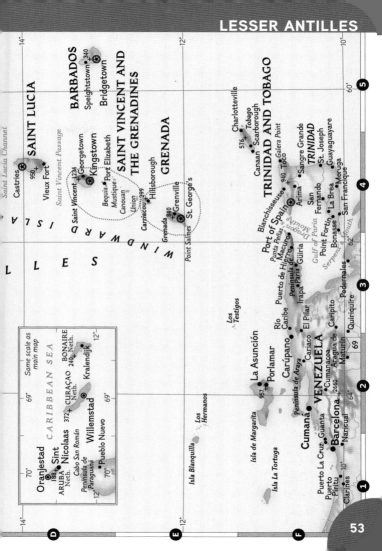

SAINT LUCIA CHANNEL

BARBADOS

SAINT LUCIA

SAINT VINCENT AND THE GRENADINES

GRENADA

Charlotteville
Tobago
Scarborough
Canaan
Galera Point
Sangre Grande
Toco
Blanchisseuse
Arima
Port of Spain
San Fernando
La Brea
Point Fortin
Bonasse
Pedernales
Quiriquire

TRINIDAD AND TOBAGO
576
TRINIDAD
940
St. Joseph
Guayaguayare
Moruga
San Francique
62

Speightstown 340
Bridgetown

Castries
950
Vieux Fort

Saint Vincent Passage
Georgetown
Kingstown
Port Elizabeth
Bequia
Mustique
Canouan
Union
Carriacou
Saint Vincent 1234
299
Hillsborough
810
Grenville
Grenada
St. George's
Point Salines

ISLA
WINDWARD

LLES

Dragon Mouths
Punta Peñas
Macuro
Güiria
Peninsula de Paria
Irapa
Peninsula de Hierro
Gulf of Paria
Serpent's Mouth

Los Testigos

Río Caribe
Carúpano
Cariaco
El Pilar
Carúpano

Puerto de Hierro

VENEZUELA

La Asunción
Porlamar
957
Isla de Margarita

Los Hermanos

Península de Araya
Araya
Cumaná
2660
Aragua de Maturín
69

Cumaná
Barcelona
Narirual
64
Maturín

Isla Blanquilla

Isla La Tortuga

Puerto La Cruz
Guanta
Puerto Píritu
Clarines
10

53

Lake Maracaibo

Bogotá

SURINAME

Amazon

Purus

B R A Z

Lima

Lake Titicaca

Paraná

Cerro Aconcagua
6,959 m
(22,831 ft)

Buenos Aires

Laguna del Carbón
-105 m
(-344 ft)

SOUTH AMERICA

GEOGRAPHIC EXTREMES

CONTINENTAL POLITICAL FACTS

TOTAL NUMBER OF COUNTRIES: 12

LARGEST COUNTRY BY AREA: Brazil
8,514,877 sq km (3,287,612 sq mi)

SMALLEST COUNTRY BY AREA:
Suriname   163,265 sq km
(63,037 sq mi)

MOST POPULOUS COUNTRY: Brazil
203,430,000

LEAST POPULOUS COUNTRY: Suriname
492,000

LARGEST CITIES BY POPULATION:
São Paulo, Brazil   20,260,000
Buenos Aires, Argentina   13,100,00
Rio de Janeiro, Brazil   12,000,000
Lima, Peru   8,950,000
Bogotá, Colombia   8,500,000

CONTINENTAL PHYSICAL FACTS

AREA: 17,819,000 sq km (6,880,000 sq mi)

HIGHEST POINT: Cerro Aconcagua,
Argentina   6,959 m (22,831 ft)

LOWEST POINT: Laguna del Carbón,
Argentina   -105 m (-344 ft)

LONGEST RIVERS:
Amazon   6,679 km (4,150 mi)
Paraná   4,695 km (2,917 mi)
Purus   3,400 km (2,113 mi)

LARGEST NATURAL LAKES (SURFACE AREA):
Lake Maracaibo *(recognized by some as a
lake)*   13,280 sq km (5,127 sq mi)
Lake Titicaca   8,372 sq km
(3,232 sq mi)

Rio de Janeiro
São Paulo

I   L

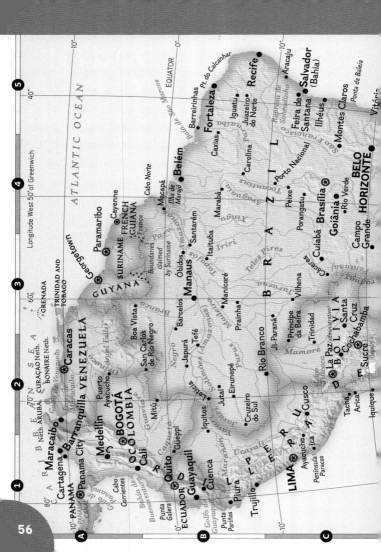

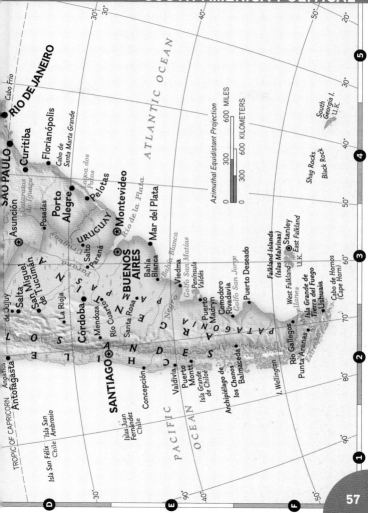

ATLANTIC OCEAN

RIO DE JANEIRO

Cabo Frio

SAO PAULO

Curitiba

Florianópolis

Cabo de Santa Marta Grande

Asunción

Lagoa dos Patos

Cataratas del Iguazú

Curitiba

Porto Alegre

Posadas

Pelotas

Montevideo

URUGUAY

Salto

Paraná

Mar del Plata

Río de la Plata

Paraná

BUENOS AIRES

Bahía Blanca

Bahía Blanca

de Jujuy

Salta

San Miguel de Tucumán

La Rioja

Mendoza

Santa Rosa

Río Cuarto

Córdoba

Viedma

Golfo San Matías

Península Valdés

Puerto Madryn

Golfo San Jorge

Comodoro Rivadavia

Puerto Deseado

Río Negro

PATAGONIA

Falkland Islands (Islas Malvinas)

Stanley

East Falkland U.K.

West Falkland

Azimuthal Equidistant Projection

600 MILES

600 KILOMETERS

300

300

0

0

South Georgia I. U.K.

Shag Rocks

Black Rock

ANDES

SANTIAGO

Concepción

Valdivia

Puerto Montt

Isla Grande de Chiloé

Archipiélago de los Chonos

I. Wellington

Balmaceda

Río Gallegos

Punta Arenas

Estrecho de Magallanes

Isla Grande de Tierra del Fuego

Ushuaia

Cabo de Hornos (Cape Horn)

TROPIC OF CAPRICORN

Angamos

Antofagasta

Isla San Ambrosio

Isla San Félix Chile

Islas Juan Fernández Chile

PACIFIC

OCEAN

57

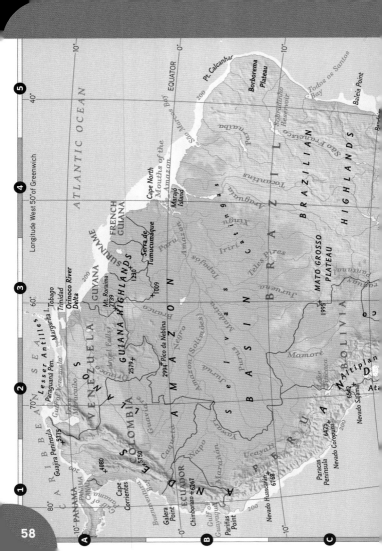

ATLANTIC OCEAN

Longitude West 50° of Greenwich

EQUATOR

Pt. Calcanhar

Borborema Plateau

Todos os Santos Bay

Sobradinho Reservoir

Baleia Point

São Marcos Bay

Mouths of the Amazon

Cape North

Marajó Island

B R A Z I L I A N

São Francisco

Parnaíba

Tocantins

Araguaia

Xingu

Iriri

Tapajós

Teles Pires

H I G H L A N D S

MATO GROSSO PLATEAU

1995

Juruena

Paraguay

Pantanal

B O L I V I A

Altiplano

Nevado Sajama 6542

Ata

Lake Titicaca

Mamoré

P E R U

6425 Nevado Coropuna

Paracas Peninsula

Nevado Huascarán 6768

Ucayali

Madre de Dios

A M A Z O N

B A S I N

S e l v a s

Madeira

Purus

Juruá

Javari

Marañón

Napo

Yavari

ECUADOR

Chimborazo 6267

Gulf of Guayaquil

Galera Point

Pariñas Point

Buenaventura Bay

Cape Corrientes

4080

E S

C O L O M B I A

5750

Caquetá

Guaviare

Vaupés

Japurá

Negro

Branco

Pico da Neblina 2994

2579

GUIANA HIGHLANDS

Mt. Roraima 2739

Angel Falls

Orinoco

V E N E Z U E L A

70°N

Guajira Peninsula 5775

Paraguaná Pen.

Gulf of Venezuela

Lake Maracaibo

Orinoco River Delta

Trinidad

Tobago

Margarita I.

Lesser Antilles

C A R I B B E A N   S E A

PANAMA

CANAL

Gulf of Panama

GUYANA

SURINAME

FRENCH GUIANA

Serra de Tumucumaque

1030

Serra

1009

Serra dos Parecis

A   B   C

1   2   3   4   5

Cape Frio

Cape Santa Marta Grande

ATLANTIC OCEAN

Iguaçu Falls

Palos Lagoon

Punta del Este
River Plate
Cape San Antonio

Magotes Point

URUGUAY

Blanca Bay

San Matías Gulf

Valdés Peninsula

Cape Tres Puntas

Gulf of San Jorge

Laguna del Carbón
-105 m
(-344 ft) South America
Lowest point in

East Falkland

West Falkland

Falkland Islands

South Georgia

Shag Rocks

Black Rock

Azimuthal Equidistant Projection

600 MILES

300

600 KILOMETERS

0 · 300 · 600

ARGENTINA

P A M P A S

Gran Chaco

Río Negro

P A T A G O N I A

Cape Horn

Tierra del Fuego

Magellan Strait

Llullaillaco Volcano 6723

6880

6380

Domuyo Volcano 4709

Cerro del Toro

Lengua de Vaca Point

Cerro Aconcagua (22831 ft) 6959
Highest point in South America

Islas Juan Fernández

Desert

Arauco Gulf

A N D E S

4035

Isla Grande de Chiloé

Chonos Archipelago

Tres Montes Peninsula

Monte San Valentín

Wellington I.

Queen Adelaida Archipelago

PACIFIC OCEAN

TROPIC OF CAPRICORN

Point

Isla San Félix

Isla San Ambrosio

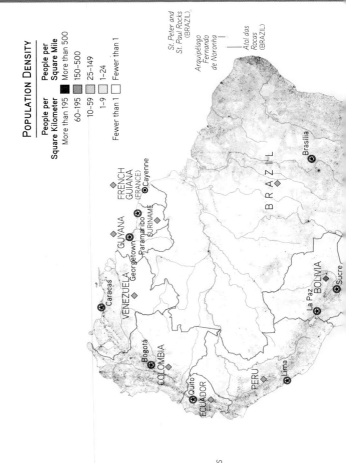

POPULATION DENSITY

People per Square Kilometer	People per Square Mile
More than 195	More than 500
60–195	150–500
10–59	25–149
1–9	1–24
Fewer than 1	Fewer than 1

Caracas
VENEZUELA
GUYANA
Georgetown
SURINAME
Paramaribo
FRENCH GUIANA (FRANCE)
Cayenne
Bogotá
COLOMBIA
Quito
ECUADOR
PERU
Lima
BRAZIL
Brasília
La Paz
BOLIVIA
Sucre

GALÁPAGOS ISLANDS (ECUADOR)

St. Peter and St. Paul Rocks (BRAZIL)

Arquipélago Fernando de Noronha

Atol das Rocas (BRAZIL)

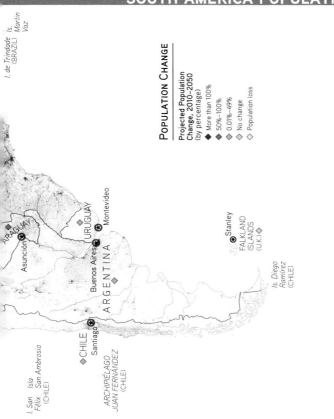

I. de Trindade
(BRAZIL)

Is. Martin
Vaz

POPULATION CHANGE

**Projected Population
Change, 2010–2050**
(by percentage)

◆ More than 100%
◆ 50%–100%
◆ 0.01%–49%
◇ No change
◇ Population loss

PARAGUAY

Asunción

URUGUAY

Montevideo

A R G E N T I N A

Buenos Aires

●Stanley

FALKLAND
ISLANDS
(U.K.)◇

Is. Diego
Ramírez
(CHILE)

CHILE
Santiago

I. San
Félix
(CHILE)

Isla
San Ambrosio

ARCHIPIÉLAGO
JUAN FERNÁNDEZ
(CHILE)

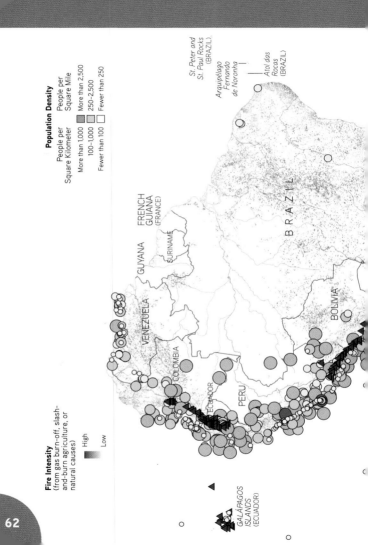

Fire Intensity
(from gas burn-off, slash-and-burn agriculture, or natural causes)

High

Low

Population Density

People per Square Kilometer	People per Square Mile
More than 1,000	More than 2,500
100–1,000	250–2,500
Fewer than 100	Fewer than 250

GUYANA

VENEZUELA

FRENCH GUIANA (FRANCE)

SURINAME

COLOMBIA

ECUADOR

PERU

B R A Z I L

BOLIVIA

GALÁPAGOS ISLANDS (ECUADOR)

St. Peter and St. Paul Rocks (BRAZIL)

Arquipélago Fernando de Noronha

Atol das Rocas (BRAZIL)

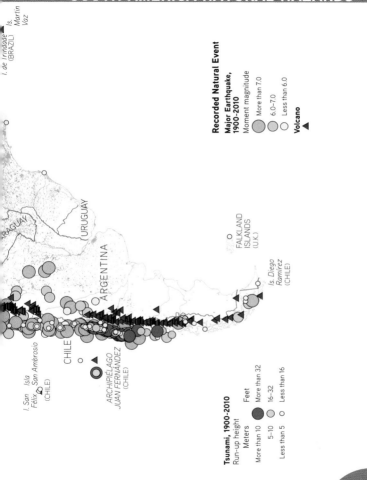

Recorded Natural Event

Major Earthquake, 1900-2010
Moment magnitude

○ More than 7.0
○○○ 6.0-7.0
○ Less than 6.0

Volcano
▲

Tsunami, 1900-2010
Run-up height

Meters	Feet
More than 10	More than 32
5-10	16-32
Less than 5	Less than 16

I. de Irindade (BRAZIL)

Is. Martin Vaz

PARAGUAY

URUGUAY

ARGENTINA

CHILE

I. San Félix

Isla San Ambrosio (CHILE)

ARCHIPIÉLAGO JUAN FERNÁNDEZ (CHILE)

FALKLAND ISLANDS (U.K.)

Is. Diego Ramírez (CHILE)

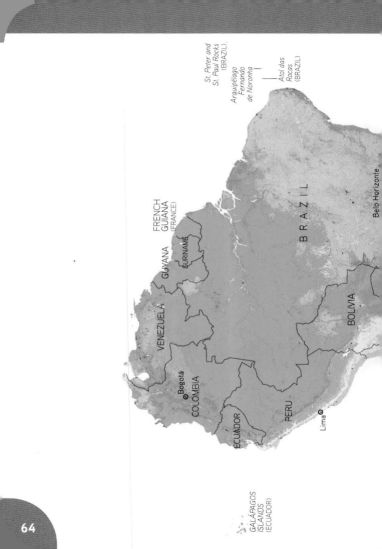

St. Peter and
St. Paul Rocks
(BRAZIL)

Arquipélago
Fernando
de Noronha

Atol das
Rocas
(BRAZIL)

FRENCH
GUIANA
(FRANCE)

GUYANA

SURINAME

VENEZUELA

B R A Z I L

Belo Horizonte

BOLIVIA

Bogotá

COLOMBIA

ECUADOR

PERU

Lima

GALÁPAGOS
ISLANDS
(ECUADOR)

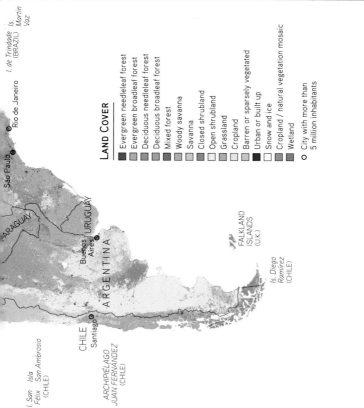

LAND COVER

- Evergreen needleleaf forest
- Evergreen broadleaf forest
- Deciduous needleleaf forest
- Deciduous broadleaf forest
- Mixed forest
- Woody savanna
- Savanna
- Closed shrubland
- Open shrubland
- Grassland
- Cropland
- Barren or sparsely vegetated
- Urban or built up
- Snow and ice
- Cropland / natural vegetation mosaic
- Wetland
- ○ City with more than 5 million inhabitants

I. de Trindade Is.
(BRAZIL) Martin Vaz

Rio de Janeiro

São Paulo

PARAGUAY

Buenos Aires URUGUAY

ARGENTINA

FALKLAND ISLANDS
(U.K.)

Is. Diego Ramírez
(CHILE)

CHILE
Santiago

I. San Isla
Félix San Ambrosio
(CHILE)

ARCHIPIÉLAGO
JUAN FERNÁNDEZ
(CHILE)

SOUTH AMERICA CLIMATE

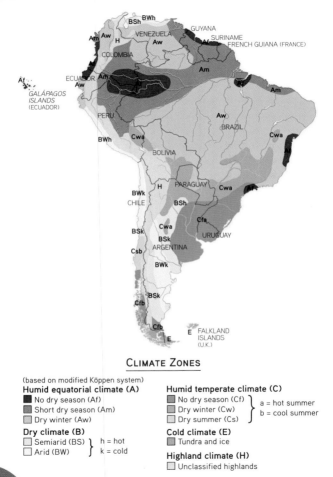

CLIMATE ZONES

(based on modified Köppen system)

Humid equatorial climate (A)
- ■ No dry season (Af)
- ■ Short dry season (Am)
- □ Dry winter (Aw)

Dry climate (B)
- □ Semiarid (BS) } h = hot
- □ Arid (BW) } k = cold

Humid temperate climate (C)
- □ No dry season (Cf)
- □ Dry winter (Cw) } a = hot summer
- □ Dry summer (Cs) } b = cool summer

Cold climate (E)
- ■ Tundra and ice

Highland climate (H)
- □ Unclassified highlands

WATER AVAILABILITY

(in millimeters per-person
per-year)

- More than 750
- 251–750
- 26–250
- Less than 26

Azimuthal Equidistant Projection

0   200   400 MILES

0   200   400 KILOMETERS

53

60°

GRENADA

Dragon's Mouths

Isla de Margarita

•Cumaná

TRINIDAD AND TOBAGO

Port of Spain

•Maturín

Serpent's Mouth

ATLANTIC

OCEAN

50°

Orinoco

Ciudad Guayana

•Ciudad Bolívar

E L A

Caura

Boca Grande

•Morawhanna
Shell Beach

Cuyuni

G U Y A N A

Georgetown
•Nieuw
•Amsterdam

Paramaribo

Pointe Isère
Saint-Laurent du Maroni

Angel Falls

Tiboku Falls

•Luepa

Pakaraima Mts.
2739▲
Mt. Roraima

•Nieuw Nickerie

Kourou•

Cayenne

Sierra Pacaraima

79
rro Marahuaca

Uraricoera

SURINAME
+1230

Lethem•

Boa Vista•

Cottica•

FRENCH GUIANA
France

Cabo Orange

•Oiapoque

Coroline

Essequibo

Boundaries claimed by Suriname

Serra de Tumucumaque

•Calçoene

•Amapá

Cabo Norte

•Caracaraí

•Caroebé

1009
✕

Japaperi

Mapuera

Trombetas

Paru

Jari

EQUATOR

Macapá•

•Ballique

•Chaves

0°

Negro

•Barcelos

Unini

•Carvoeiro

Negro

Represa da Balbina

•Óbidos

Amazonas (Amazon)

•Gurupá

•Curralinho

•Tefé

Manaus

•Coari

•Itacoatiara

•Parintins

•Santarém

Tapajós

Iriri

Xingu

Tocantins

Represa de Tucuruí

B R A Z I L

coari

Purus

•Borba

•Itaituba

Madeira

Roosevelt

Theodore

Aripuanã

Juruena (São Manuel)

Tele Pires (São Manuel)

Iriri

Sa. da Seringa

Serra dos Carajás

•Canutama

•Manicoré

•Jacareacanga

71

•Lábrea

•Prainha

•Humaitá

•Calama

•Barra do São Manuel

Jiparaná

Madeira

•Porto Velho

Longitude West 60° of Greenwich

50°

•Cachimbo

10°

4   5   6

69

A

B

C

D

E

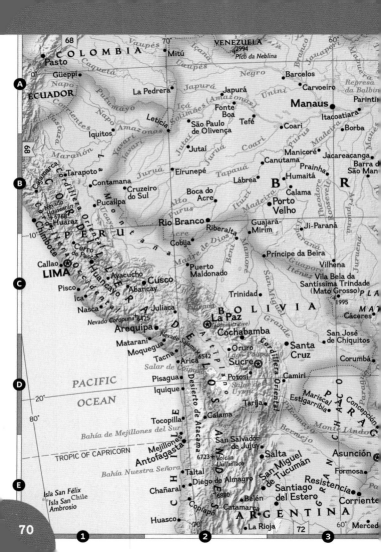

COLOMBIA
Pasto
Güeppi
ECUADOR
Napo
Iquitos
Cajamarca
Tarapoto
Contamana
Cruzeiro do Sul
Pucallpa

0°

Mitú
Icana
Vaupés
Vaupés
VENEZUELA
2994
Pico da Neblina
Negro

La Pedrera
Japurá
Japurá

Putumayo
Leticia
São Paulo de Olivença
Fonte Boa
Tefé

Barcelos
Carvoeiro
Unini
Represa da Balbin
Parinti

Manaus
Itacoatiara
Borba

Marañón
Amazonas
Solimões (Amazonas)
Coari
Purus
Madeira

Yavari
Jutaí
Juruá
Coari
Manicoré
Jacareacanga
Barra do São Man

Napo
Corrientes
Pastaza
Tigre

Eirunepé
Tapauá
Canutama
Prainha
Humaitá

Lábrea

B
R

Cordillera Oriental
CO

Boca do Acre
Alto Purus
Ituxi

Calama
Porto Velho
Theodore Roosevelt

Nevado Huascarán 6768
Huaraz

Rio Branco
Acre
Ribera/ta
Madre de Dios
Guajará-Mirim

Ji-Paraná

10°
Chimbote
PERU
Cerro de Pasco

Cobija
Beni

Príncipe da Beira
Guaporé
Iténez

Vilhena
Vila Bela da Santíssima Trindade (Mato Grosso)

Callao
LIMA
Huancayo
Ayacucho
Cusco
Abancay
Puerto Maldonado
Mamoré

1995
PLA

Pisco
Ica
Nasca
Nevado Coropuna 6425
Juliaca

Trinidad
San
Grande

Cáceres
MA

Arequipa
Nevado Sajama 6542
BOLIVIA
La Paz (administrative)
Cochabamba

San José de Chiquitos

Matarani
Moquegua
Tacna
Arica

Oruro
Lago Poopó
Sucre
Santa Cruz
Cordillera Oriental

Corumbá

Salar de Coipasa
Altiplano

PACIFIC
Pisagua
Iquique

Potosí
Salar de Uyuni

Camiri

20°
80°

Tarija

Mariscal Estigarribia

P
A
R
A
G

Concepción

OCEAN
Tocopilla
Calama

San Salvador de Jujuy

Pilcomayo
Bermejo

Monte Lindo

Bahía de Mejillones del Sur
Mejillones
Antofagasta
6723 Volcán Llullaillaco

Salta
San Miguel de Tucumán

Asunción
Formosa

TROPIC OF CAPRICORN

Bahía Nuestra Señora
Taltal

Diego de Almagro

CH
6880

Resistencia

Corriente

Isla San Félix
Isla San Chile
Ambrosio

Chañaral
Copiapó

Belén
Santiago del Estero
Catamarca
ARGENTINA

Pa

Huasco
70°
La Rioja
72
60°
Merced

1   2   3

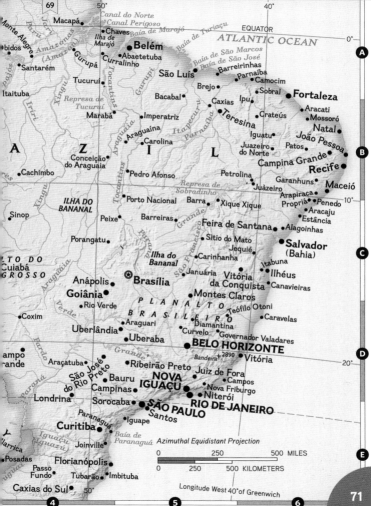

69

Canal do Norte
Canal Perigoso
Macapá
Monte Alegre
bidos
Santarém
Itaituba
•Chaves
Ilha de
Marajó
Baía de Marajó
Belém
Abaetetuba
Curralinho
Gurupá
Tucuruí
Bacabal
Marabá
Imperatriz
Araguaína
Carolina
Conceição
do Araguaia
Cachimbo
Pedro Afonso
Represa de
Tucuruí
Represa de
Sobradinho

EQUATOR
ATLANTIC OCEAN

Baía de Turiaçu
Baía de São Marcos
Baía de São José
São Luís
Barreirinhas
Parnaíba
Camocim
Sobral
Fortaleza
Aracati
Mossoró
Natal
João Pessoa
Campina Grande
Recife
Maceió
Penedo
Aracaju
Estância
Alagoinhas
Salvador
(Bahia)
Itabuna
Ilhéus
Canavieiras

São Luís
Brejo
Caxias
Ipu
Crateús
Teresina
Iguatu
Juazeiro
do Norte
Patos
Petrolina
Garanhuns
Juàzeiro
Arapiraca
Propriá

ILHA DO
BANANAL
Sinop
Porto Nacional
Barra
Xique Xique
Peixe
Barreiras
Porangatu
Grande

Feira de Santana
Sítio do Mato
Carinhanha
Januária
Vitória
da Conquista
Teófilo Otoni
Caravelas

LTO DO
Cuiabá
GROSSO
Coxim

Ilha do
Bananal

Anápolis
Goiânia
Rio Verde
Brasília
Montes Claros
PLANALTO
BRASILEIRO
Uberlândia
Araguari
Uberaba
Curvelo
Diamantina
Governador Valadares
BELO HORIZONTE
Bandeira+2890
Vitória

ampo
rande
Araçatuba
São José
do Rio Preto
Londrina
Ribeirão Preto
Bauru
Campinas
Sorocaba
SÃO PAULO
Paranaguá
Curitiba
Joinville
Iguape
Santos
Juiz de Fora
Campos
Nova Friburgo
NOVA
IGUAÇU
Niterói
RIO DE JANEIRO

Baía de
Paranaguá

Azimuthal Equidistant Projection

0   250   500 MILES
0   250   500 KILOMETERS

Longitude West 40° of Greenwich

larrica
Posadas
Passo
Fundo
Caxias do Sul
Florianópolis
Tubarão
Imbituba

50°
40°
0°
A
B
10°
C
D
20°
E

4
5
6

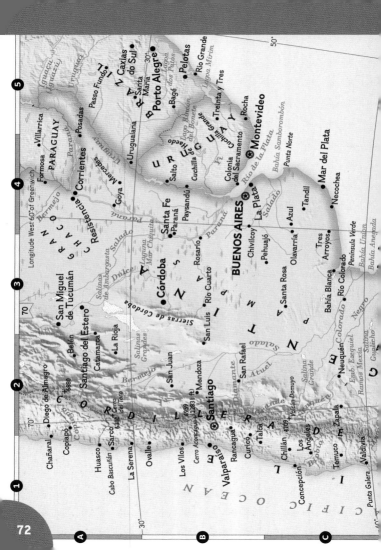

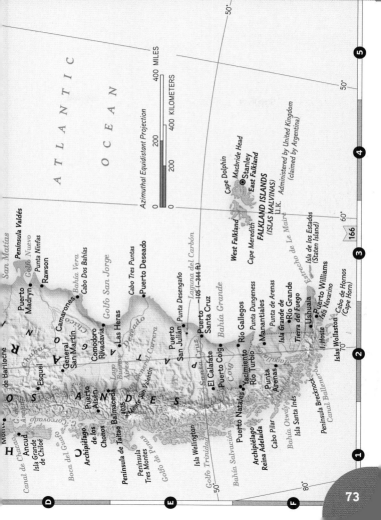

ATLANTIC

OCEAN

Azimuthal Equidistant Projection

400 MILES

400 KILOMETERS

200

200

0

0

San Matías

Península Valdés

Golfo Nuevo

Punta Ninfas

Puerto
Madryn

Rawson

Chubut

Camarones

Bahía Vera

Cabo Dos Bahías

General
San Martín

Golfo San Jorge

Comodoro
Rivadavia

Las Heras

Cabo Tres Puntas

Deseado

Puerto Deseado

Punta Desengaño

*Laguna del Carbón
-105 (-344 ft)*

Puerto
San Julián

Puerto
Santa Cruz

Bahía Grande

Santa Cruz

Río Gallegos

Punta Dungeness

Coig

Puerto Coig

Punta de Arenas

Manantiales

Puerto
Natales

Isla Grande de
Tierra del Fuego

Río Grande

Ushuaia

Cape Dolphin

Macbride Head

Stanley
East Falkland

FALKLAND ISLANDS
(ISLAS MALVINAS)
U.K.

Administered by United Kingdom
(claimed by Argentina)

West Falkland

Cape Meredith

Isla de los Estados
(Staten Island)

Estrecho de Le Maire

166

Puerto Williams

Isla
Hoste

Isla Navarino

Islas Wollaston

Cabo de Hornos
(Cape Horn)

A
N
D
E
S

S

A
N
T
A
C
R
U
Z

4035

Monte San Valentín

Lago
Buenos
Aires

El Calafate

Puerto
Yacimiento
Río Turbio

Punta
Arenas

Península Brecknock

Bahía Otway

Canal Ballenero

Isla Santa Inés

Cabo Pilar

Bahía Salvación

Golfo de Penas

Isla Trinidad

Isla Wellington

Archipiélago
Reina Adelaida

Península
Tres Montes

Península de Taitao

Golfo
de
Ancud

Chonos

Archipiélago
de los
Chonos

Aisén

Puerto
Aisén

Balmaceda

Esquel

de Bariloche

R

O

S

O

Canal de Chacao

Ancud

Isla Grande
de Chiloé

Montt

Corcovado

Boca del Guafo

H

70°

50°

80°

50°

60°

73

D   E   F

1   2   3   4   5

EUROPE

GEOGRAPHIC EXTREMES

CONTINENTAL POLITICAL FACTS

TOTAL NUMBER OF COUNTRIES: 46

LARGEST COUNTRY BY AREA: Russia
17,075,400 sq km (6,592,850 sq mi)

SMALLEST COUNTRY BY AREA:
Vatican City   0.4 sq km (0.2 sq mi)

MOST POPULOUS COUNTRY: Russia
138,740,000

LEAST POPULOUS COUNTRY: Vatican City
830

LARGEST CITIES BY POPULATION:
Moscow, Russia   10,550,000
Istanbul, Turkey   10,525,000
Paris, France   10,485,000
London, United Kingdom   8,630,000
Madrid, Spain   5,850,000

CONTINENTAL PHYSICAL FACTS

AREA: 9,947,000 sq km (3,841,000 sq mi)

HIGHEST POINT: El'brus, Russia   5,642 m
(18,510 ft)

LOWEST POINT: Caspian Sea   -28 m
(-92 ft)

LONGEST RIVERS:
Volga   3,685 km (2,290 mi)
Danube   2,848 km (1,770 mi)
Dnieper   2,285 km (1,420 mi)

LARGEST NATURAL LAKES:
Caspian Sea   371,000 sq km
(143,200 sq mi)
Lake Ladoga   17,872 sq km
(6,900 sq mi)
Lake Onega   9,842 sq km
(3,800 sq mi)

London

Paris

Madrid

VATICAN
CITY

Lake
Onega

Lake
Ladoga

R U S S I A

Volga

• Moscow

Kaliningrad
(Russia)

Dnieper

Caspian
Sea
(-92 ft) -28 m
See p. 79

Danube

İstanbul

El'brus
5,642 m
(18,510 ft)

Azimuthal Equidistant Projection

0   200   400 MILES
0   200   400 KILOMETERS

A commonly accepted division between Asia and Europe—here marked by a green line—is formed by the Ural Mountains, Ural River, Caspian Sea, Caucasus Mountains, and the Black Sea with its outlets, the Bosporus and Dardanelles.

NORWEGIAN SEA

Hólmavík • • Húnaflói
Þistilfjördur
Reykjavík ⊛ ICELAND • Akureyri
Faxaflói • Langanes
Vopnafjördur
• Höfn
Vestfjorden
Tromsø
Narvik •
Svolvær •
• Bodø
Mo i Rana •
N O R W A Y

Meridian of Greenwich (London)

Tórshavn • • Faroe Islands
Denmark
Shetland Islands
• Lerwick
Namsos •
Trondheim •
Örnsköldsvik
S C A N D I N A V I A

Isle of Lewis • Orkney Is.
Wick •
Inverness •
Moray Firth
Lillehammer •
Bergen •
Skien •
⊛
S W E D E N
Gävle •

Belfast •
Glasgow •
Edinburgh •
Kristiansand •
Oslo ⊛
Stockholm ⊛
Göteborg
Gotland

ATLANTIC OCEAN

(Baile Átha Cliath)
(ÉIRE) IRELAND
Dublin ⊛ UNITED
(Sionainn) Shannon • KINGDOM
Irish Sea
NORTH SEA
DENMARK
København ⊛
(Copenhagen)
Skagerrak
BALT

Cork • Cardiff •
(Corcaigh) Manchester •
Birmingham ⊛
CELTIC SEA
Land's End
U.K. Channel Is.
LONDON ⊛
English Channel
NETH.
Amsterdam ⊛
Hamburg •
Elbe
Gdańsk •
POL
Poznań •

Brest •
Pointe de Saint-Mathieu
Rennes •
Seine
BELG.
Bruxelles (Brussels)
LUX.
GERMANY
Berlin ⊛
Praha ⊛
(Prague)
CZECH R
(CZECHIA
Łódz •

Nantes •
Loire
PARIS ⊛
Strasbourg •
München •
(Munich)
Bratislava ⊛
Wien ⊛
(Vienna)
SLOV. HU

A Coruña •
Vigo •
BAY OF BISCAY
FRANCE
SWITZ.
LIECH.
AUSTRIA
Bordeaux •
Lyon •
Bern ⊛
Milano •
(Milan)
Ljubljana ⊛
CROAT.
Zagr
BOSN. & HERZG.
Sarajevo •

(Oporto) Porto •
Bilbao •
Pamplona •
Pyrenees
Massif Central
Rhône
Po
ADRIATIC
Podgor
MONT

Coimbra •
Toulouse •
ANDORRA
MONACO
SAN MARINO
Tiran
(Tiran
ALBA

PORTUGAL
Lisboa ⊛
(Lisbon)
Valladolid •
MADRID ⊛
Golfe du Lion
Marseille •
Corsica
VATICAN CITY ⊛
Roma ⊛
(Rome)
ITALY

Cabo de São Vicente
Setúbal •
SPAIN
Cap de Tortosa
Napoli
(Naples)

Sevilla •
Córdoba •
Valencia •
BARCELONA ⊛
Sardinia
TYRRHENIAN SEA
Palermo •

Strait of Gibraltar
(Tangier)
Cádiz •
Granada ⊛
Cartagena •
Balearic Islands
Cagliari •
Sicily •
Catania •
IONI
SEA

Longitude West of Greenwich
Casablanca •
Rabat ⊛
Tanger •
GIBRALTAR U.K.
Ceuta Sp.
Oran •
Alger ⊛
(Algiers)
Tunis ⊛
M E D I T E R R
Valletta ⊛
MALTA

MOROCCO
Fès (Fez) •
Melilla Sp.
MOROCCO
A T L A S
M O U N T A I N S
TUNISIA
ALGERIA
Longitude East 10° of Greenwich

Hammerfest
Tanafjorden 40°
Vadsø
Varangerfjorden 70°
50°
Alta
Kirkenes
Ostrov
Kolguyev
ARCTIC
CIRCLE
70°
Polnovat
Surgut
Ivalo
Murmansk
Pol.
Kanin
Indiga
Usinsk
Sos´va
Khanty-
Mansiysk
Kandalaksha
Kol´skiy
Poluostrov
Volonga
Mezen´
Pechora
Nyagan
Severoural´sk
Tobol´sk
A

Kemi
Keret´
BELOYE
Arkhangel´sk
(Archangel)
Sosnogorsk
Berezniki
Yekaterinburg
Tyumen´
Irtysh
70°

Oulu
Kem´
Onezhskaya
Guba
Onega
Zheleznodorozhnyy
Syktyvkar
Gayny
Perm´
A

FINLAND
Petrozavodsk
Plesetsk
Kotlas
Kamskoye
Vdkhr.
Kirov
Kama
Chelyabinsk

Vaasa
Onezhskoye
Ozero
Konosha
Kazan´
Ufa
Rüdnyy
B

Helsinki
(Helsingfors)
Ladozhskoye
Ozero
Nizhniy
Novgorod
Magnitogorsk

rku
Turku
Gulf of Finland
Sankt-Peterburg
(St.Petersburg)
Yaroslavl´
R
U
S
S
I
A
Ul´yanovsk
Samara
Orenburg
Orsk
50°

ESTONIA
Tallinn
Pskov
Rybinskoye
Vdkhr.
Vladimir
Volga
Oral

LATVIA
Rīga
Tver
MOSKVA
(Moscow)
Saransk
Balakovo
Oktyabr´sk
Aqtöbe
KAZAKHSTAN
60°

THUANIA
LITHUANIA
Smolensk
Tula
Penza
Saratov
Shalqar

alingrad
Kaliningrad
Russia
Vilnius
Orel
Tambov
Ural
C

D
Minsk
BELARUS
Homyel´
Kursk
Voronezh
Volgogradskoye
Vdkhr.
Aral Sea

Warszawa
(Warsaw)
Pinsk
Marshes
Sumy
Don
Volgograd
(Stalingrad)
Caspian Depression
Beyneu

Kyiv
(Kiev)
Kharkiv
UZB.

L´viv
Dnipro
UKRAINE
Astrakhan´
Aqtau

IA
udapest
Budapest
Dnipropetrovs´k
Donets´k
Oral
CASPIAN
Zhangaözen

MOLD.
Chişinău
Sea of
Azov
Krasnodar
Stavropol´
Garabogaz
TURKM.
40°

ROMANIA
Odesa
CRIMEA
Caucasus Mts.
Groznyy
Bakı
(Baku)

RBIA
Beograd
(Belgrade)
Bucureşti
(Bucharest)
Sevastopol´
Sochi
GEORGIA
T´bilisi
(Tbilisi)
SEA
D

os.
Prishtina (Priština)
BULGARIA
BLACK
SEA
ARMENIA
AZERB.
Yerevan
Azerb. Neftçala

Skopje
Sofiya (Sofia)
İSTANBUL
(Constantinople)
Trabzon
Erzurum
Van
Tabrīz
TEHRĀN
(Tehran)

ACED.
Thessaloníki
Kuzey Anadolu Dağları
Van
Qom
E

GREECE
Bursa
Ankara (Angora)
TURKEY
IRAN

Athína
(Athens)
İzmir
(Smyrna)
Konya
Adana
Gaziantep
Al Mawşil
Kirkūk
Hamadān
Zagros Mountains
50°

eloponnesus
Antalya
Toros Dağları
Halab
(Aleppo)
Tigris
Euphrates

Kalamáta
Ródos
(Rhodes)
CYPRUS
Hims
(Homs)
SYRIA
Baghdad

Crete
Iráklio (Candia)
Nicosia
(Lefkosia)
LEBANON
Dimashq
(Damascus)
IRAQ

AN
SEA
30°
Sea of
Crete
AEGEAN SEA

77

60°
(North Cape) Horn
Húnaflói
30°
20°
10°
0°
70°
10°

Faxaflói
ICELAND
Thistilfjördur
NORWEGIAN SEA

Langanes
Vestfjorden

A

Azimuthal Equidistant Projection

0   200   400 MILES
0   200   400 KILOMETERS

30°

Faroe
Islands

Meridian of Greenwich
(London)

200

Shetland
Islands

Galdhøpiggen
2469

S C A N D I

A commonly accepted division
between Asia and Europe—here
marked by an orange line—is
formed by the Ural Mountains,
Ural River, Caspian Sea,
Caucasus Mountains, and the
Black Sea with its outlets, the
Bosporus and Dardanelles.

B

Isle of Lewis
Orkney Is.

200

Hebrides
Moray Firth

50°

IRELAND
(EIRE)

Ben Nevis
1343

BRITISH
ISLES

Great Britain

NORTH
SEA

Skagerrak
Kattegat

JUTLAND

Gotland

BALT

UNITED KINGDOM

DENMARK

1041

Irish
Sea

C

A T L A N T I C
20°

CELTIC
SEA

Land's End

O C E A N

Point Saint-Mathieu

English Channel
Channel Is.

NETH.

N O R T H E

POL

Elbe

Oder

BELG.

GERMANY

Rhine

LUX.

CZECH REP.
(CZECHIA)

Seine

LIECH.

SLO

Loire

SWITZ.

AUSTRIA

HUN

Cape Finisterre

200

BAY OF
BISCAY

FRANCE

A L P S

SLOV

Mt. Blanc
4810

Po

CROATIA

40°

D

PORTUGAL

Douro

Massif
Central

Pyrenees

ANDORRA

Rhône

BOSN. &
HERZG.

MON

Cape St. Vincent

IBERIAN

Duero

SPAIN

PENINSULA

Golf of
Lions

Corsica

A p e n n i n e s

ITALY

ADRIATIC
SEA

ALBAN

Cape Tortosa

Strait of Gibraltar

Cape Gata

Balearic Islands

Sardinia

Vesuvius
1281

TYRRHENIAN
SEA

Longitude West
of Greenwich

10°

E

200

M E D I T E R R A N

Sicily
Etna
3315

IONIA
SEA

MOROCCO

A L G E R I A

A T L A S   M O U N T A I N S

TUNISIA

MALTA

Longitude East 10° of Greenwich

78

1   2   3

North Cape
Nordkapp
Tanafjorden 40° Varangerfjorden 70° 50°
BARENTS SEA
60°
Kolguyev I.
Kanin Pen.
ARCTIC CIRCLE
Narodnaya 1895
West Siberian Plain
URAL MOUNTAINS
SIBERIA
Kola Peninsula
WHITE SEA
Chesha Bay
Mezen Bay
Timan Ridge
Kanin Reservoir
Irtysh
Suomen Ridge
FINLAND
Salpaus Ridge
Dvina Bay
Onega Bay
Lake Onega
70°
ESTONIA
Gulf of Finland
Lake Ladoga
Rybinsk Res.
EUROPEAN PLAIN
RUSSIA
Kama
50°
LATVIA
Volga
Ural
LITHUANIA
BELARUS
Pinsk Marshes
Don
Volgograd Reservoir
KAZAKHSTAN
60°
Caspian Depression
Aral Sea
Dnieper
Volga
Ustyurt Plateau
UZB.
Carpathian Mountains
UKRAINE
Sea of Azov
Caspian Sea:
Surface elevation
(−92 ft) −28
Lowest point
in Europe
MOLD.
CRIMEA
CASPIAN SEA
Garabogaz Bay
TURKM.
ROMANIA
2543
Caucasus Mountains
40°
SERBIA
BALKAN
BULGARIA
BLACK SEA
Bosporus
Elbrus 5642
(18510 ft)
Highest point
in Europe
GEORGIA
ARM. AZERBAIJAN
200
MACED.
PENINSULA
2917
Olympus
Kuzey Anadolu Dağları
Dardanelles
Sea of Marmara
ANATOLIA
TURKEY
(ASIA MINOR)
Tigris
IRAN
GREECE
Peloponnesus
AEGEAN SEA
3585
Taurus Mts.
SYRIA
Zagros Mountains
50°
Sea of Crete
Crete
Rhodes
CYPRUS 30°
LEBANON
Euphrates
IRAQ
MEDITERRANEAN SEA
40°

A
B
C
D
E

4   5   6

79

Reykjavík
ICELAND

FAROE ISLANDS
(DENMARK)

NORWAY

SWEDEN

FINLAN

Helsinki

Oslo

Tallinn

Stockholm   ES

IRELAND

U.K.

DEN.

Riga

Dublin

Copenhagen

RUSS.

LITH

Vilnius

London

NETH.

Amsterdam

Berlin

Warsaw

BELG.

POLAND

CHANNEL IS.
(U.K.)

Brussels

GERMANY

Paris

LUX.

LIECH.

Prague

CZECH
REP.

SLOVAKIA

FRANCE

Bern

Vienna

Bratislava

SWITZ.

AUSTRIA

Budapest

HUNGARY

Ljubljana

SLOV.

Zagreb

PORTUGAL

ANDORRA

MONACO

SAN MARINO

CROATIA

BOSN. &
HERZG.

SERBIA

Belgrade

Sarajevo

Sofia

Lisbon

Madrid

SPAIN

ITALY

Rome

Podgorica

MONTENEGRO

Tirana

Prishtina

KOS.

Skopje

MACED.

VATICAN
CITY

ALBANIA

GREEC

GIBRALTAR
(U.K.)

MALTA   Valletta

80

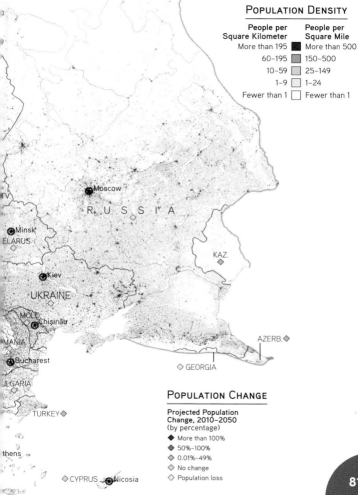

POPULATION DENSITY

People per Square Kilometer	People per Square Mile
More than 195	More than 500
60–195	150–500
10–59	25–149
1–9	1–24
Fewer than 1	Fewer than 1

POPULATION CHANGE

Projected Population Change, 2010–2050 (by percentage)

- More than 100%
- 50%–100%
- 0.01%–49%
- No change
- Population loss

81

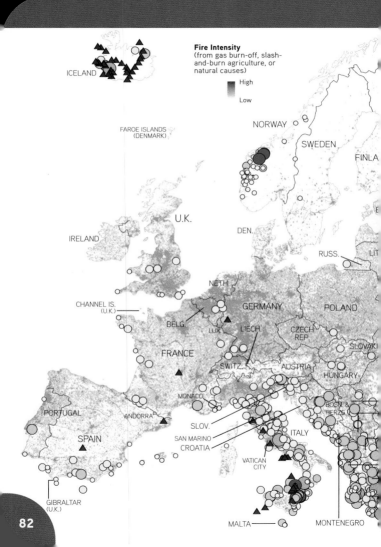

Fire Intensity
(from gas burn-off, slash-and-burn agriculture, or natural causes)

High

Low

ICELAND

FAROE ISLANDS
(DENMARK)

NORWAY

SWEDEN

FINLA

U.K.

IRELAND

DEN.

RUSS.

LIT

NETH

GERMANY

POLAND

CHANNEL IS.
(U.K.)

BELG.

LUX.

LIECH.

CZECH
REP

SLOVAKI

FRANCE

SWITZ.

AUSTRIA

HUNGARY

MONACO

SLOV.

SAN MARINO

CROATIA

BOSN. &
HERZG.

ITALY

PORTUGAL

ANDORRA

SPAIN

VATICAN
CITY

GIBRALTAR
(U.K.)

MALTA

MONTENEGRO

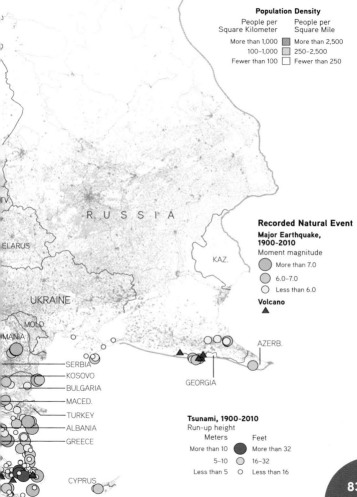

Population Density

People per Square Kilometer		People per Square Mile
More than 1,000		More than 2,500
100–1,000		250–2,500
Fewer than 100		Fewer than 250

RUSSIA

KAZ.

ELARUS

UKRAINE

MOLD.

MANIA

SERBIA
KOSOVO
BULGARIA
MACED.
TURKEY
ALBANIA
GREECE

GEORGIA

AZERB.

CYPRUS

Recorded Natural Event

Major Earthquake, 1900–2010

Moment magnitude

More than 7.0

6.0–7.0

Less than 6.0

Volcano ▲

Tsunami, 1900–2010

Run-up height

Meters		Feet
More than 10		More than 32
5–10		16–32
Less than 5	○	Less than 16

ICELAND

FAROE ISLANDS
(DENMARK)

NORWAY

SWEDEN

FINLAN

ES

U.K.

DEN.

RUSS.

LIT

IRELAND

NETH.

London

BELG.

CHANNEL IS.
(U.K.)

GERMANY

POLAND

Paris

LUX.

LIECH.

CZECH
REP.

SLOVAKIA

FRANCE

SWITZ.

AUSTRIA

HUNGARY

SLOV.

CROATIA

MONACO

BOSN. &
HERZG.

SERBIA

PORTUGAL

ANDORRA

SAN MARINO

Madrid

KOS.

SPAIN

Barcelona

ITALY

MONTENEGRO

MACED.

ALBANIA

VATICAN
CITY

GREEC

GIBRALTAR
(U.K.)

MALTA

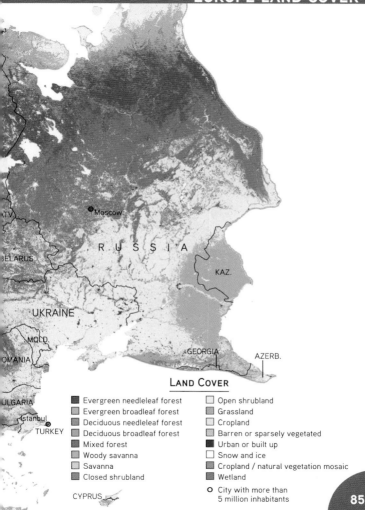

Land Cover

- ■ Evergreen needleleaf forest
- ■ Evergreen broadleaf forest
- ■ Deciduous needleleaf forest
- ■ Deciduous broadleaf forest
- ■ Mixed forest
- ■ Woody savanna
- ■ Savanna
- ■ Closed shrubland

- □ Open shrubland
- ■ Grassland
- ■ Cropland
- ■ Barren or sparsely vegetated
- ■ Urban or built up
- □ Snow and ice
- ■ Cropland / natural vegetation mosaic
- ■ Wetland

- ○ City with more than 5 million inhabitants

85

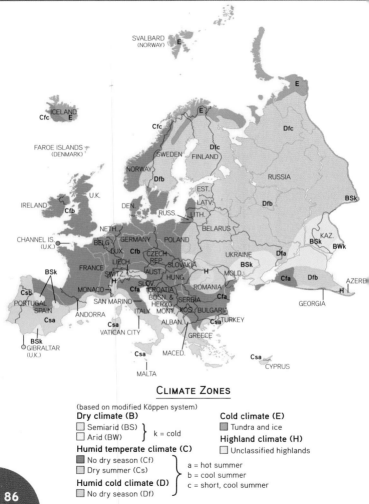

CLIMATE ZONES

(based on modified Köppen system)

Dry climate (B)
- Semiarid (BS)
- Arid (BW) } k = cold

Humid temperate climate (C)
- No dry season (Cf)
- Dry summer (Cs)

Humid cold climate (D)
- No dry season (Df)

Cold climate (E)
- Tundra and ice

Highland climate (H)
- Unclassified highlands

a = hot summer
b = cool summer
c = short, cool summer

SVALBARD
(NORWAY)

ICELAND

FAROE ISLANDS
(DENMARK)

SWEDEN   FINLAND

NORWAY

RUSSIA

U.K.

EST.

LATV.

IRELAND

DEN.

RUSS.   LITH.

BELARUS

NETH.

CHANNEL IS.
(U.K.)

BELG.   GERMANY   POLAND

KAZ.

LUX.

CZECH
REP.

LIECH.

SLOVAKIA

UKRAINE

FRANCE

SWITZ.   AUST.

HUNG.

MOLD.

SLOV.

AZERB.

CROATIA

ROMANIA

'PORTUGAL

BOSN. &
HERZG.   SERBIA

GEORGIA

SPAIN

ANDORRA   ITALY

MONT.   KOS.   BULGARIA

ALBAN.   TURKEY

GIBRALTAR
(U.K.)

MONACO

SAN MARINO

GREECE

VATICAN CITY

MACED.

CYPRUS

MALTA

WATER AVAILABILITY

(in millimeters per-person
per-year)

- More than 750
- 251–750
- 26–250
- Less than 26
- No data available

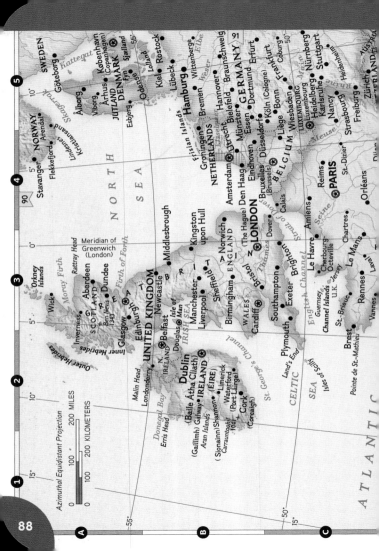

SWEDEN

Kattegat

Göteborg

NORWAY

Arendal

Stavanger

Flekkefjord

Kristiansand

Skagerrak

Ålborg

Viborg

Århus

DENMARK

JUTLAND

Esbjerg

København
(Copenhagen)

Odense

Fyn

Sjælland

Lolland

Kiel

Lübeck

Rostock

Wittenberge

Weser

Elbe

91

Hamburg

Bremen

Braunschweig

Wittenberg

Hannover

Bielefeld

GERMANY

Erfurt

Nürnberg

Coburg

Stuttgart

Münster

Dortmund

Düsseldorf

Essen

Köln (Cologne)

Bonn

Frankfurt

Wiesbaden

Main

Heidelberg

Karlsruhe

AUSTRIA

Friesian Islands

Groningen

Utrecht

Amsterdam

NETHERLANDS

Eindhoven

Den Haag
(The Hague)

BELGIUM

Bruxelles
(Brussels)

Liège

LUXEMBOURG

Luxembourg

Nancy

Strasbourg

Freiburg

Zürich

Rhine

Heidenheim

Meuse

NORTH

SEA

90

Orkney
Islands

Wick

Rattray Head

Meridian of
Greenwich
(London)

Middlesbrough

Kingston
upon Hull

Norwich

Calais

Strait of Dover

Dover

Amiens

Reims

St-Dizier

Dun

PARIS

Seine

Orléans

Chartres

Le Mans

Laval

Rennes

Vannes

St-Brieuc

Brest

Pointe de St-Mathieu

Le Havre

Cherbourg

Octeville

Jersey

Guernsey

Channel Islands
U.K.

Inverness

Moray Firth

Aberdeen

Dundee

Ben Nevis
1343

SCOTLAND

Glasgow

Edinburgh

Firth of Forth

Newcastle

Outer Hebrides

Inner Hebrides

Malin Head

Londonderry

N.
IRELAND

Belfast

Isle of
Man

Douglas

IRISH SEA

Liverpool

Manchester

Sheffield

Birmingham

ENGLAND

Bristol

Cardiff

WALES

UNITED KINGDOM

Donegal Bay

Erris Head

Galway
(Gaillimh)

Aran Islands

Shannon
(Sionainn)

Limerick

IRELAND
(EIRE)

Dublin
(Baile Átha Cliath)

Waterford
(Port Láirge)

Cork
(Corcaigh)

Carrauntoohil
1041

St. George's Channel

CELTIC

SEA

Isles of Scilly

Land's End

Plymouth

Exeter

Southampton

Brighton

English Channel

ATLANTIC

Azimuthal Equidistant Projection

200 MILES

200 KILOMETERS

100

0

100

88

OCEAN

BAY OF BISCAY

FRANCE

Lausanne
Genève
Mont Blanc 4810
Lyon
Vichy
Limoges
Brive
Bordeaux
La Rochelle
Biarritz
Toulouse
MASSIF CENTRAL
Loire
Garonne
Valence
Avignon
Nîmes
Arles
Marseille
Toulon
Marcantour 3143
Cannes
Nice
Îles d'Hyères
Golfe du Lion

ITALY
Milano (Milan)
Torino (Turin)
Genova (Genoa)
La Spezia
LIGURIAN SEA
Bastia
CORSICA France
Ajaccio
Porto-Vecchio
MONACO

SARDINIA Italy
Sassari
Oristano
Cagliari

MEDITERRANEAN SEA

Constantine
(Bône) Annaba
Skikda
Bejaïa (Bougie)
Sétif
ATLAS MOUNTAINS
Dellys Oujou
Bouira
Médéa
Alger (Algiers)
Blida
Chlef
Mostaganem
Oran

Cap de Creus
PYRENEES
Pico de Aneto 3404 ANDORRA
Perpignan
Narbonne
BARCELONA
Castellón de la Plana
Tortosa
Cabo de la Nao
Ebro
Lleida
Zaragoza

Torre de Cerredo 2648
A Coruña
Cabo Finisterre
Santiago de Compostela
Vigo
Ourense
Braga
Porto (Oporto)
Coimbra
PORTUGAL
Lisboa (Lisbon)
Setúbal
Lagos
Cabo de São Vicente
Faro

Gijón
Oviedo
Santander
Bilbao
Donostia-San Sebastián
Burgos
Logroño
Valladolid
Salamanca
Duero
SPAIN
MADRID
Cuenca
Cáceres
Badajoz
Tajo (Tagus)
Mulhacén 3481
Linares
Córdoba
Sevilla (Seville)
Huelva
Jerez de la Frontera
Cádiz
Guadalquivir
Guadiana
Guadiana
Duero

Valencia
Albacete
Murcia
Lorca
Alicante (Alacant)
Cartagena
Cabo de Gata
Almería
Granada
Málaga
ALBORÁN
Gibraltar U.K.
Ceuta Sp.
Tánger (Tangier)
Tétouan (Tetuán)
Melilla Sp.
Strait of Gibraltar
MOROCCO

BALEARIC ISLANDS
Menorca (Minorca)
Mahón
Palma de Mallorca
Mallorca (Majorca)
Ibiza (Iviza)
BALEARIC SEA

92
SARDINIA Italy 40°
Longitude East 5° of Greenwich
Longitude West 5° of Greenwich
138

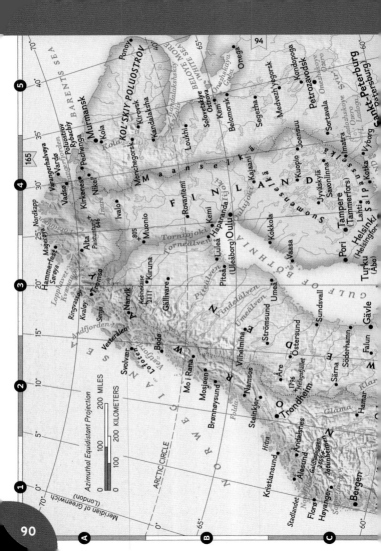

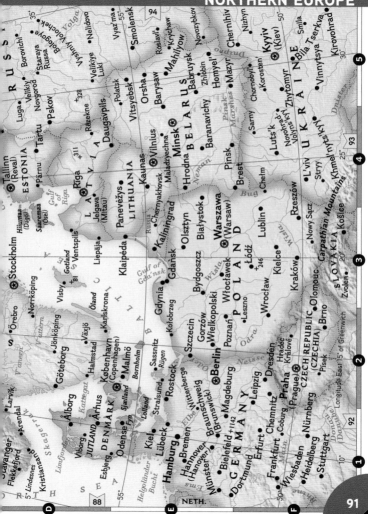

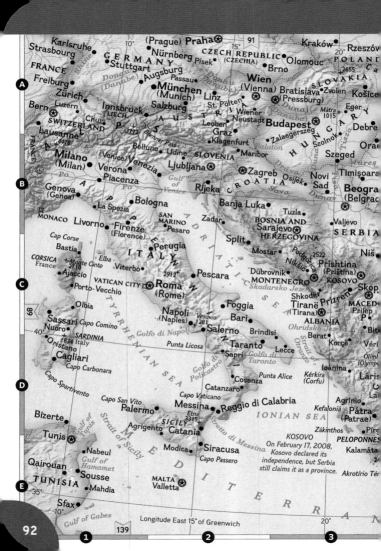

Karlsruhe
Strasbourg
FRANCE
Freiburg
Zürich
Bern
Luzern
SWITZERLAND
4478
Lausanne
FRANCE
Milano
(Milan)
Genova
(Genoa)
MONACO
Livorno
Cap Corse
Bastia
CORSICA
France
Ajaccio
Porto-Vecchio
Olbia
Sassari
Nuoro
SARDINIA
1834 Italy
Oristano
Cagliari
Capo Carbonara
Capo Spartivento
Bizerte
Tunis
TUNISIA
Qairouan
Sfax

(Prague) Praha
Nürnberg
Pisek
GERMANY
Stuttgart
Augsburg
Passau
München
(Munich)
Linz
Salzburg
St. Pölten
Innsbruck
LIECH.
3772
Chur
Brenner Pass
Belluno
Udine
Verona
Venezia
(Venice)
Piacenza
Po
Bologna
La Spezia
SAN MARINO
Pesaro
Firenze
(Florence)
Perugia
Elba
Monte Cinto
2710
Viterbo
2912
Roma
(Rome)
VATICAN CITY
Napoli
(Naples)
Vesuvio
1281
Golfo di Napoli
Salerno
Punta Licosa
Golfo di Policastro
Sapri
Cosenza
Punta Alice
Catanzaro
Capo Vaticano
Capo San Vito
Palermo
SICILY
Agrigento
Catania
Etna
3315
Modica
Siracusa
Capo Passero
Nabeul
Sousse
Mahdia
MALTA
Valletta

CZECH REPUBLIC
(CZECHIA)
Brno
Olomouc
Wien
(Vienna)
Bratislava
(Pressburg)
Zvolen
Mátra
1015
Wiener
Neustadt
Leoben
Graz
Budapest
Klagenfurt
Maribor
Zalaegerszeg
Balaton
Szolnok
SLOVENIA
Ljubljana
Zagreb
Osijek
CROATIA
Rijeka
Sava
Novi
Sad
Banja Luka
Tuzla
Zadar
BOSNIA AND
HERZEGOVINA
Sarajevo
Split
Mostar
Podgorica
2522
Nikšić
MONTENEGRO
Dubrovnik
Skadarsko Jezero
Shkodër
Tiranë
(Tirana)
ALBANIA
Berat
Foggia
Bari
Brindisi
Lecce
Taranto
Golfo di
Taranto
Strait of
Otranto
Ohridsko Jezero
Korçë
Ioánina
Kérkira
(Corfu)
Messina
Reggio di Calabria
Stretto di Messina
IONIAN SEA
Kefaloniá
Zákinthos

Kraków
Rzeszów
POLAND
2655
SLOVAKIA
Košice
Eger
Debre
Szeged
Oradea
Timişoara
SERBIA
Valjevo
Beograd
(Belgrade)
Niš
Prishtina
(Priština)
KOSOVO
Prizren
Skop
MACED
Prilep
P
Bit
Véri
Olimb
(Olymp
Lárisa
Agrínio
La
Pátra
(Patrae)
Pírg
PELOPONNE
Kalamáta
Akrotírio Tér

A
B
C
D
E

1
2
3

SEA
ADRIATIC
TYRRHENIAN SEA
MEDITERRANEAN

Gulf of
Venice

Golfo di
Napoli

KOSOVO
On February 17, 2008,
Kosovo declared its
independence, but Serbia
still claims it as a province.

Gulf of
Tunis
Strait of Sicily
Gulf of
Hamamet
Gulf of Gabes

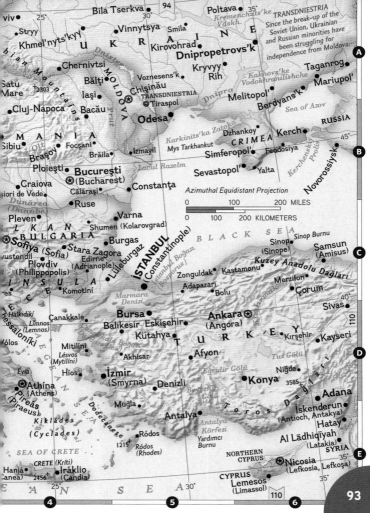

viv
Stryy
Khmel'nyts'kyy
U   K   R   A   I   N   E
Bila Tserkva
94
Poltava   35°
Kremenchuts'ke   Vdskh.
TRANSDNIESTRIA
Since the break-up of the Soviet Union, Ukrainian and Russian minorities have been struggling for independence from Moldova.

Vinnytsya
Smila
Kirovohrad
Dnipropetrovs'k
Kryvyy Rih

Chernivtsi
Bălţi
MOLDOVA
Voznesens'k
Taganrog
Satu Mare   2303
Iaşi   Chişinău
Dnister
Mariupol'
Cluj-Napoca
Bacău
TRANSDNIESTRIA
Tiraspol
Melitopol'
Berdyans'k
RUSSIA

Odesa
Dnipro
Sea of Azov
M   A   N   I   A
Focşani
Karkinits'ka Zatoka
Kakhovs'ke Vodokhranilishche
Dzhankoy
Kerch
Sibiu
Prut
Braşov
Brăila
Izmayil
Mys Tarkhankut
CRIMEA
Simferopol'
Feodosiya
45°
Novorossiysk
Ploieşti
Bucureşti (Bucharest)
Lacul Razelm
Sevastopol'
Yalta
Kerchens'
Proliv
B

Craiova
siori de Vede
Călăraşi
Azimuthal Equidistant Projection
Dunărea (Dunăre)
Ruse
Constanţa
0   100   200 MILES
0   100   200 KILOMETERS

Pleven
Varna
BLACK   SEA
Sinop Burnu
L   K   A   N
Shumen (Kolarovgrad)
Sinop (Sinope)
Samsun (Amisus)
Sofiya
Burgas
C
BULGARIA
Stara Zagora
İSTANBUL
(Constantinople)
Zonguldak
Kuzey Anadolu Dağları
ustendil
Sofiya (Sofia)
Edirne (Adrianople)
Lüleburgaz
İstanbul Boğazı
(Bosporus)
Kastamonu
Merzifon
Çorum
Plovdiv (Philippopolis)
INSULA
Komotini
Adapazarı
Bolu
Sivas
es
Halkidiki
Marmara Denizi
40°
Thessaloniki
Límnos (Lemnos)
Çanakkale
Bursa
Ankara (Angora)
110
Balıkesir
Eskişehir
Kırşehir
Kayseri
ólos
Mitilíni
Lésvos (Mytilíni)
Kütahya
T   U   R   K   E   Y
D
Évia
Akhisar
Híos
İzmir (Smyrna)
Afyon
Eğridir Gölü
Niğde   3585
Konya
Tuz Gölü
Athína (Athens)
reás (Piraeus)
Denizli
Beyşehir Gölü
Adana
Kikládes (Cyclades)
Muğla
Dodecanese
Antalya
Toros Dağları
İskenderun (Antioch, Antakya)
Hatay
Ródos
1215
Ródos (Rhodes)
Antalya Körfezi
Yardımcı Burnu
Al Lādhiqīyah (Latakia)
SYRIA
35°
SEA OF CRETE
CRETE (Kríti)
NORTHERN CYPRUS
Nicosia (Lefkosia, Lefkoşa)
E
Haniá
anea)
2456
Iráklio (Candia)
CYPRUS
Lemesos (Limassol)
110
35°

E   A   N   25°   S   E   A   30°   A
4   5   6

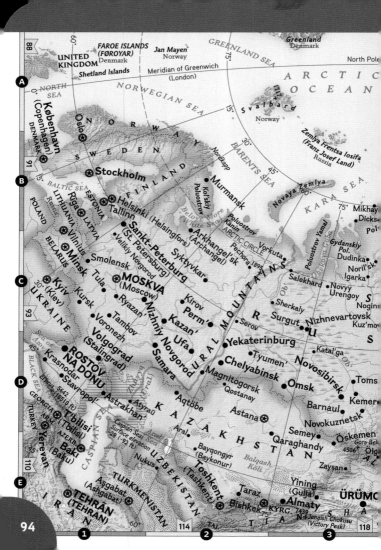

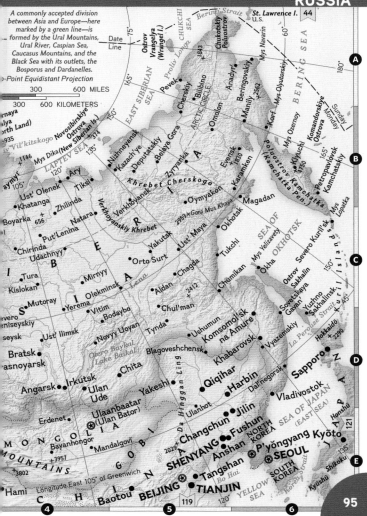

A commonly accepted division between Asia and Europe—here marked by a green line—is formed by the Ural Mountains, Ural River, Caspian Sea, Caucasus Mountains, and the Black Sea with its outlets, the Bosporus and Dardanelles.

Yenisey

Angara

*Caspian
Sea*

*Lake
Balkhash*

Dead Sea
-422 m (-1,385 ft)

C H I

Delhi

Mumbai
(Bombay)

Kolkata
(Calcutta)

Mount Everest
8,850 m
(29,035 ft)

MALDIVES

ASIA

GEOGRAPHIC EXTREMES

CONTINENTAL POLITICAL FACTS

TOTAL NUMBER OF COUNTRIES: 46

LARGEST COUNTRY BY AREA: China
9,596,961 sq km (3,705,407 sq mi)

SMALLEST COUNTRY BY AREA:
Maldives 298 sq km (115 sq mi)

MOST POPULOUS COUNTRY: China
1,336,720,000

LEAST POPULOUS COUNTRY:
Maldives 395,000

LARGEST CITIES BY POPULATION:
Tokyo, Japan 36,669,000
Delhi, India 22,157,000
Mumbai (Bombay), India 20,041,000
Shanghai, China 16,575,000
Kolkata (Calcutta), India 15,552,000

CONTINENTAL PHYSICAL FACTS

AREA: 44,570,000 sq km
(17,208,000 sq mi)

HIGHEST POINT: Mount Everest,
China-Nepal 8,850 m (29,035 ft)

LOWEST POINT: Dead Sea,
Israel-Jordan -422 m (-1,385 ft)

LONGEST RIVERS:
Chang Jiang (Yangtze) 6,244 km
(3,880 mi)
Yenisey-Angara 5,810 km (3,610 mi)
Huang (Yellow) 5,778 km (3,590 mi)

LARGEST NATURAL LAKES:
Caspian Sea 371,000 sq km
(143,200 sq mi)
Lake Baikal 31,500 sq km
(12,200 sq mi)
Lake Balkhash 18,000 sq km
(6,900 sq mi)

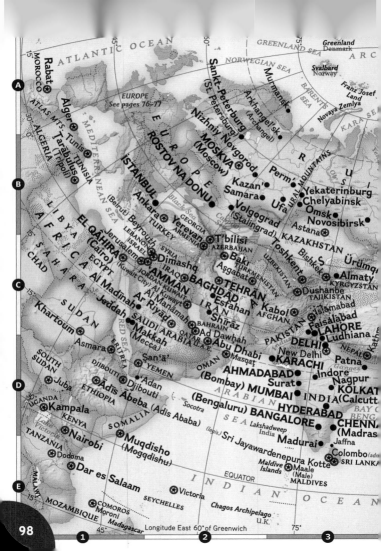

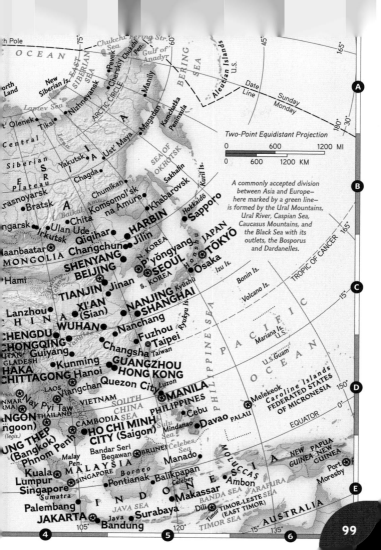

ATLANTIC OCEAN

GREENLAND SEA

Greenland

ARC

15°

45°

60°

75°

Ireland
BRITISH
ISLES
Great
Britain
North
Sea

NORWEGIAN SEA

Svalbard

Franz Josef
Land

A

MOROCCO

IBERIAN
PENINSULA

SCANDINAVIA

BARENTS
SEA

Novaya Zemlya

200

ATLAS
MOUNTAINS

G. of Bothnia

Kola
Pen.

White Sea

ALGERIA

30°

Baltic Sea

NORTHERN EUROPEAN PLAIN

R

KARA
SEA

ALPS

EUROPE

TUNISIA

MEDITERRANEAN

BALKAN
PENINSULA

Crimea

U

URAL MOUNTAINS

Volga

West
Siberian
Plain

Ob

B

A

F

LIBYA

World's lowest
point

TURKEY
ANATOLIA
(ASIA MINOR)

Black Sea

Caucasus Mts.

Elbrus
5642

Caspian
Depression

THE STEPPES

Kazakh

Uplands

Belukha

15°

Dead
Sea
(-1365 ft)

-5421

Cyprus
LEB.
ISRAEL

SYRIA

Mt. Ararat
5137

KAZAKH.

Lake
Balkhash

450

R

I

EGYPT

JORDAN

Sinai

Syrian
Desert

IRAQ

Mesopotamia

IRAN

Turan Lowland

TURKMEN

UZBEK.

Jengish Chokusu
(Victory Pk.)
7439

Bogda Feng
5445

Sha

C

C

A

SAHARA

SUDAN

CHAD

15°

RED SEA

KUWAIT
BAHRAIN
QATAR
U.A.E.

Zagros Mts.

Persian Gulf

AFGHAN.

Gulf of Oman

Hindu Kush
7649

TAJIK.
KYRGYZ.

Tian Shan

Kunlun Shan

Taklimakan
Desert

Kongur Shan
7719

8611 K2
(Godwin Austen)

PLAT

S. SUDAN

SAUDI
ARABIA

ARABIAN
PENINSULA

Rub al Khali

OMAN

Ra's al Hadd

PAKISTAN

Great Indian
Desert

HIMAL

Mt. Everest
(29035 ft) 8850

D

0°

UGANDA

ETHIOPIAN
HIGHLANDS

ETHIOPIA

ERITREA

DJIBOUTI

YEMEN

Gulf of Aden

Gulf of
Masira

World's
highest
point

Ganges

INDIA

DECCAN
PLATEAU

KENYA

Lake
Victoria

Kilimanjaro
5895

Somali Peninsula

SOMALIA

Socotra

ARABIAN

SEA

Lakshadweep

Laccadive Sea

Western Ghats

Eastern Ghats

BANGLA

TANZANIA

EQUATOR

Maldive
Islands

MALDIVES

Sri
Lanka
SRI LANKA

BE

E

15°

MALAWI

MOZAMBIQUE

COMOROS
Comoro Is.

Seychelles
SEYCHELLES

INDIAN

Cape Comorin

Chagos Archipelago
U.K.

OCEA

Madagascar

45°

Longitude East 60° of Greenwich

75°

100

1

2

3

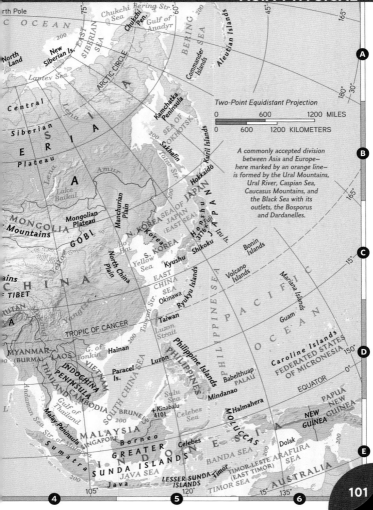

North Pole

ARCTIC OCEAN

Chukchi Sea

Bering Str.

Gulf of Anadyr

BERING SEA

Commander Islands

Aleutian Islands

North Land

New Siberian Is.

EAST SIBERIAN SEA

Laptev Sea

ARCTIC CIRCLE

Central

Siberian

Plateau

Lena

Kamchatka Peninsula

SEA OF OKHOTSK

Sakhalin

Kuril Islands

Two-Point Equidistant Projection

| 0 | 600 | 1200 MILES |

| 0 | 600 | 1200 KILOMETERS |

A commonly accepted division between Asia and Europe—here marked by an orange line—is formed by the Ural Mountains, Ural River, Caspian Sea, Caucasus Mountains, and the Black Sea with its outlets, the Bosporus and Dardanelles.

Amur

Lake Baikal

MONGOLIA

Mountains

Mongolian Plateau

Manchurian Plain

Hokkaido

SEA OF JAPAN (EAST SEA)

Honshu

JAPAN

N. KOREA

Koje

S. KOREA

Fuji 3776

Yellow Sea

North China Plain

Kyushu

Shikoku

Bonin Islands

CHINA

TIBET

Yangtze

EAST CHINA SEA

Okinawa

Ryukyu Islands

Volcano Islands

PACIFIC

Mariana Islands

TROPIC OF CANCER

Taiwan

Hainan

Luzon Strait

Guam

OCEAN

MYANMAR (BURMA)

LAOS

G. of Tonkin

VIETNAM

Paracel Is.

PHILIPPINE SEA

Luzon

PHILIPPINES

Babelthuap

PALAU

Caroline Islands

FEDERATED STATES OF MICRONESIA

INDOCHINA PENINSULA

THAILAND

CAMBODIA

SOUTH CHINA SEA

Sulu Sea

Mindanao

Halmahera

EQUATOR

Gulf of Thailand

BRUNEI

Kinabalu 4101

Celebes Sea

PAPUA NEW GUINEA

Malay Peninsula

MALAYSIA

NEW GUINEA

Andaman Sea

Str. of Malacca

SINGAPORE

Borneo

Celebes

MOLUCCAS

Dolak

Sumatra

GREATER

SUNDA ISLANDS

I N D O N E S I A

BANDA SEA

ARAFURA SEA

JAVA SEA

LESSER SUNDA ISLANDS

Timor

TIMOR-LESTE (EAST TIMOR)

Java

TIMOR SEA

AUSTRALIA

POPULATION DENSITY

People per Square Kilometer	People per Square Mile
More than 195 ■	More than 500
60–195 ■	150–500
10–59 ☐	25–149
1–9 ☐	1–24
Fewer than 1 ☐	Fewer than 1

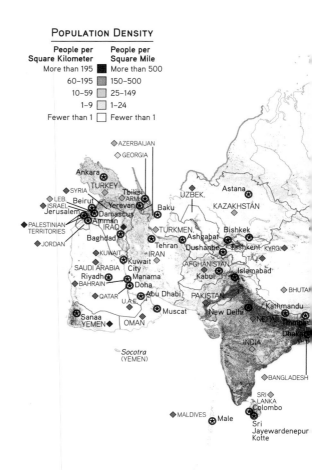

◇ AZERBAIJAN
◇ GEORGIA
Ankara ✪
TURKEY
◆ SYRIA
Tbilisi ✪ ◇ ARM.
UZBEK.
Astana ✪
◆ LEB. Beirut ✪ Yerevan ✪
◆ ISRAEL
Jerusalem ✪ Damascus ✪ Baku ✪
KAZAKHSTÁN
✪ Amman
◆ PALESTINIAN TERRITORIES
IRAQ
◇ TURKMEN. Ashgabat ✪ Bishkek ✪
◆ JORDAN
Baghdad ✪
Tehran ✪ Dushanbe ✪ Tashkent ✪ KYRG. ◇
◆ KUWAIT
IRAN
AFGHANISTAN TAJ. ◇
SAUDI ARABIA ✪ Kuwait City
Riyadh ✪ ✪ Manama
Kabul ✪ Islamabad ✪
◆ BAHRAIN
✪ Doha
◇ QATAR ◇ Abu Dhabi
◇ BHUTAN
U.A.E. PAKISTAN
✪ Muscat New Delhi ✪ Kathmandu ✪
Sanaa ✪
OMAN NEPAL ◇ Thimphu ✪
YEMEN ◆
Dhaka ✪
INDIA
Socotra (YEMEN)
◇ BANGLADESH
◆ MALDIVES ✪ Male
SRI ◇ LANKA Colombo ✪
Sri Jayewardenepur Kotte

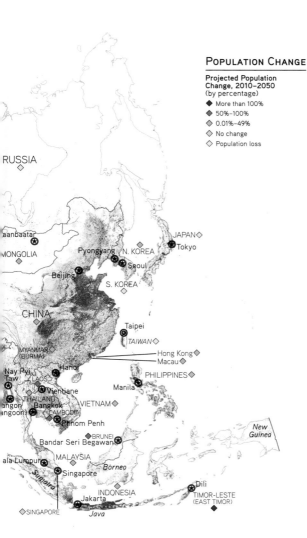

POPULATION CHANGE

**Projected Population
Change, 2010–2050**
(by percentage)
◆ More than 100%
◆ 50%–100%
◇ 0.01%–49%
◇ No change
◇ Population loss

RUSSIA ◇

Ulaanbaatar
MONGOLIA ◇

Pyongyang N. KOREA
Seoul
S. KOREA ◇

Beijing

CHINA

JAPAN ◇
Tokyo

Taipei
TAIWAN ◇

MYANMAR ◇
(BURMA)

Hong Kong ◇
Macau ◇

Nay Pyi
Taw LAOS

Hanoi

PHILIPPINES ◇

Vientiane

Manila

Yangon
(Rangoon)

THAILAND
Bangkok
CAMBODIA

VIETNAM ◇

Phnom Penh

◆ BRUNEI
Bandar Seri Begawan

New
Guinea

Kuala Lumpur

MALAYSIA

Borneo

Singapore

Sumatra

INDONESIA
Jakarta

Dili
TIMOR-LESTE
(EAST TIMOR)
◆

Java

◇ SINGAPORE

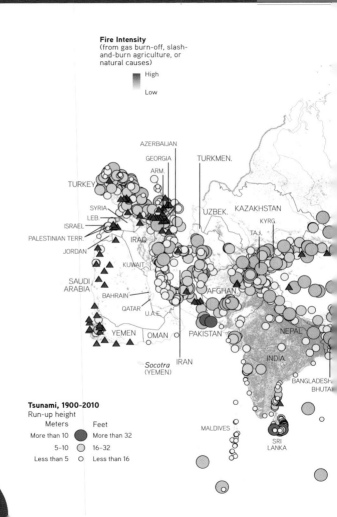

Fire Intensity
(from gas burn-off, slash-and-burn agriculture, or natural causes)

High

Low

AZERBAIJAN
GEORGIA
ARM.
TURKEY
TURKMEN.
SYRIA
LEB.
ISRAEL
PALESTINIAN TERR.
JORDAN
IRAQ
KUWAIT
SAUDI
ARABIA
BAHRAIN
QATAR
U.A.E.
YEMEN
OMAN
Socotra
(YEMEN)
IRAN
UZBEK.
KAZAKHSTAN
KYRG.
TAJ.
AFGHAN.
PAKISTAN
NEPAL
INDIA
BANGLADESH
BHUTAN
MALDIVES
SRI
LANKA

Tsunami, 1900-2010
Run-up height

Meters	Feet
More than 10	More than 32
5-10	16-32
Less than 5	Less than 16

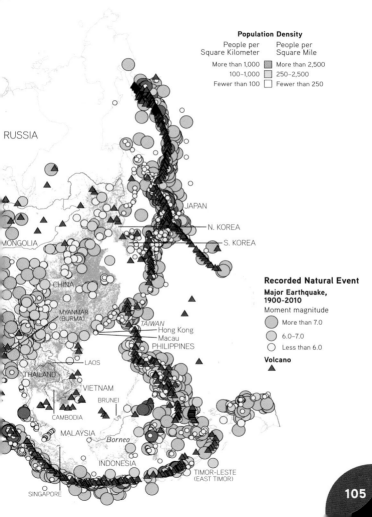

Population Density

People per Square Kilometer		People per Square Mile
More than 1,000	▨	More than 2,500
100–1,000	▨	250–2,500
Fewer than 100	☐	Fewer than 250

RUSSIA

JAPAN

N. KOREA

S. KOREA

MONGOLIA

CHINA

MYANMAR
(BURMA)

TAIWAN
Hong Kong
Macau
PHILIPPINES

LAOS

THAILAND

VIETNAM

BRUNEI

CAMBODIA

MALAYSIA

Borneo

INDONESIA

TIMOR-LESTE
(EAST TIMOR)

SINGAPORE

Recorded Natural Event

Major Earthquake, 1900-2010
Moment magnitude

○ More than 7.0
○ 6.0–7.0
○ Less than 6.0

Volcano

▲

LAND COVER

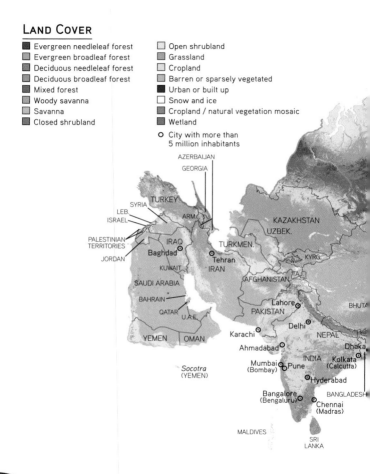

- ■ Evergreen needleleaf forest
- ■ Evergreen broadleaf forest
- ☐ Deciduous needleleaf forest
- ☐ Deciduous broadleaf forest
- ☐ Mixed forest
- ☐ Woody savanna
- ☐ Savanna
- ■ Closed shrubland
- ☐ Open shrubland
- ■ Grassland
- ☐ Cropland
- ■ Barren or sparsely vegetated
- ■ Urban or built up
- ☐ Snow and ice
- ■ Cropland / natural vegetation mosaic
- ■ Wetland
- ○ City with more than 5 million inhabitants

AZERBAIJAN
GEORGIA
TURKEY
SYRIA
LEB.
ISRAEL
ARM.
PALESTINIAN
TERRITORIES
IRAQ
JORDAN
Baghdad
KUWAIT
SAUDI ARABIA
BAHRAIN
QATAR
U.A.E.
YEMEN
OMAN
TURKMEN.
Tehran
IRAN
KAZAKHSTAN
UZBEK.
KYRG.
AFGHANISTAN
Lahore
PAKISTAN
Delhi
Karachi
NEPAL
BHUTA
Ahmadabad
Dhaka
INDIA
Mumbai
(Bombay)
Pune
Kolkata
(Calcutta)
Socotra
(YEMEN)
Hyderabad
Bangalore
(Bengaluru)
BANGLADESH
Chennai
(Madras)
MALDIVES
SRI
LANKA

RUSSIA

MONGOLIA

CHINA

Shenyang

Beijing Tianjin

N. KOREA

Seoul

S. KOREA

JAPAN

Tokyo

Osaka-Kobe

Shanghai

Wuhan

Chongqing

Dongguan

Guangzhou
(Canton)

Shenzhen

TAIWAN

Hong Kong

ANMAR
URMA) LAOS

THAILAND

Bangkok

CAMBODIA

VIETNAM

Ho Chi Minh City
(Saigon)

PHILIPPINES

Manila

New
Guinea

BRUNEI

MALAYSIA

Borneo

Sumatra

SINGAPORE

INDONESIA

Jakarta

Java

TIMOR-LESTE
(EAST TIMOR)

107

ASIA CLIMATE

CLIMATE ZONES

(based on modified Köppen system)

Humid equatorial climate (A)
- No dry season (Af)
- Short dry season (Am)
- Dry winter (Aw)

Dry climate (B)
- Semiarid (BS) } h = hot
- Arid (BW) } k = cold

Humid temperate climate (C)
- No dry season (Cf)
- Dry winter (Cw)
- Dry summer (Cs)

a = hot summer
b = cool summer
c = short, cool summer
d = very cold winter

Humid cold climate (D)
- No dry season (Df)
- Dry winter (Dw)

Cold climate (E)
- Tundra and ice

Highland climate (H)
- Unclassified highlands

WATER AVAILABILITY

(in millimeters per-person
per-year)

- More than 750
- 251–750
- 26–250
- Less than 26
- No data available

109

BULGARIA • Burgas

Edirne
(Adrianople)

GREECE

Lüleburgaz

Marmara
Denizi

Zonguldak

İSTANBUL
(Constantinople)

BLACK SEA

40°

ABKHAZIA

(Sokhum) Sokhumi

K'ut'ai

GEORGIA

Bat'umi

Kastamonu

Kuzey

Sinop (Sinope)

Samsun
(Amisus)

Bursa

Balıkesir

Eskişehir

Çorum

Anadolu Dağları

Trabzon

Lésvos • Mitilíni

Kütahya

Ankara
(Angora)

T U R K E Y

Sivas

Erzincan

Akhisar

İzmir
(Smyrna)

Afyon

A N A T O L I A

(ASIA MINOR)

Kayseri

Elazığ

Bitlis

Muğla

Híos

Denizli

Tuz Gölü

Konya
(Iconium)

3916

Malatya

Diyarba

3585

Antalya

Toros D.

Adana

Gaziantep

Mardin

AEGEAN SEA

93

Ródos
1215

Ródos
(Rhodes)

Kárpathos
(Carpathos)

Kríti
(Crete)

İskenderun
(Antioch)

Hatay

Al Lādhiqīyah
(Latakia)

Halab
(Aleppo)

Al Hasak

Al Furāt

Euphrates

NORTHERN CYPRUS
(Lefkosia)
Nicosia

CYPRUS

Dayr az Zawr

SYRIA

Hamāh
(Hamath)

Albers Conic Equal-Area Projection

0   100   200 MILES

0   100   200 KILOMETERS

(Beirut) Beyrouth

Ḥimṣ (Homs)

Ḥuşaybah

Trâblous (Tripoli)

MEDITERRANEAN

LEBANON

SEA

(Haifa) Hefa

Dimashq
(Damascus)

Ar Ruṭbah

El Iskandarîya
(Alexandria)

(Al Quds, Yerushalayim)

Tel Aviv-Yafo

ISRAEL

(Gaza City) Ghazzah

Jerusalem

GAZA STRIP

S Y R I A N

DESERT

El 'Alamein

Bûr Sa'îd

WEST
BANK

Az Zarqā'

JORDAN

Ṭanṭa

El Mansûra

Amman
(Philadelphia)

Munkhafad el Qattâra
(Qattara Depression)

El Gîza

Ismâ'ilîya

Dead
Sea

Wadi as Sirhān

Ṭurayf

'Ar'ar

EL QÂHIRA
(Cairo)

Ma'ān

El Faiyûm

Beni Suef

SINAI

Elat

Al 'Aqabah

Dawmat al Jandal
(Al Jawf)

Sakākah

140

Beni Mazâr

El Minya

Mallawi

Bahr el Nile

Asyûṭ

Gebel Mûsa (Mt. Sinai)
2285

Gemsa

Sharm el Sheikh
Râs Muhammad

Gulf of Aqaba

Tabûk

Gulf of Suez

An Nafūd

Taymā'

Ḥā'il

Jabal Shamma

E G Y P T

El Qaṣr

Hurghada

Bûr Safâga

Eastern Desert

Quṣeir

Al Wajh

Al 'Ulá
Şafājah

S

Girga

Luxor

Western Desert

El Khârga

Bârîs

Idfu

RED SEA

Hadīyah

A

Aswân

Umm Lajj

140

1   2   3

30°

Longitude East 40° of Greenwich

Groznyy

KAZ.

Ustyurt

50° | 114

60°

Daşoguz

Makhachkala

Shynvali

CASPIAN

UZB.

S. OSSETIA

MOUNTAINS

Derbent

Qazaq
Shyghanaghy

Plateau

Garabogaz
Aylagy

A

S. OSSETIA

T'bilisi
(Tbilisi)

Sumqayıt

Türkmenbaşy

Turkey, Cyprus, Syria, Lebanon, Israel,
Jordan, Egypt, Iraq, Iran, and the countries
of the Arabian Peninsula form the heart
of the Middle East region.

TURKMENISTAN

40°

114

Gyumri

Gäncä

Bakı
(Baku)

AZERBAIJAN

ARMENIA

Stepanakert

Garagum

Balkanabat

Gyzylarbat

Yerevan

Ağrı Dağı
(t. Ararat)
5137

Xankändi

NAGORNO-
KARABAKH

SEA

Bäherden

Aşgabat
(Ashgabat)

Khoy

Länkäran

Gyzyletrek

Esenguly

Bojnürd

B

Van
Gölü

Tabrız

Ardabıl

Quchän

Mashhad

Orümiyeh
(Urmia)

Marägheh

Bandar-e Anzalı

Rasht

Bandar-e Torkaman

Sabzevär

Neyshäbur

Cheekha Där
3611

Daryächeh-ye
Orümiyeh

Zanjän

Bäbol

Eshteh-ye Alborz

Al Mawşil (Mosul)

Qazvın

(Elburz Mountains)

Torüd

Käshmar

Arbıl (Irbil)

TEHRAN

Koh-e Dämävand
5671

Gonäbäd

As Sulaymänıyah

Sanandaj

Qom (Qum)

Dasht-e Kavir
(Kavir Desert)

Qä'en

Karkük
(Kirkuk)

Hamadän (Ecbatana)

I   R   A   N

Birjand

C

Ar Ramädı (Ramadi)

Kermänshäh

Aräk

Käshän

Dasht-e Lut

Al Fallüjah (Fallujah)

Borüjerd

Baghdad

Dezfül

Esfahan (Isfahan)

Yazd

Karbalä'

Masjed Soleymän

Najafäbäd

A

Q

Al Hillah

'Al Amärah

Bäfq

An Najaf
(Najaf)

Ahväz

Äbädeh

Anär

Kerman

An Näşirıyah
(Nasiriyah)

Behbahän

Deh Bid

Rafsanjän

(Basra) Al Başrah

Khorramshahr

30°

Äbädän

Shıräz

Sırjän

D

Rafhä'

KUWAIT

Al Kuwayt
(Kuwait City)

Boräzjän

Büshehr

Bam

113

Hafar al Bätin

Al Ahmadı

Jahrom

Kahnüj

Maun

Bandar-e
Abbäs

Mınäb

An Nu'ayrıyah

Manıfah

Bandar-e
Lengeh

Strait of
Hormuz

UDI

Al Jubayl

Ad Dammäm

Al Manämah
(Manama)

GULF

Khaşab

Oman Jäsk

Sharjah

GULF OF
OMAN

E

Buraydah

BAHRAIN

Dubai

ABIA

Al Hufüf
(Hofuf)

QATAR

UNITED
ARAB EMIRATES

OMAN

Unayzah

Gulf of
Bahrain

Al Ain

Shaqrä'

Ar Riyäd
(Riyadh)

Ad Dawhah
(Doha)

Abu Dhabi

112

50°

5

6

113

4

Jerusalem • 'Ammān (Philadelphia) | 110 | 40° | Karbalā' • Al Hillah •
GAZA STRIP • Ghazzah (Gaza City) | S Y R I A N | An Najaf (Najaf) •
Būr Sa'īd (Port Said) | WEST BANK | D E S E R T | I R A Q | An Nāşirīyah (Nasiriyah) •
•EL QĀHIRA (Cairo) | ISRAEL JORDAN | Ma'ān | Ar'ar | Al Furāt (Euphrates) | (Basra) Al Başrah •
Elat • Al 'Aqabah (Aqaba) | Dawmat al Jandal (Al Jawf) • | KUWAIT Al Kuwayt (Kuwait City) •
SINAI | Gulf of Aqaba | Sakākah • | Rafḥā' • | Ḥafar al Bāţin • | Al Ahmad •
Gebel Mūsā (Mt. Sinai) 2285 | Tabūk • | An Nafud |
Sharm el Sheikh | Rās Muḥammad | Tayma' • | Ḥā'il • | Az Zilfī • |
Gemsa • Rās Muwaylih | Jabal Shammar | Buraydah • | Ar Riyād (Riyadh) •
Hurghada | Al 'Ulā • | 'Unayzah • | Ad Dahnā |
Qena • Būr Safāga | Şafāyah • | Al Majma'ah • |
Luxor • Quşeir • | Al Wajh • | Hadiyah • | Shaqrā' • |
Idfu • | Abū Madd | Umm Lajj • | Al Madīnah (Medina) • | S A U D I
140 | Aswān • Berenice • | Ra's | 'Afīf • | (Hauta) Al Hillah •
Lake Nasser | Rās Banās | Yanbu'al Baḥr • | Mahd adh Dhahab • |
Boundary claimed by Sudan | Gezaīr Marir (Mirear) | Foul Bay | Rābigh • | Şufaynah • |
Halayeb • | Siyal Is. | Al Khurmah • | A R A B I
Jebel Is. 1850 | Ra's Hadarba (Cape Elba) | Jeddah • | Nafūd ad Daḥy |
Gebeit • | Ra's Ḥātibah | Makkah (Mecca) • | At Ţā'if •
Muhammad Qol • | Ras Abu Shagara | Al Līth • | Qal'at Bīshah • | As Sulayyil • |
Nubian Desert | 20° | Al Qunfudhah • | Al Lidām • | AR |
Abu Hamed • Port Sudan • | Suakin • | Jabal Sawda 3133 | Khamīs Mushayţ • |
Shereiq • Suakin Sinkat • | Archipelago | Al Birk • | Abhā • | Najrān •
El Bauga • Atbara • Haiya • | Ras Kasar | Ra's aţ Ţarfā | Şabyā • | Najrān • Şa'dah •
SUDAN | Tokar • | Jazā'ir Farasān | Jīzān • | Maydī • |
Ed Damer • Derudeb • | Algena • | Jabal Zuqar | Al Luḥayyah • | 'Amrān •
Kabushiya • | Dahlak Archipelago | Kamarān • | Şan'ā' (Sanaa) • | Shabwa •
Shendi • Abu Deleiq • | Keren • ERITREA | Mits'iwa (Massawa) • | Bājil • | Jabal an Nabi Shu'ayb 3667 |
Kassala • | Asmara (Asmera) • | Al Ḥudaydah • | Dhamār •
Khashm el Qirba • | Jazīrat | 'Īdī | Zabid • | Ibb • | Y E
Gedaref • | Aksum • 'Ādwa • | Zuqar | Ta'izz • | Shaqrā' •
Doka • Qallabat • | Mek'ele • | 116° | Al Mukhā • | Lahij • | Ahwar •
Galegu • | Gonder • ETHIOPIA | Aseb • | Denakil | 'Adan (Aden) •
Tana Hayk' | Korem • | 40° | Bāb al Mandab | GULF OF
112 | Bahir Dar • | 141 | Obock • | DJIBOUTI

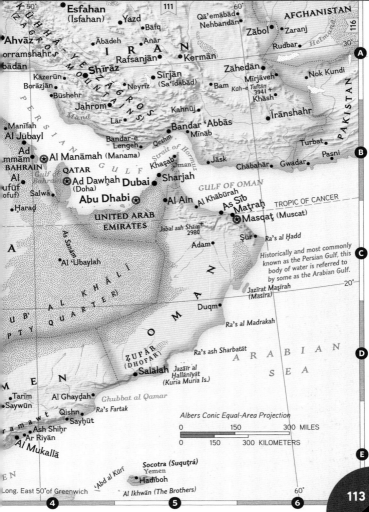

KŪHHĀ-YE

50°

Esfahan
(Isfahan)

Yazd

Bāfq

Ābādeh

Anār

Qā'emābād
Nehbandān

60°

AFGHANISTAN

Zābol

Zaranj

Helmand

Ahvāz

rramshahr

bādān

I R A N

Shīrāz

ZAGROS

Kāzerūn

Borāzjān

Būshehr

Jahrom

Rafsanjān

Neyrīz
(Sa'īdābād)

Kermān

Sīrjān

Kahnūj

111

Rudbar

30

Zāhedān

Mīrjāveh

Kūh-e Taftān
3941 +
Khāsh

Bam

Nok Kundi

Īrānshahr

116

PAKISTAN

MOUNTAINS

A

Lār

Manīfah

Al Jubayl

Ad
mmām

Al
ufūf

ofuf

Ḥarad

Salwá

BAHRAIN

Al Manāmah (Manama)

QATAR

Ad Dawḥah
(Doha)

Abu Dhabi

Bandar-e
Lengeh

Hand

Dubai

Qeshm

Bandar 'Abbās

Mīnāb

Jāsk

Chābahār

Turbat

Gwadar

Pasni

MOUNTAINS

PERSIAN

GULF

Gulf of
Bahrain

Khaṣab

Sharjah

Al Ain

Al Khābūrah

UNITED ARAB
EMIRATES

Jabal ash Shām +
2980

Adam

As Sīb

Matrah

Masqaṭ (Muscat)

Ṣūr

Ra's al Ḥadd

GULF OF OMAN

Strait of
Hormuz

TROPIC OF CANCER

B

C

As Sawān

Al 'Ubaylah

A

UB' AL KHĀLĪ
PTY QUARTER)

O

M

A

N

Duqm

Historically and most commonly
known as the Persian Gulf, this
body of water is referred to
by some as the Arabian Gulf.

20°

Ra's al Madrakah

ZUFĀR
(DHOFAR)

MEN

Ṣalālah

Tarīm

Al Ghaydah

Saywūn

Qishn

Ra's Fartak

ramawt

Ash Shiḥr

Ar Riyān

Al Mukallā

Ra's ash Sharbatāt

Jazā'ir al
Ḥallānīyāt
(Kuria Muria Is.)

Ghubbat al Qamar

Sayḥūt

A R A B I A N

S E A

D

E

Albers Conic Equal-Area Projection

0   150   300 MILES

0   150   300 KILOMETERS

EN

Long. East 50° of Greenwich

4

Socotra (Suquṭrá)
Yemen
Ḥadīboh

'Abd al Kūrī

Al Ikhwān (The Brothers)

5

60°

6

113

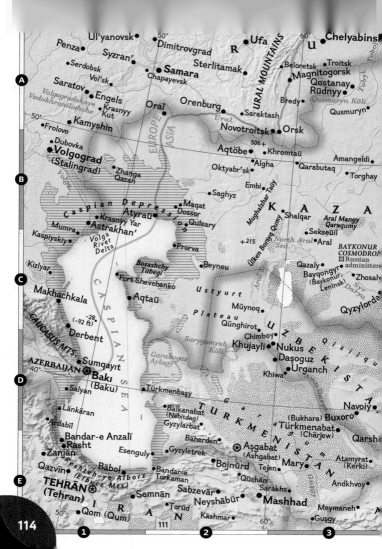

A

Ul'yanovsk • 50° Dimitrovgrad • • Ufa 60° • Chelyabinsk
Penza • Syzran' • R U
Serdobsk • Vol'sk • Sterlitamak • Beloretsk • Troitsk
Saratov • Samara • Magnitogorsk • Qostanay
Engels • Chapayevsk • Vodokhranilishche Krasnyy Kut • Oral • Orenburg • URAL MOUNTAINS • Rūdnyy
Kamyshin • Saraktash • Bredy • Qusmuryn Köli
50° Frolovo • Ural • Novotroitsk • Orsk • Qusmuryn
• Dubovka EUROPE ASIA • 506+ • Khromtaū
Volgograd (Stalingrad) • Aqtöbe • Amangeldi
• Zhanga Qazan • Oktyabr'sk • Algha • Qarabutaq • Torghay

B

50° • Saghyz • Embi • K A Z A
Caspian Depression • Maqat • Dossor • Mughalzhar Taūy • Shalqar • Aral Mangy Qaraqumy
Mumra • Krasnyy Yar • Atyraū • Qulsary • Ülken Borsyq Qumy • Sekseūil
Astrakhan' • North Aral • Aral
Kaspiyskiy • Volga River Delta • Prorva • +215 • Sea • BAYKONUR COSMODRO
Kizlyar • Bozashchy Tübegi • Beyneu • ☒ Russian administere
C A S P I A N • Fort Shevchenko • Qazaly • Bayqongyr
• Ustyurt • (Baykonur, Lenīnsk) • Zhosal
Makhachkala • Aqtaū • Müynoq • Plateau • UZBEK Syr Darya
• -28 (-92 ft) • Qŭnghirot • Qyzylorda

C

Derbent • Sarygamysh Köli • Chimboy • Khujayli • Nukus
CAUCASUS MTS. • S E A • Garabogaz Aylagy • Dashoguz
AZERBAIJAN • Sumqayıt • Khiwa • Urganch
40° • Bakı (Baku) • U Z B E K I S T A

D

Salyan • Türkmenbaşy • Navoiy
Länkäran • Balkanabat (Nebitdag) • (Bukhara) Buxoro
Ardabīl • Gyzylarbat • TURKMENISTAN • Türkmenabat (Chärjew)
Bandar-e Anzalī • Bäherden • Qarsh
Rasht • Esenguly • Gyzyletrek • Aşgabat (Ashgabat) • Mary • Atamyrat (Kerki)
Zanjān • Bojnürd • Tejen
Qazvīn • Bābol • Bandar-e Torkaman • Quchān • Sarähs • Andkhvoy
Reshteh-ye Alborz (Elburz Mts.) • Sabzevär • Neyshäbür • Mashhad • Meymaneh

E

TEHRĀN (Tehran) • I R A N • Semnān • Torüd • Gushgy
50° • Qom (Qum) • Kāshmar
111 • 60°

1 • 2 • 3

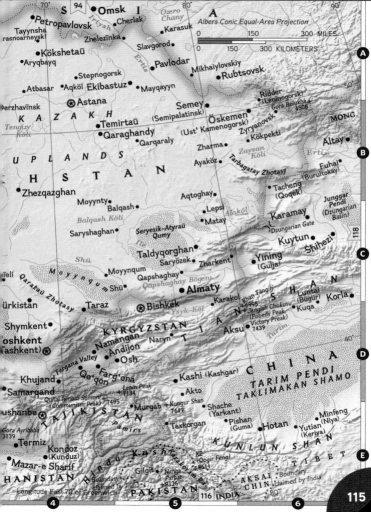

Albers Conic Equal-Area Projection

0   150   300 MILES
0   150   300 KILOMETERS

A
B
C
D
E

94

S   Omsk
•Petropavlovsk   Irtysh
Tayynsha   •Cherlak
rasnoarmeyskiy   •Karasuk
•Kökshetaū   Zheleznīnka
•Aryqbayq   Ertis   Slavgorod
          •Pavlodar   •Mikhaiylovskiy
•Stepnogorsk   •Rubtsovsk
•Atbasar   •Aqköl Ekibastuz •Mayqayyn
          Ridder
•Derzhavīnsk   (Leninogorsk)
⊛Astana   Semey   Gora Belukha
K A Z A K H   •Temirtaū   (Semipalatinsk)   4506
          Öskemen   MONG.
Tengzy   •Qaraghandy   (Ust' Kamenogorsk)   •Zyryanovsk
Köli   •Qarqaraly   •Kökpekti   •Altay
U P L A N D S   Zharma   Zaysan   Ertis
H S T A N   •Ayaköz   Tarbagatay Zhotasy   •Fuhai
          (Burultokay)
•Zhezqazghan   •Aqtoghay   •Tacheng   Junggar
•Moyynty   •Balqash   •Lepsi   (Qoqek)   Pendi
          •Matay   (Dzungarian Basin)
Balqash Köli   Seryesik-Atyraū   Alaköl   •Karamay
•Saryshaghan   Qumy   •Dzungarian Gate   118
          Ili   •Taldyqorghan   Kuytun•   •Shihezi
Shū   •Saryözek   •Zharkent   Yining   Shihezi•
Teli Qarataū Zhotasy •Moyynqum   Shū   (Gulja)
ürkistan   •Qapshaghay   Karakol   Khan Tängiri
          Almaty   Qapshaghay Bögeni   6995
Shymkent   Ysyk-Köl   Jengish Chokusu   •Luntai
⊛Bishkek   (Pobedy Peak)   (Bügür)   •Korla
oshkent   Victory Peak   •Kuqa   T A
ashkent)⊛   KYRGYZSTAN   Aksu   7439
•Namangan   Naryn   T I A N   S H A N   40°
Khujand   •Andijon   •Osh   C H I N A
•Samarqand   Fergana Valley   •Kashi (Kashgar)   TARIM PENDI
ushanbe•   Farg'ona   TAKLIMAKAN SHAMO
Qulla Ismoili Somoni   •Akto
Communism Peak   7495   •Shache
Gora Ayribaba   •Murgab   Kongur Shan   (Yarkant)   •Hotan   •Minfeng
3139   TAJIKISTAN   7649   •Pishan   •Yutian   (Niya)
•Termiz   Pamirs   •Taxkorgan   (Guma)   (Keriya)
Kondoz   K U N L U N   S H A N
(Kunduz)   Hindu Kush   (Qogir Feng)
•Mazar-e Sharif   Boundary   K2   8611   T I B E T
HANISTAN   Longitude East 70° of Greenwich   claimed by India   AKSAI   Boundary
          Gilgit   Nanga   Karakoram Ra.   CHIN   claimed by India
PAKISTAN   Parbat   8126   80°
116   INDIA

4   **5**   **6**

Mashhad
Kāshmar
Kavir Desert
Esfahan
(Isfahan)
Yazd
Bīrjand
Herat
Dasht-e Lūt
Kermān
Zābol
Zaranj
Lashkar Gah
Farah
I R A N
Shīrāz
Bam
Zāhedān
Mīrjāveh
Kūh-e Taftān
4042
Rudbar
Bandar
'Abbās
Nok Kundi
Īrānshahr
PERSIAN
GULF
Strait of
Hormuz
Khasab
Dubai
Abu Dhabi
U.A.E.
Jabal ash Sham
2980
As Sīb
Matrah
Masqat
(Muscat)
Ra's al Hadd
O M A N
Jazīrat Maşīrah
Ra's ash Sharbatāt
Jazā'ir al Hallānīyāt
(Kuria Muria Is.)

TURKM.
Mazar-e Sharif
Kondoz
Hindu Kush
Novshak
7492
K2
8611
Karakoram R.
KASH
Boundary claimed
by India
Kabol
(Kabul)
Jalalabad
Peshawar
Islamabad
Srinag
Rawalpindi
AFGHANISTAN
Harirud
Qalat
(Kalat)
Kandahar
Chaman
Faisalabad
Gujranw
Quetta
LAHORE
Amrits
Multan
Ludhiana
Chandigarh
Bahawalpur
DELHI
Larkana
Sukkur
Thar Desert
(Great Indian Desert)
Bikaner
New
Delhi
Jaipur
Agra
Turbat
Jodhpur
Ajmer
Kota
Gwalic
Pasni
Gwadar
Sonmiani Bay
Hyderabad
Udaipur
KARACHI
TROPIC OF CANCER
Rann of Kutch
Bhopal
AHMADABAD
Ujjain
Gulf of Kutch
Indore
I
Rajkot
Vadodara
N
Porbandar
Surat
Amravati
Gulf of Khambhat
Aurangabad
Jalna
Thane
Kalyan
(Bombay) MUMBAI
Nanded
PUNE
Sholapur
Kolhapur
Kurnoc
Belgaum
Bellary
Marmagao
Hubli
Davangere
(Bengaluru) BANGALORE
Mangalore
Mysore
Coimbatore
Thrissur
(Trichur)
Madura
(Cochin) Kochi
Tirunelveli
(Trivandrum) Thiruvananthapuram
Cape Comorin

ARABIAN
SEA

Lakshadweep
India

Nine Degree Channel

Eight Degree Channel

I N D I A

MALDIVES

Longitude East 70° of Greenwich

Azimuthal Equidistant Projection
0   250   500 MILES
0   250   500 KILOMETERS

60°
70°
30°
20°
10°
111
113
A
B
C
D
E
1
2
3

Hotan

+Muztag
6638
Muztag Feng
6973
Boundary claimed
by India

Hoh Xil Shan

Golmud

Madoi

Hezuo

Minxian

Wuli

Bayan Har Shan

Huang (Yellow)

Tongtian

Yushu
(Gyêgu)

Deyang

QING ZANG GAOYUAN
(PLATEAU OF TIBET)

Tanggula Shan

Amdo
(Pagnag)

Baqên

Ngamda

CHENGDU

Ya'an

Qagcaka

Rutog

+6595
Nganglong Kangri

Nyima

Baingoin

Gangdise Shan

Boundary
claimed
by China

TIBET

Paryang

Xigaze
(29035 ft) 8850

Gyangzê

Mount Everest

oradabad

Bareilly

NEPAL

Kathmandu

Kangchenjunga
+8586

Nyainqêntanglha Shan

Lhasa

Boundary
claimed
by China

Brahmaputra

Thimphu

Dibrugarh

Hkakabo Razi
5881

Xichang

Panzhihua

Dali

Lucknow

Allahabad

Varanasi
(Banaras)

Patna

BHUTAN

Tezpur

Guwahati

Shillong

Dimapur

Jorhat

Kohima

Myitkyina

Tengchong

Bhamo

Kunming

Yuxi

anpur

Gaya

BANGLADESH

Rajshahi

Imphal

TROPIC OF CANCER

Ganga (Ganges)

Ranchi

Korba

Haora

Khulna

DHAKA

Narayanganj

Mogok

Lashio

Jabalpur

KOLKATA
(Calcutta)

CHITTAGONG

Mandalay

Kengtung

Bhilai

Nagpur

Raipur

D I A

Cuttack

Mouths of the
Ganges

1052 +Mowdok
Mual

Monywa

MYANMAR
(BURMA)

LAOS

Chandrapur

Bhubaneshwar

Sittwe
(Akyab)

Nay Pyi Taw
(administrative)

Chiang
Mai

Warangal

Brahmapur

Arakan Yoma

Cheduba I.

Taungoo

Phitsanulok

HYDERABAD

Vizianagaram

Vishakhapatnam

BAY

Hinthada

Bago

YANGON
(Rangoon)
(legislative)

Mawlamyine

Nakhon
Sawan

Vijayawada

Guntur

OF

Irrawaddy

Gulf
of
Martaban

THAILAND

Nellore

BENGAL

Preparis I.

KRUNG THEP
(Bangkok)

CHENNAI (Madras)

North Andaman

Kadan Kyun

Myeik

Puducherry (Pondicherry)

Middle Andaman

India Andaman Islands

South Andaman

Port
Blair

ANDAMAN

Mergui
Archipelago

Gulf
of
Thailand

lem

iruchchirappalli

Little Andaman

SEA

Isthmus
of
Kra

Strait

Jaffna

Vavuniya

Trincomalee

Ten Degree Channel

(Ban Don) Surat Thani

Nakhon Si Thammarat

SRI LANKA
(CEYLON)

Nicobar
Islands
India

Phuket

Ko Phuket

MALAY
PEN.

Colombo
(administrative)

+2524
Sri Jayewardenepura Kotte
(legislative)

Little Nicobar

Great Nicobar

O C E A N

Great Channel

Banda Aceh

INDONESIA

Sumatra

St. of Malacca

117

Map Labels

Zhezqazghan • Astana • Pavlodar • Barnaul • Novokuznetsk

Temirtau • Ekibastuz • Rubtsovsk

Qaraghandy

KAZAKH UPLANDS

R U S S I A

Kyzyl

Qyzylorda • Öskemen • Semey • Ayaköz • Nayramadin Uul (Youyi Feng) 4374 • Ulaangom • Mörön • Hödrögö

KAZAKHSTAN

Balqash • Balqash Köl • Zaysan Köli • Tarbagatay Zhotasy • A L T A Y • Olgiy

Türkistan • Lepsi • Fuhai • Altay • Uliastay • Bayanhongor

Shymkent • Taldyqorghan • Junggar Pendi (Dzungarian Basin) • Fuyun • M O U N T A I N S

Taraz • Zharkent • Karamay • Ih Bogd Uul +3

Toshkent (Tashkent) • Bishkek • Almaty • Shihezi (Gujja) • Ürümqi • +3802

UZB. • Farg'ona • Yining (Gulja) • +2584

Namangan • KYRGYA • Aksu • Jengish Chokusu (Pobedy Peak) (Victory Peak) 7439 • Luntai • Turpan Pendi • Hami (Kumul) • Ejin Qi

Dushanbe • Kashi (Kashgar) • -154 • Kuqa • Korla

TAJIKISTAN +7495 • Akto • Shache (Yarkant)

AFGHAN. • Taxkorgan • Pishan (Guma) • TAKLIMAKAN SHAMO • Dunhuang • Yumen (Laljunmiao) • Jiayuguan

Hindu Kush 7119 • Ruoqiang (Qarklilk) • Lenghu • Da Qaidam • Qilian Shan

Peshawar • Hotan • Yutian (Keriya) • Qiemo (Qarqan) • Mangnai • Paidam Pendi • Xinir

K2 8611 • Minfeng (Niya) • A L T U N S H A N

Islamabad • Srinagar • K U N L U N 6973 • Muztag Feng • Golmud • Qinghai Hu • S H A

PAK. Rawalpindi • Boundary claimed by India • Hoh Xil Shan • Wuli • Madoi • Bayan Har Shan

LAHORE • Amritsar • Rutog 6720+ • Dogaicoring • C • Bayan Har Shan

Ludhiana • Qagcaka • QING ZANG GAOYUAN • Nyima (Pagnag) • Amdo • Tongtian • Yushu (Gyêgu)

Chandigarh • (Plateau of Tibet) • Baqên (Dartang)

DELHI • Moradabad • Gangdise Shan • Balngoin • Ngamda

New Delhi • Bareilly • NEPAL • Nyainqêntanglha Shan • Lhasa • Boundary claimed by China

Jaipur • Agra • Kathmandu • Thimphu • Xichan

Ajmer • Kanpur • Lucknow • Mount Everest 8850 (29035 ft) • BHUTAN • Dibrugarh

Kota • Allahabad • Jorhat • Panzhihua • Myitkyina

Ujjain • Varanasi (Banaras) • Patna • Guwahati • Kohima • Tengchong • Dali

INDIA • Jabalpur • Ranchi • Shillong • Imphal • Bhamo • Mogok

Indore • Bhopal • Ganga (Ganges) • Khulna • BANGLADESH • DHAKA

Amravati • HAORA • Narayanganj • CHITTAGONG • Mandalay

Albers Conic Equal-Area Projection • KOLKATA (Calcutta) • Sittwe (Akyab) • MYANMAR (BURMA)

0 — 250 — 500 MILES

0 — 250 — 500 KILOMETERS • Bhubaneshwar • BAY OF BENGAL • Nay Pyi Taw (admin.) • THAILAND

Hyderabad • Longitude East 90° of Greenwich • Taungoo

Angarsk
Irkutsk
Ulan Ude
Chita
S S
R
A
Sühbaatar
Darhan
Erdenet
Bulgan
Ulaanbaatar
(Ulan Bator)
Choybalsan
rvayheer Undurhaan
Baruun
Urt
Mandalgovĭ
Saynshand
(Buyant-Uhaa)
Dalandzadgad
Xilinhot
Erenhot
Duolun
(Dolonnur)
Taibus Qi
(Baochang)
Hanggin
Houqi
Hohhot
Jining
Zhangjiakou
Baotou
Datong
Shizuishan
nchuan
uwei
Huang He
(Yellow)
Shijiazhuang
Taiyuan
Handan
Zhengzhou
(Chengchow)
Lanzhou
Hezuo
Minxian
N
A
XI'AN
Luoyang
Hanzhong
Guangyuan
Deyang
CHENGDU
CHONGQING
Ya'an
zhou
bin
Changsha
Zunyi
Pingxiang
Zhaotong
Shaoyang
Hengyang
Guiyang
Guilin
Shaoguan
Ganzhou
Kunming
Liuzhou
GUANGZHOU
uxi
Gejiu
Wuzhou
SHENZHEN
Nanning
Beihai
HONG
Macau
KONG
VIETNAM
Hanoi
Zhanjiang
G. of
Tonkin
Basuo
Dongfang
Haikou
Hainan
+1867
Sanya
110°

Heilong
Jiang
Amur
Ostrov
Sakhalin
Tatarskiy
Proliv
Da Hinggan Ling
Hailar
Yakeshi
Nehe
Zalantun
Arxan
Hulun
Nur
Daqing
Qiqihar
Baicheng
Jiamusi
Qitaihe
Jixi
HARBIN
Didao
Mudanjiang
Changchun
Jilin
Songhua
Hu
Tongliao
Liaoyuan
SHENYANG
Fushun
Anshan
Dandong
Zhangjiakou
BEIJING
Tangshan
Korea
Bay
Bo Hai
Dalian
(Dairen)
Jinan
Zibo
Yantai
Tai'an
Qingdao
Xuzhou
Huainan
NANJING
Hefei
Wuxi
SHANGHAI
Yichang
WUHAN
Hangzhou
Huangshi
Jiujiang
Ningbo
Dongting
Hu
Nanchang
Wenzhou
Nanping
Woyi Shan
Fuzhou
Quanzhou
Xiamen
Shantou

Amur
Jagdaqi
Blagoveshchensk
Khabarovsk
Xiao Hinggan Ling
Yichun
Fujin
Khrebet Sikhote Alin'
Vladivostok
Ch'ŏngjin
SEA OF JAPAN
(EAST SEA)
NORTH
KOREA
P'yŏngyang
JAPAN
SEOUL
SOUTH KOREA
Incheon
Daejeon
Daegu
Busan
(Pusan)
KOBE
Hiroshima
Honshū
Gwangju
(Kwangju)
Fukuoka
Jeju-Do
S. Korea
Nagasaki
Kyūshū
YELLOW
SEA
Korea Strait
EAST
CHINA
SEA
Yaku Shima
Tanega Shima
30°
Amami Ō
Shima
Nansei Shotō
(Ryukyu Islands)
Tokuno Shima
Okinawa
Naha
PHILIPPINE SEA
Taipei (Taibei)
Iriomote Jima
Ishigaki Shima
Miyako Jima
Taichung
TAIWAN
TROPIC OF CANCER
Kaohsiung
TAIWAN
Bashi Channel
Taiwan Strait
Batan Is.
Babuyan Is.
Cape Bojeador
Laoag
Tuguegarao
PHILIPPINES
Luzon
SOUTH CHINA SEA
Qiongzhou Haixia
Dongsha
(Pratas I.)

The People's Republic of China
claims Taiwan as its 23rd province.
Taiwan's government maintains that there
are two political entities.

MONGOLIA

Argun

Nehe

130°

140°

50°

40°

30°

110° 95 120 130°

121

123 120°

A B C D E

4 5 6

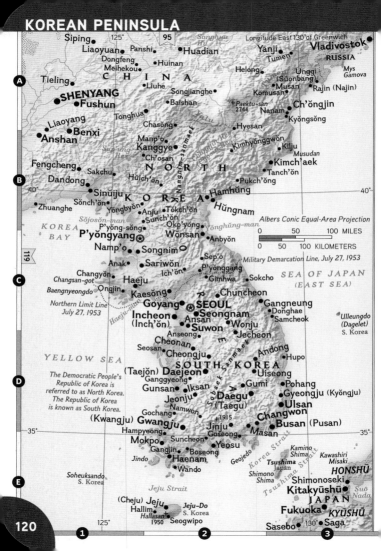

KOREAN PENINSULA

130°   95   135°   140°   Ostrov   145°
                                              Sakhalin
Yichun   SEA OF
Hegang Amur Khor   Yuzhno   OKHOTSK
Hailun   Heilong   Sakhalinsk
              Jiang   Svetlaya
                                    Kholmsk
CHINA   Jiamusi Bikin   Korsakov
        Hulin   Zaliv
Suihua   Dal'nerechensk   Amgu   Aniva   Mys Aniva
        Jixi   Lesozavodsk   Mys Kril'on
                                La Perouse Strait
        Mudanjiang Spassk Dal'niy Terney Rebun Tō Wakkanai
                                          Rishiri Tō Sōya Misaki
        Ussuriysk   Nayoro
                                                      Abashiri Wan
        Vladivostok   Asahikawa   Kitami
              Zaliv   Kamui Misaki HOKKAIDŌ +2290 Kushiro
        Nakhodka Petra   Otaru Obihiro
        Velikogo   Sapporo   Kunashir
Dunhua (Peter the   Tomakomai (Kunashiri)
        Great Bay)   Okushiri Tō Uchiura Wan Russia
                                              Erimo Misaki
Ch'ŏngjin   Hakodate
                                   Shirakami Misaki
NORTH   Tsugaru Kaikyō
KOREA   SEA OF JAPAN   Mutsu Wan Z
                                   Hirosaki Aomori
         (EAST SEA)   Hachinohe
                                   Nyūdō Zaki Morioka
Military Demarcation Line,   Akita Kamaishi
July 27, 1953   Tobi Shima Sakata Ichinoseki
         Ulleungdo   Yamagata U
         (Dagelet)   Niigata Sendai
         S. Korea   Sado Ishinomaki Wan
SOUTH   Fukushima
KOREA   Dokdo (Takeshima,   Maebashi
         Liancourt Rocks)   Nagano Utsunomiya
Daegu   S. Korea   Toyama Mito
(Taegu) Oki Shotō Wakasa Wan   Kanazawa Saitama
         Miho Wan   Matsumoto Kōfu TŌKYŌ
Korea St. Tottori Hinomi Saki   H Nagoya Kawasaki
         Matsue   KYŌTO +Fuji Yokohama
         Yamaguchi Takamatsu   KŌBE 3776 Tōkyō Wan
Hiroshima   OSAKA Shizuoka Sagami Nada
Tsushima Kitakyūshū SHIKOKU   Toyohashi Ise Wan
Fukuoka   Ōita Matsuyama   Wakayama Hamamatsu
Nagasaki Kumamoto Kōchi   Shiono Misaki Kumano Nada
Gotō   KYŪSHŪ Tokushima   Hachijō Jima
Rettō   Miyazaki Bungo Suidō   Aoga Shima
Noma   Kagoshima J   Beyoneisu Retsugan
Misaki   Kanoya   Sumisu Jima (Smith)
Ōsumi Shotō Osumi Kaikyō   Tori Shima
Yaku Shima (Van Diemen Strait)
Tanega Shima Albers Conic Equal-Area Projection
Tokara Kaikyō
(Colnett Strait)
Tokara Rettō Nakano Shima

PHILIPPINE SEA

Sōfu Gan
(Lot's Wife)

0   100   200 MILES
0   100   200 KILOMETERS

Longitude East 135° of Greenwich

Monywa • **Mandalay**
Kengtung
MYANMAR
(BURMA)
Arakan Yoma
Pyinmanaa •
Pyu
(Pyè) •
Hinthada •
Pathein •
YANGON
(Rangoon)
(legislative)

Louangphrabang •
Thai Nguyen •
119
Nanning •
110°
CHINA
GUANGZHO
Macau •
HONG
Zhanjiang
KONG
Qiongzhou Haixia
Haiphong ⊕
Nam Dinh •
Haikou •
Thanh Hoa •
Dongfang •
Vinh •
Hainan
Sanya •

Fan Si Pan
3142±
Hanoi ⊕
Phu
Bia ±2818
Nay Pyi Taw
administrative

Chiang Mai •
Doi Inthanon
2565±

Viangchan
(Vientiane) ⊕
LAOS
Phitsanulok •
Huê ⊕
Da
Nang •

Paracel
Islands

Sar

Mawlamyine •
THAILAND
Nakhon
Sawan •
Khon
Kaen •
Pakxé •

Ye •
Nakhon
Pathom •
Dawei •
Myeik •
KRUNG THEP
(Bangkok) ⊕
Samut
Prakan •
CAMBODIA
±1813
Tônlé Sap
Buon Me Thuot •
Phnom Aural
Pleiku •
Qui Nhon •
Nha Trang •
Da Lat •
Cam Ranh •
Phnom Penh ⊕
Bien Hoa •
HO CHI MINH CITY
(Saigon)

Nakhon Ratchasima •

Tenasserim
Gulf of Martaban

ANDAMAN
SEA
Isthmus
of Kra
Gulf of
Thailand
Dao Phu
Quoc
Can
Tho •
Rach
Gia •
Mekong River Delta

10°
Surat Thani •
Ko Samui
Nakhon Si
Thammarat •
Mui Bai Bung

Spratly Islands

Palaw
2100

Nicobar
Islands
India
Phuket •
Ko Phuket

Hat Yai •

Balabac
Bangg
Balabac Strait
Kota Kinabalu
Kina
+4101

Great Channel

Banda
Aceh •
George
Town •
Taiping •
Ipoh •
MALAYSIA
Kuala
Terengganu •
Kota Baharu •
Kep.
Anambas
Indonesia
Kep.
Natuna
Besar
Kep.
Natuna
Selatan
Bandar Seri
Begawan ⊕
BRUNEI
Miri •
Sandaka
Tawa

Medan •
Kuantan •
Bintulu •
MALAYSIA
Tarakan •

Pematangsiantar •
Simeulue
Kuala Lumpur ⊛
Seremban •
Sibu •
Kuching •
BORNEO

Kep. Banyak
Nias
Johor Bahru •
SINGAPORE
Singapore
(KALIMANTAN)
+2987
Bonta
Samarinda •

0°
Kepulauan Batu
Pekanbaru •
Singkawang •
Pontianak •
Balikpapan •

Padang •
Kep.
Lingga
S
Kerinci
+3800
Jambi •
Selat Karimata
Kep. Karimata
G R E A T E R
Palangkaraya •

Siberut
Kep. Mentawai
Sipura
Pagai Utara
Pagai Selatan
Palembang •
Selat Gelasa
Belitung
Bangka
Banjarmasin •
Martapura •
Laut

Bengkulu •
Lahat •
S U N D A
I S L A

Enggano
Kotabumi •
Krui •
Tanjungkarang-Telubketung
JAKARTA ⊛
Bekasi •
Semarang •
Madura
Surabaya •
Kep. Kange

INDIAN
OCEAN
Selat Sunda
Bogor •
Bandung •
Tasikmalaya •
Surakarta •
Malang •
Yogyakarta
Bali
BALI SEA
Lessε
Sum
Denpasar •
Banyuwangi •

JAVA
(JAWA)
Pekalongan

10°
Christmas Island
Australia
Longitude East 110°of Greenwich

INDONESIA
Selat Karimata

1
100°
2
3

PACIFIC OCEAN

120°
TAIWAN
•Kaohsiung
Bashi Channel
130°
140°
20°

LUZON
STRAIT
Batan Islands

A

oag•
•Aparri
gan• •Tuguegarao
do• Mount Pulog 2934
guio• LUZON
Mt. Pinatubo 1780
•les•
•Quezon City
MANILA

Catanduanes
•Legazpi Sorsogon

Babuyan Islands

160

B

FEDERATED STATES
OF MICRONESIA
Ulithi Atoll
10°

tangas•
Mindoro
ip
•Masbate

Calbayog
Masbate• Samar
•Tacloban
Roxas• Panay Cebu •Leyte
Iloilo• •Cebu
•Bacolod
Negros Bohol

Yap Islands

Fais

Sorol Atoll

erto
incesa
ULU SEA

Siargao

Bohol Sea
Butuan
•Cagayan de Oro
•Iligan MINDANAO
•Pagadian
mboanga Mount Apo
•Basilan 2954 •Davao
Davao Gulf
•General Santos

Ngulu Atoll

CAROLINE ISLANDS

PALAU
⊗Melekeok
Babelthuap

C

Sulu Arch.
•Tawi Tawi
el Bay

Sonsorol Islands

Pulo Anna
Merir

ELEBES SEA
•Manado
•Tolitoli
•Gorontalo
*Teluk
Tomini*

Kepulauan
Talaud

Tobi•
•Helen Island

•Morotai
1635+
Halmahera
•Ternate

EQUATOR

0°

Teluk
Tomini
Bacan
Peleng Mangole Obi
Taliabu
Kep. Sula

Halmahera
Sea
Salawati Waigeo
Misool
•Sorong

D

ULAWESI
CELEBES)
55+

Supiori
Biak

Tanjung D'Urville
Yapen •Sarmi
•Jayapura

•Parepare •Kendari
S Wowoni
•Bone Buton
•Makassar (Ujungpandang)
ayar

Buru

Ceram
•Ambon

Teluk Berau
•Fakfak
Teluk
Cenderawasih

•Aitape

Puncak Jaya
4884+
•Timika

NEW GUINEA

Kalao

Baubau

BANDA SEA

Kep. Kai
Tual
Kep.
Aru

Wokam
Kobroor
Trangan

Teluk
Flamingo

PAPUA
NEW
GUINEA
•Kepi

•Muting

E

•Makassar (Ujungpandang)

Kep. Tanimbar

FLORES SEA
•Ruteng
•Flores
NDA ISLANDS
•Waingapu
ba •Sawu

Lomblen
Pantar Damar Romang
Alor Wetar Babar
Moa

Yamdena
Selaru

Dolak
•Merauke
Tanjung Vals

Dili
TIMOR-LESTE
(EAST TIMOR)

ARAFURA
SEA

120°
Roti
•Kupang

130°
TIMOR SEA
AUSTRALIA
149

SEA

140°
10°

123

Azimuthal Equidistant Projection
0   250   500 MILES
0   250   500 KILOMETERS

4   5   6

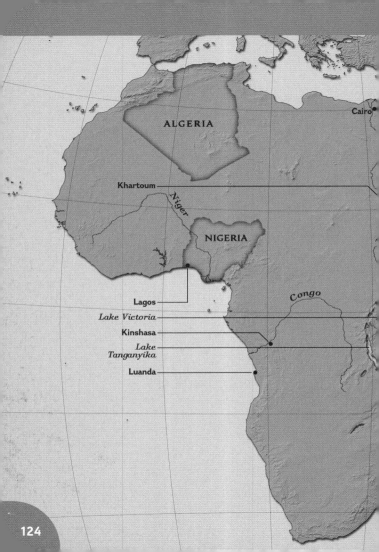

ALGERIA

Cairo

Khartoum

Niger

NIGERIA

Lagos

Lake Victoria

Congo

Kinshasa

Lake Tanganyika

Luanda

AFRICA

GEOGRAPHIC EXTREMES

Lake Assal
-156 m
(-512 ft)

Kilimanjaro
5,895 m
(19,340 ft)

SEYCHELLES

Lake Malawi
(Lake Nyasa)

CONTINENTAL POLITICAL FACTS

TOTAL NUMBER OF COUNTRIES: 54

LARGEST COUNTRY BY AREA: Algeria
2,381,740 sq km (919,595 sq mi)

SMALLEST COUNTRY BY AREA:
Seychelles 455 sq km (176 sq mi)

MOST POPULOUS COUNTRY: Nigeria
155,216,000

LEAST POPULOUS COUNTRY: Seychelles
89,000

LARGEST CITIES BY POPULATION:
Cairo, Egypt 11,000,000
Lagos, Nigeria 10,580,000
Kinshasa, Dem. Rep. Congo 8,750,000
Khartoum, Sudan 5,175,000
Luanda, Angola 4,770,000

CONTINENTAL PHYSICAL FACTS

AREA: 30,065,000 sq km
(11,608,000 sq mi)

HIGHEST POINT: Kilimanjaro,
Tanzania 5,895 m (19,340 ft)

LOWEST POINT: Lake Assal, Djibouti
-156 m (-512 ft)

LONGEST RIVERS:
Nile 6,695 km (4,160 mi)
Congo 4,700 km (2,900 mi)
Niger 4,170 km (2,591 mi)

LARGEST NATURAL LAKES:
Lake Victoria 69,500 sq km
(26,800 sq mi)
Lake Tanganyika 32,600 sq km
(12,600 sq mi)
Lake Malawi (Lake Nyasa) 28,900 sq
km (11,200 sq mi)

125

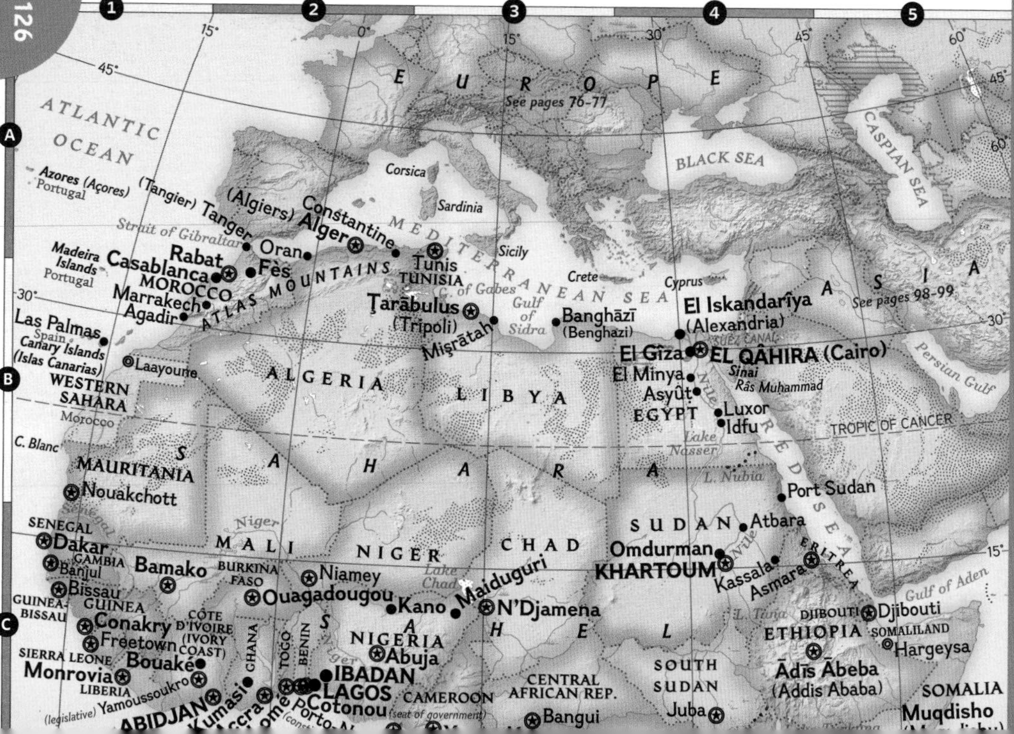
EUROPE
See pages 76-77
ATLANTIC OCEAN
Azores (Açores) Portugal
Madeira Islands Portugal
Las Palmas
Spain
Canary Islands (Islas Canarias)
Strait of Gibraltar
(Tangier) Tanger
(Algiers) Alger
Constantine
Oran
Rabat
Casablanca
Fès
MOROCCO
Marrakech
Agadir
ATLAS MOUNTAINS
Corsica
Sardinia
Sicily
Crete
Cyprus
MEDITERRANEAN SEA
Tunis
TUNISIA
G. of Gabes
Ţarābulus (Tripoli)
Mişrātah
Gulf of Sidra
Banghāzī (Benghazi)
BLACK SEA
CASPIAN SEA
ASIA
See pages 98-99
El Iskandarîya (Alexandria)
SUEZ CANAL
El Gîza
EL QÂHIRA (Cairo)
Sinai
Râs Muhammad
Persian Gulf
El Minya
Asyûţ
EGYPT
Luxor
Idfu
Lake Nasser
TROPIC OF CANCER
RED SEA
L. Nubia
Port Sudan
Laayoune
WESTERN SAHARA
Morocco
C. Blanc
ALGERIA
LIBYA
SAHARA
MAURITANIA
Nouakchott
Senegal
SENEGAL
Dakar
GAMBIA
Banjul
Bissau
GUINEA-BISSAU
GUINEA
Conakry
Freetown
SIERRA LEONE
Monrovia
LIBERIA
CÔTE D'IVOIRE (IVORY COAST)
Bouaké
Yamoussoukro (legislative)
ABIDJAN
Kumasi
Accra
GHANA
TOGO
BENIN
Porto-Novo
Cotonou (seat of government)
Bamako
MALI
Niger
BURKINA FASO
Ouagadougou
Niamey
NIGER
SAHEL
NIGERIA
Abuja
IBADAN
LAGOS
Kano
Maiduguri
Lake Chad
CHAD
N'Djamena
CAMEROON
CENTRAL AFRICAN REP.
Bangui
SUDAN
Atbara
Omdurman
KHARTOUM
Nile
Kassala
Asmara
ERITREA
SOUTH SUDAN
Juba
L. Tana
ETHIOPIA
Ādīs Ābeba (Addis Ababa)
DJIBOUTI
Djibouti
Gulf of Aden
SOMALILAND
Hargeysa
SOMALIA
Muqdisho
45°
30°
15°
0°
60°

EQUATOR

Nairobi
Mwanza Mombasa
RWANDA **Kigali** *Ungoma Bay*
Bujumbura **Arusha** Pemba I.
BURUNDI **Dodoma** Zanzibar
DEMOCRATIC TANZANIA **Dar es Salaam**
REPUBLIC (legislative)
Lake
OF THE CONGO Tanganyika L. Malawi
Kananga **Likasi** Kitwe MALAWI **Nampula**
(Léopoldville) **KINSHASA** Ndola **Lilongwe**
Mbuji-Mayi **Lumbashi** **Blantyre**
Kolwezi **Harare**
Luanda ZAMBIA ZIMBABWE
ANGOLA **Lusaka** **Bulawayo**
CABINDA **Huambo** Okavango Delta MOZAMBIQUE
Angola *Bengo Bay*
BOTSWANA
Windhoek **Gaborone**
NAMIBIA Etosha Pan
Makgadikgadi
Johannesburg
SOUTH **Bloemfontein**
AFRICA **Maseru**
Pretoria (Tshwane) (administrative)
Mbabane (administrative)
SWAZILAND
Maputo
LESOTHO
Durban
Port Elizabeth
Algoa Bay
(judicial)
St. Helena Bay Mossel Bay
(legislative) **Cape Town** False Bay
Cape of Good Hope Cape Agulhas

Brazzaville
GABON
CONGO
SÃO TOMÉ
AND PRÍNCIPE

SEYCHELLES
Cape d'Ambre
Antananarivo
COMOROS **Moroni** MADAGASCAR
Cape Ste. Marie
Mozambique Channel

I N D I A N
O C E A N

A T L A N T I C

O C E A N

Ascension
U.K.

Saint Helena
U.K.

Tristan da
Cunha Group
U.K.

TROPIC OF CAPRICORN

Meridain of Greenwich (London)

Longitude East 15° of Greenwich

Azimuthal Equidistant Projection

0   500   1000 MI
0   500   1000 KM

127

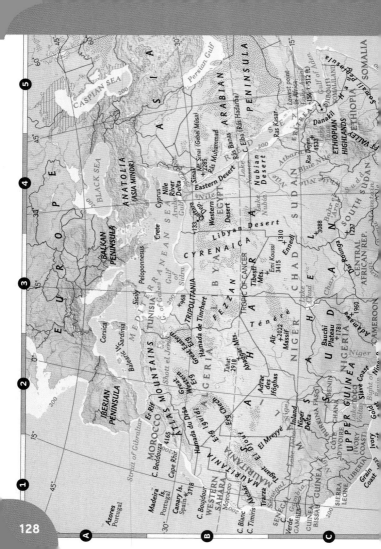

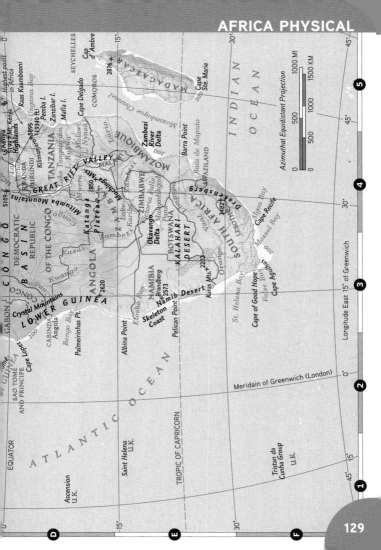

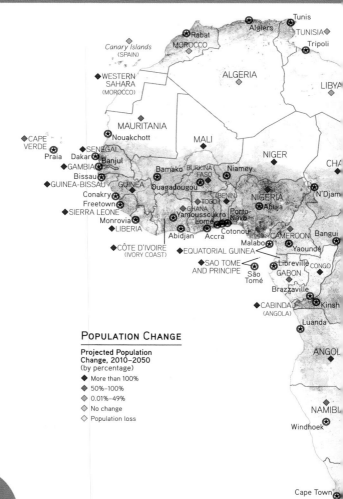

POPULATION CHANGE

Projected Population Change, 2010–2050 (by percentage)

◆ More than 100%
◆ 50%–100%
◇ 0.01%–49%
◇ No change
◇ Population loss

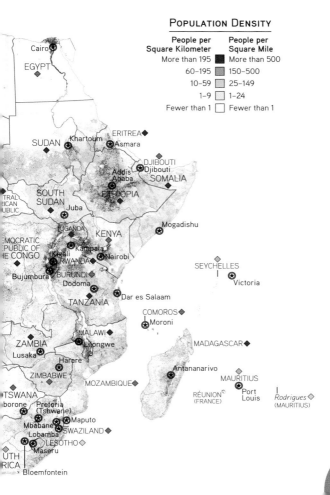

POPULATION DENSITY

People per Square Kilometer		People per Square Mile
More than 195	■	More than 500
60–195	■	150–500
10–59	■	25–149
1–9	□	1–24
Fewer than 1	□	Fewer than 1

EGYPT
Cairo

SUDAN
Khartoum
ERITREA
Asmara
DJIBOUTI
Djibouti
Addis Ababa
ETHIOPIA
SOMALIA

CENTRAL AFRICAN REPUBLIC
SOUTH SUDAN
Juba

DEMOCRATIC REPUBLIC OF THE CONGO

UGANDA
Kampala
KENYA
Kigali
RWANDA
Nairobi
BURUNDI
Bujumbura
Dodoma
TANZANIA
Dar es Salaam

Mogadishu

SEYCHELLES
Victoria

MALAWI
Lilongwe
COMOROS
Moroni

ZAMBIA
Lusaka
Harare
ZIMBABWE
MOZAMBIQUE

MADAGASCAR
Antananarivo

MAURITIUS
Port Louis
RÉUNION
(FRANCE)
Rodrigues
(MAURITIUS)

BOTSWANA
Gaborone
Pretoria (Tshwane)
Mbabane
Maputo
Lobamba
SWAZILAND
LESOTHO
Maseru
SOUTH AFRICA
Bloemfontein

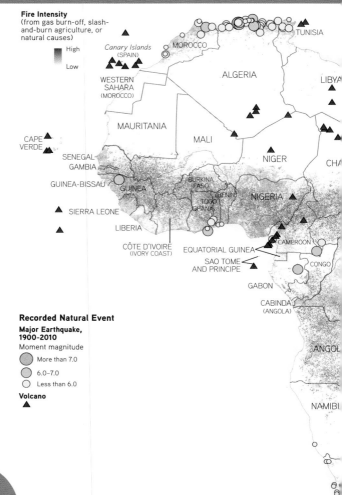

Fire Intensity
(from gas burn-off, slash-and-burn agriculture, or natural causes)

High

Low

Canary Islands
(SPAIN)

MOROCCO

WESTERN
SAHARA
(MOROCCO)

ALGERIA

TUNISIA

LIBYA

CAPE
VERDE

MAURITANIA

MALI

NIGER

CHA

SENEGAL

GAMBIA

GUINEA-BISSAU

GUINEA

BURKINA
FASO

BENIN

TOGO

GHANA

NIGERIA

SIERRA LEONE

LIBERIA

CÔTE D'IVOIRE
(IVORY COAST)

EQUATORIAL GUINEA

SAO TOME
AND PRINCIPE

GABON

CABINDA
(ANGOLA)

CAMEROON

CONGO

ANGOL

NAMIBI

Recorded Natural Event

**Major Earthquake,
1900-2010**

Moment magnitude

More than 7.0

6.0–7.0

Less than 6.0

Volcano

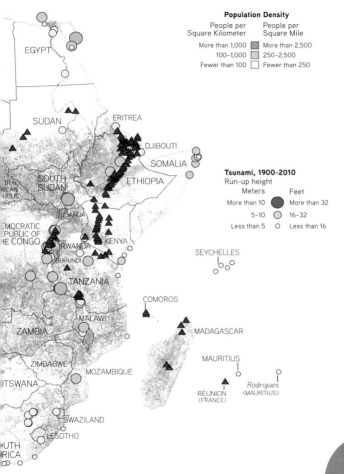

Population Density

People per Square Kilometer		People per Square Mile
More than 1,000		More than 2,500
100–1,000		250–2,500
Fewer than 100		Fewer than 250

EGYPT

SUDAN

ERITREA

DJIBOUTI

SOMALIA

SOUTH SUDAN

ETHIOPIA

CENTRAL AFRICAN REPUBLIC

UGANDA

DEMOCRATIC REPUBLIC OF THE CONGO

RWANDA

BURUNDI

KENYA

SEYCHELLES

Tsunami, 1900–2010
Run-up height

Meters		Feet
More than 10		More than 32
5–10		16–32
Less than 5		Less than 16

TANZANIA

COMOROS

MALAWI

ZAMBIA

MADAGASCAR

MAURITIUS

ZIMBABWE

MOZAMBIQUE

BOTSWANA

Rodrigues (MAURITIUS)

RÉUNION (FRANCE)

SWAZILAND

LESOTHO

SOUTH AFRICA

LAND COVER

- ▪ Evergreen needleleaf forest
- ▪ Evergreen broadleaf forest
- ▪ Deciduous needleleaf forest
- ▪ Deciduous broadleaf forest
- ▪ Mixed forest
- ▪ Woody savanna
- ▪ Savanna
- ▪ Closed shrubland

- □ Open shrubland
- □ Grassland
- □ Cropland
- □ Barren or sparsely vegetated
- ▪ Urban or built up
- □ Snow and ice
- ▪ Cropland / natural vegetation mosaic
- ▪ Wetland

- O City with more than 5 million inhabitants

CLIMATE ZONES

(based on modified Köppen system)

Humid equatorial climate (A)
- No dry season (Af)
- Short dry season (Am)
- Dry winter (Aw)

Dry climate (B)
- Semiarid (BS) } h = hot
- Arid (BW) } k = cold

Humid temperate climate (C)
- No dry season (Cf) } a = hot summer
- Dry winter (Cw)
- Dry summer (Cs) } b = cool summer

Highland climate (H)
- Unclassified highlands

WATER AVAILABILITY

(in millimeters per-person per-year)

- More than 750
- 251–750
- 26–250
- Less than 26
- No data available

Azimuthal Equidistant Projection

0 250 500 MILES

0 250 500 KILOMETERS

20° 10° 0° (Philip

SPAIN

Málaga

Cádiz GIBRALTAR U.K.

Strait of Gibraltar

(Tangier) Tanger Ceuta Sp. Melilla Oran Algers

(Port Lyautey) Kenitra Tétouan Sp. Oujda (Algiers)

Rabat Fès (Fez) Tlaret N

Casablanca Meknès M Sidi Bel Djelfa

Funchal Abbès Laghoua

Madeira Safi Marrakech Béchar Gharda

Islands Cap Beddouza

Portugal Beni

Cap Rhir Abbès El

ATLANTIC Jbel Toubkal Grand Erg Occidental Golea

30° 4165 Hamada du Drâa Timimoun

Agadir Plateau

OCEAN Tabelbala Tadem

Lanzarote

Fuerteventura Goulimine A

Tenerife C. Juby Tarfaya Tindouf L G

La Palma (Villa Bens) Erg Iguidi I-n-Salah

Santa Cruz de Tenerife Laayoune Reggane

Canary Islands Gran Smara Tadjmo

(Islas Canarias) Canaria

Spain Boujdour Erg Chech

WESTERN SAHARA Bir Mogreïn A

Western Sahara (in gray) is in (Fort Trinquet)

dispute and has been administered

by Morocco since 1979. Mdennah

Ad Dakhla

TROPIC OF CANCER Zouîrat

Cap Barbas 915 Taoudenni

Nouadhibou Techla (Smeïda) Tessalit

(Port Étienne) Akchâr Adrar Ti-n-Zaouâtene

Cap Blanc Ouadane (Ft. Pierre Bordes)

Baie du Lévrier Adrar des

Cap Timiris Atar Ifôghas

20° (Mirik) Akjoujt Kidal

MAURITANIA Araouane Anefis

Nouakchott i-n-Daran

Tidjikja El Mreyyé Ménaka

Rosso Tombouctou Niger Gao

Saint-Louis Kaédi Kiffa (Timbuktu) L Hombori

Mbout Timbedgha Néma Ménaka

Dakar Thiès SENEGAL Nioro du Sahel 1155

Mbour Diourbel Nara Mopti Niamey

Kaolack Kayes Markala A

GAMBIA Banjul Koulikoro Ségou S BURKINA FASO

Ziguinchor M Ouagadougou Dosso

GUINEA-BISSAU Kédougou Bamako

Bissau Fouta +952 Gaya

Arquipélago Djallon Sikasso Bobo Dioulasso

dos Bijagós Boké Labé Bawku Kandi

Îles Tristao Fria GUINEA Kankan GHANA BENIN Parako

Kindia Tamale Toco

Conakry Kabala Korhogo Porto-

SIERRA Kissidougou (seat of Novo

Freetown LEONE Guéckédo CÔTE D'IVOIRE government) Cotonou LAGO

Yawri Bay Nzérékoré (IVORY COAST) Bouaké Kumasi

Sherbro I. Kenema Man Daloa Lomé

Robertsport Gbarnga Lake Accra

Monrovia Ganta Yamoussoukro Volta Divo ABIDJAN Slave Co

Buchanan Zwedru (legislative) (administrative)

Greenville LIBERIA (administrative) Gold Coast Bight of

Harper C. Palmas Ivory Coast Sekondi-Takoradi GULF OF GUINE

Longitude West 10° of Greenwich

1 2 3

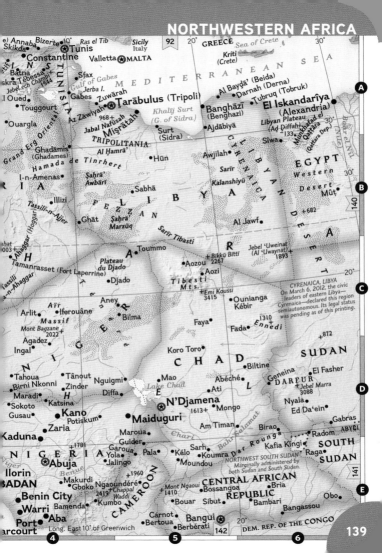

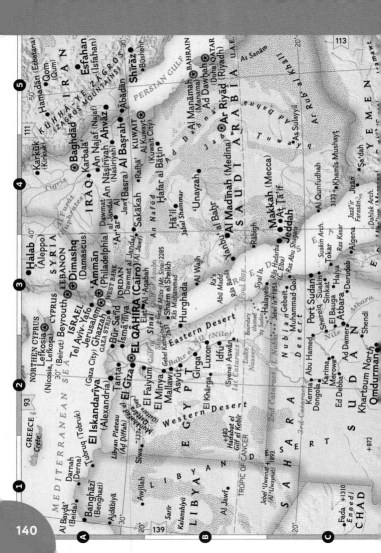

I R A N

Ḥamadān (Ecbatana)
(Qom)
Esfahan (Isfahan)

KÜH-HĀ-YE ZAGROS (ZAGROS MOUNTAINS)

Karkūk (Kirkuk)
Baghdād
Karbalā'
An Najaf (Najaf)
Ahwāz
Ābādān
Būsheh

Shīrāz

PERSIAN GULF

BAHRAIN
Al Manāmah
Manamah
(Doha) QATAR
Ad Dawḥah
U.A.E.

As Sanām

I R A Q

Al Furāt
(Euphrates)

Dawmat
An Nāṣirīyah
(Nasīrīyah)
Al Baṣrah

Jaw (Basra)

KUWAIT
Al Kuwayt (Kuwait City)

Ar Riyāḍ (Riyadh)

Ar Rub' al Khālī

Baḥra

Ḥalab 40°
(Aleppo)

S Y R I A

Dimashq (Damascus)

LEBANON

Beyrouth (Beirut)

NORTHERN CYPRUS
Lefkoşia
(Nicosia, Lefkoşa)
CYPRUS

ISRAEL
Tel Aviv-Yafo

Ammān
JORDAN

Rafḥa'
Ḥafar al Bāṭin

Sakākah
Ar'ar
Jawf (Al Jawf)
Dawmat al Jandal

An Nafūd

Ḥā'il
Jabal Shammar

Buraydah

SAUDI ARABIA

'Unayzah

Al Madīnah (Medina)

As Sulayyil

Ṭuwa

GREECE
Crete
93

MEDITERRANEAN SEA

Damah (Derna)

Tubruq (Tobruk)

Al Bayḍā' (Beida)

Banghāzī (Benghazi)

Ajdābiyā

Awjilah

Sarīr

Kalanshiyū

Al Jawf

L I B Y A N

Jebel 'Uweinat (Al'Uwayrāt) +1893

S A H A R A

Fada +1310
Ennedi
CHAD

Damāh

Jerusalem
Būr Saïd
Ismā'īlīya
GAZA STRIP
Gaza City
Ghazzah
WEST BANK
(Philadelphia)

EL QĀHIRA (Cairo)
El Gīza
El Faiyûm
El Minya
Mallawi
Asyûṭ
El Khārga

E G Y P T

Western Desert

Libyan Plateau
(Ad Diffah)

Qattara
Muṭṭabat

Siwa

−133

Ḥaṭīabet el Gilf el Kebir

TROPIC OF CANCER

Elat
Al 'Aqabah

Gulf of Aqaba

Gebel Mûsa (Mt. Sinai) 2285
Gebel Kathrîn
Sinai
Sharm el Sheikh
Râs Muḥammad

Al Wajh

Yanbu' al Baḥr

Rābigh

MAKKAH (Mecca)
Jeddah
At Ṭā'if

Al Qunfudhah

3133 +
Khamīs Mushayṭ

Ṣa'dah

Y E M E N

Ḥurghada

Râs Gharib
Foul Bay
Abu Ramâd

Siyal Is.
Râs Banâs
Jebel Is +1651
(C. Elba)
Ras Hadarba

Ra's Madd
Abū Ramād

Gebel Shâyib

Râ's
Shâgara

Ras Kasar

Algena

Jazā'ir
Farasān

Dahlak Arch.

Dahlak Archipelago

'amawt

Luxor
(Nile)
Idfu
Aswân
(Syene) Aswân
1st Cataract

Bir d El Nile

Lake Nasser

Boundary claimed by Sudan

Nubian
Desert

Suakin Arch.

Port Sudan
Suakin
Sawākin
Tokar
Muhammad Gol
Halya

Derudeb

Kerma
Abu Hamed

S U D A N

Dongola
Karima
Merowe
Ed Debba

Sherejq
Sinkat
El Bauga
Atbara
Ad Damer

Kassala

3rd Cataract
2nd Cataract
Bir el Cataract

Nile

Atbara

Shendi

Khartoum North
Omdurman

+872

Tanta
Alexandria
El Iskandarîya

139

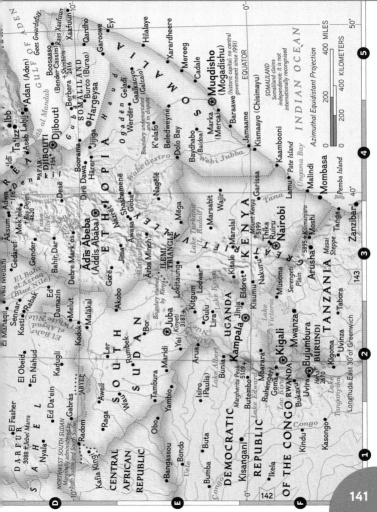

MILES

KILOMETERS

INDIAN OCEAN

SOMALILAND
Somaliland claims
independence, but it is not
internationally recognized

Azimuthal Equidistant Projection

EQUATOR

SOMALIA

Muqdisho (Mogadishu)
(historic capital; no central
government since 1991)

GULF OF ADEN

Gulf of Aden

Adan (Aden)
'Aseb Lahij
Ta'izz
Ibb

Bab al Mandab

DJIBOUTI
Djibouti

Bender Cassim (Boosaaso)
Raas Xaafuun
Xaafuun
Gees Gwardafuy
Raas Maskan

Eyl
Hilalaye
Qardho
Garoowe

Xarardheere
Mereeg
Cadale

Muqdisho (Mogadishu)
Marka (Merca)
Baraawe

Berbera (Burao)
Burco
Hargeysa
Galaakacyo (Galcaio)
Werder
Shimbiris
2416
Geladi

G u b a n

O g a d ē n
Boundary undemarcated
and in dis, in dispute

Jijiga
Booraama
Dirē Dawa
Hārer
Wabē Gestro

K'elafo
Beledweyne
Dolo Bay
Baydhabo (Baidoa)
Baraawe
Jamaame
Kismaayo (Chisimayu)

ERITREA
Adwa
Aksum
Mek'elē
Adigrat

Mitsiwa'

AFAR
DEPRESSION
-156'

Ras Dejen
4620

Trans-Aksum

Gonder
Bahir Dar
Debre Mark'os
Desē

Nazrēt
Shashemenē
Gorē
Jima
Goba
Ārba Minch'
Mēga
Marsabit
Moyale

Āwasa
Nagēlē

ETHIOPIA

Adīs Abeba (Addis Ababa)

El Obeid
El Fasher
Ed Da'ein
Nyala
Tekeze
Gedaref
El Baḥr el Azraq (Blue Nile)
Rabak
Kosti
Sennar
Ed Damazin
Melut
Malakal
Kodok

SAHEL

DARFUR
Jebel Marra
3088

Kafia Kingi

El Managil

White Nile
El Baḥr el Abyad

NORTHWEST SOUTH SUDAN
Marginally administered
by both Sudan and South Sudan

ABYEI

Kadugli
En Nahud

SOUTH SUDAN

Awiel
Raga
Wau

Bor
Akobo
Ler
Rumbek
Tambura
Yambio
Obo
Yei
Maridi
Juba
Kinyeti
3187
Marīdi

Bunia
Isiro (Paulis)
Butembo
Kindu
Kasongo
Bumba
Buta
Bondo

Bangassou

CENTRAL
AFRICAN
REPUBLIC

DEMOCRATIC
REPUBLIC
OF THE CONGO

Kisangani
Ikela
Uele

Congo

Lake Albert

Lake Edward
Margherita Peak
5109
Ruwenzori

Lake Kivu
Bukavu
Goma
Uvira
Kigoma

Lake Tanganyika

RWANDA
Kigali
BURUNDI
Bujumbura
Ruhengeri

Heha
2670

UGANDA
Kampala
Jinja
Gulu
Lira
Arua
Lake Kyoga
Lake Albert

Boundary claimed
by Kenya

LEMI
TRIANGLE

Lake Turkana
(L. Rudolf)

Lokitaung
Lodwar
Kitgum

KENYA

Lake Victoria
Kisumu
Eldoret
Nakuru
Kitale
Maralal
Wajir
Garissa
Tana
Kericho
Ruiru
Thika
Nairobi
Machakos

Mount Kenya
5199

Mombasa
Malindi
Lamu
Pate Island
Kaambooni
Ungwana Bay

Pemba Island

Mwanza
Musoma
Serengeti Plain
Masai Steppe
Kilimanjaro
5895
Moshi
Arusha
Tanga
Zanzibar
Tabora
Uvinza

TANZANIA

Kigoma
Serengeti

Longitude East 30° of Greenwich

CENTRAL AFRICAN REPUBLIC

10° • Bafousam
Loum • Nkongsamba • Bertoua • Bangui ⊛ Bangassou •
Cameroon Mt. • Douala CAMEROON • Berbérati Bosobolo • Bondo •
4095+ • Yaoundé • Nola Businga • Buta •
BIOKO • Malabo Gemena • Bumba •
EQUATORIAL • Ebolowa • Sangmélima Impfondo Lisala • Basoko •
Bight of Bonny GUINEA • Bata RÍO • Bitam + Mont Nabeda Basankusu
MUNI • Oyem 1020 Ouesso
Baie de + Mont Bengoué Mbandaka EQUATOR
Mondah • Libreville • Makokou 1070 (Coquilhatville) • Boende
0° Owando • Mossaka DEMOCRA
Cap Lopez G A B O N Inongo REPUBL
Port-Gentil Moanda • Lac Mai-Ndombe
Iguéla • Franceville Congo OF THE
Tchibanga • Mossendjo Djambala Bandundu CONGO
Mayumba • Sibiti Brazzaville Lukenie Ileb o • Mweka • Mbuji-
Pointe Banda Dolisie ⊛ KINSHASA Kasai Kikwit Luebo • Mayi
Pointe-Noire (Loubomo) (Léopoldville) Kananga (Bakwanga)
Angola CABINDA Mbanza-Ngungu Lusanga Tshikapa Gandajika •
Cabinda Boma • Kimpese • Kahemba • Mwene-
Matadi Chitato Lucapa Ditu
N'zeto • Songo (Dundo) Kamina •
ATLANTIC Uíge • Capenda- Saurimo • Sandoa
OCEAN Baía do Luanda Camulemba Dilolo • Kat
Bengo
Ponta das Palmeirinhas • Catete
Dondo • Malanje
10° Calulo •
Porto Amboim ANGOLA Luena •
Azimuthal Equidistant Projection • Sumbe Zambeze
0 150 300 MI Lobito • Morro + Kuito Lungwebungu •
0 150 300 KM Benguela de Môco Huambo • Zambezi
Cabo de Santa Maria 2620
• Lucira Kuvango • Menongue
Namibe • Lubango Cuito Cuanavale Cuando Mongu •
Tombua • Z
Baía dos Tigres Humbe • Katima Mulilo
Foz do Cunene • Ondjíva Cuito Dirico CAPRIVI STRIP
NAMIBIA Okavango BOTSWAN
10° 144 Longitude East 20° of Greenwich

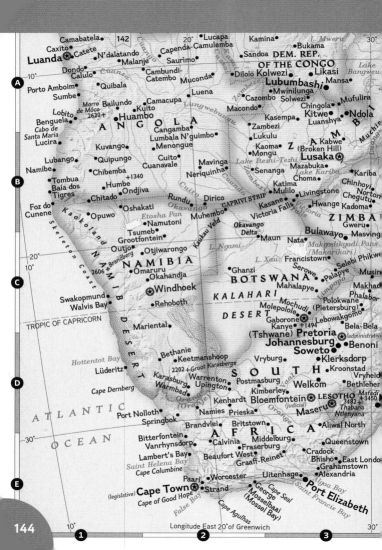

Camabatela
Caxito
Luanda
N'dalatando
Catete
Camba-Camulemba
Lucapa
Kamina
L. Mweru
Bukama
Porto Amboim
Dondo
Calulo
Malanje
Saurimo
Sandoa
DEM. REP.
OF THE CONGO
Dilolo Kolwezi
Lubumbashi
Mansa
Lake
Bangweu
Sumbe
Quibala
Cambundi-
Catembo
Muconda
Cazombo Solwezi
Mwinilunga
Likasi
Lobito
Morro
de Móco
2620
Bailundo
Camacupa
Luena
Macondo
Kasempa
Chingola
Lukulu
Kitwe
Mufulira
Luanshya
N
Benguela
Cabo de
Santa Maria
Lucira
Huambo
Kuito
Cangamba
Zambezi
Zambezi
Kaoma
Mongu
Mazabuka
Kariba
Chinhoyi
Norton
Chegutu
Kabwe
(Broken Hill)
Lusaka
Ndola
d
Lubango
Kuvango
Quipungo
Menongue
Lumbala N'guimbo
Cuito
Cuanavale
Mavinga
Lake Itezhi-Tezhi
Senanga
Lake Kariba
Choma
Namibe
Chibemba
+1340
Neriquinha
Katima
Mulilo
Livingstone
Hwange
Kadoma
Tombua
Baía dos
Tigres
Humbe
Ondjiva
Chitado
Rundu
Dirico
CAPRIVI STRIP
Kasane
Victoria Falls
Victoria
Falls
ZIMBA
Foz do
Cunene
Oshakati
Okavango
Muhembo
Gweru
Opuwo
Etosha Pan
Okavango
Delta
Maun
Nata
Makgadikgadi Pans
(Makarikari)
Bulawayo
Masving
Namutoni
Tsumeb
Kaudum Veld
Grootfontein
Brandberg
2606
Outjo
Otjiwarongo
L. Ngami
L. Xau
Francistown
Serowe
Selebi Phikw
Ghanzi
BOTSWANA
Palapye
Musin
Omaruru
Okahandja
NAMIBIA
Mahalapye
Makhad
Phalabor
Windhoek
KALAHARI
Mochudi
Molepolole
Polokwane
(Pietersburg)
Lebowakgomo
Swakopmund
Walvis Bay
Rehoboth
DESERT
Kanye
+1494
Gaborone
Bela-Bela
TROPIC OF CAPRICORN
Mariental
(Tshwane)
Pretoria
(administrati
Johannesburg
Benoni
Soweto
Klerksdorp
Bethanie
Keetmanshoop
2202
Groot Karasberge
Karasberge
Vryburg
SOUTH
Kroonstad
Vryheid
Bethlehe
Hottentot Bay
Lüderitz
Warmbad
Warrenton
Upington
Postmasburg
Welkom
Cape Dernberg
Kenhardt
Namies
Prieska
Kimberley
Bloemfontein
AFRICA
LESOTHO
(judicial)
Maseru
Mafadi
3482
3450
Thabana
Ntlenyana
ATLANTIC
Port Nolloth
Springbok
Brandvlei
Britstown
AFRICA
Aliwal North
OCEAN
Bitterfontein
Vanrhynsdorp
Calvinia
Middelburg
Fraserburg
Cradock
Queenstown
Bhisho
Lambert's Bay
Saint Helena Bay
Cape Columbine
Beaufort West
Graaff-Reinet
East Londo
Grahamstown
Alexandria
Paarl
Worcester
Uitenhage
George
Algoa Bay
Port Elizabeth
Cape Town
(legislative)
Strand
Cape of Good Hope
False Bay
Cape Seal
Mosselbaai
(Mossel Bay)
Saint Francis Bay
Cape Agulhas
Cape Francis Bay

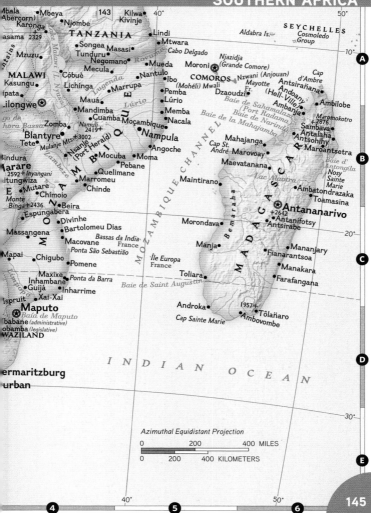

Mbala
(Abercorn)
•Mbeya
143
Kilwa
Kivinje
•Karonga
•Njombe
40°
asama 2329
Mzuzu
TANZANIA
Songea
Tunduru
Masasi
Mueda
Lindi
Mtwara
Cabo Delgado
50°

SEYCHELLES
Aldabra Is.
Cosmoledo
Group

10°

A

MALAWI
Kasungu
•Cóbuè
Lichinga
Negomano
Mecula
Nantulo
Ibo
(Mohéli) Mwali
Njazidja
(Grande Comore)
Moroni ⊕
COMOROS
Nzwani (Anjouan)
Mayotte
Dzaoudzi

Cap
d'Ambre
Antsirañana
Andoany
(Hell-Ville)
Ambanja
•Ambilobe
Maromokotro
+2876

ipata•
Lilongwe ⊛
Maná
Mandimba
Cuamba
Marrupa
Lúrio
Pemba
Memba
Nacala
Baie de Sahamalaza
(Port Radama)
Baie de Narinda

Sambava
Antalaha
Maroantsetra

•Zomba
Blantyre
Tete
Mulanje Mts.
+3002
Namuli
2419+
Moçambique
Nampula
Angoche
Moma
Baie de la
Mahajamba
Mahajanga
Cap St.
André
Marovoay
Maevatanana

Baie d'
Antongila
Nosy
Sainte
Marie
•Ambatondrazaka
Toamasina

B

Harare
2592+ Inyangani
itungwiza
Mutare
Chimoio
Monte
Binga +2436
Beira
Isanje
(Port Herald)
Mocuba
Pebane
Quelimane
Marromeu
Chinde

Lac Alaotra

Antananarivo ⊛
+2642
Antanifotsy
Antsirabe

Espungabera
Divinhe
Bartolomeu Dias

Maintirano

Morondava

Fianarantsoa
Mananjary

C

Massangena
Macovane
Ponta São Sebastião
Bassas da India
France
Manja

Manakara
Farafangana

Mapai•
Chigubo
Pomene
Île Europa
France
Toliara

Maxixe
Inhambane
Guijá•
Inharrime
Ponta da Barra
Baie de Saint Augustin

spruit
Xai-Xai
Maputo ⊛
babane (administrative)
obamba (legislative)
WAZILAND
Baía de Maputo

Androka
1957+
Cap Sainte Marie
Tôlañaro
Ambovombe

D

ermaritzburg
urban

INDIAN   OCEAN

30°

E

Azimuthal Equidistant Projection

0   200   400 MILES
0   200   400 KILOMETERS

40°

50°

4

5

6

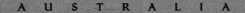

A U S T R A L I A

Brisbar

Perth

Lake Eyre
-16 m (-52 ft)

Lake
Gairdner

Lake
Torrens

Darling

Adelaide

Murray

Melbourne

Murrumbidgee

Mount Kosciuszko
2,228 m
(7,310 ft)

Sydney

NAURU

TUVALU
See p. 160
→

Aukland •

AUSTRALIA & OCEANIA

GEOGRAPHIC EXTREMES

CONTINENTAL POLITICAL FACTS

TOTAL NUMBER OF COUNTRIES: 14

LARGEST COUNTRY BY AREA: Australia
7,692,024 sq km (2,969,906 sq mi)

SMALLEST COUNTRY BY AREA:
Nauru 21 sq km (8 sq mi)

MOST POPULOUS COUNTRY: Australia
20,575,000

LEAST POPULOUS COUNTRY: Tuvalu
10,000

LARGEST CITIES BY POPULATION:
Sydney, Australia 4,429,000
Melbourne, Australia 3,853,000
Brisbane, Australia 1,970,000
Perth, Australia 1,599,000
Auckland, New Zealand 1,404,000

CONTINENTAL PHYSICAL FACTS

AREA: 7,687,000 sq km (2,968,000 sq mi)

HIGHEST POINT: Mount Kosciuszko,
New South Wales, Australia
2,228 m (7,310 ft)

LOWEST POINT: Lake Eyre, South
Australia, Australia -16 m (-52 ft)

LONGEST RIVERS:
Murray 2,375 km (1,476 mi)
Murrumbidgee 1,485 km (923 mi)
Darling 1,472 km (915 mi)

LARGEST NATURAL LAKES:
Lake Eyre 0-9,690 sq km
(0-3,741 sq mi)
Lake Torrens 0-5,745 sq km
(0-2,218 sq mi)
Lake Gairdner 0-4,351 sq km
(0-1,680 sq mi)

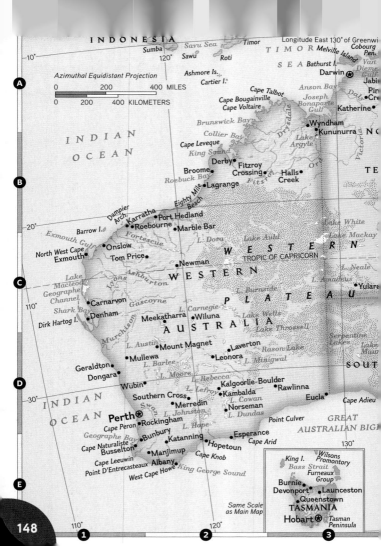

INDONESIA

Sumba
Sawu
Roti
Timor
Sayu Sea

Longitude East 130° of Greenwi

TIMOR

Melville Island
Cobourg
Pen.
Bathurst I.
Van
SEA
Darwin ⊛
Jabi
Anson Bay
Pin
Dal
Cre
Katherine

120°

−10°

A

Azimuthal Equidistant Projection

0   200   400 MILES

0   200   400 KILOMETERS

INDIAN

OCEAN

Ashmore Is.
Cartier I.

Cape Talbot
Cape Bougainville
Cape Voltaire

Joseph
Bonaparte
Gulf

Wyndham
Kununurra

NO

Brunswick Bay

Collier Bay

Drysdale

Lake
Argyle

Victoria

Cape Leveque

King Sound

Derby
Broome

Roebuck Bay

Fitzroy
Crossing

Halls
Creek

Ord

TE

B

Lagrange

Fitz

Eighty Mile Beach

Dampier
Arch.

Karratha
Roebourne

Port Hedland
Marble Bar

Lake White

Lake Mackay

−20°

Exmouth Gulf

Barrow I.

Fortescue

L. Dora

Lake Auld

WESTERN

North West Cape
Exmouth

Onslow

Tom Price

Newman

TROPIC OF CAPRICORN

L. Neale

Ashburton

WESTERN

L. Amadeus

Yulare

C

Lake
Macleod

Geographe
Channel

Lons

Carnarvon

PLATEAU

I. Burnside

110°

Shark Bay

Gascoyne

Denham

AUSTRALIA

Serpentine
Lakes

Dirk Hartog I.

Murchison

Meekatharra
Wiluna

L. Carnegie

Lake Wells

Lake Throssell

Lake
Mun

SOUT

L. Austin

Mount Magnet

Laverton

Rason Lake

Mullewa

Leonora

L. Minigwal

Geraldton

L. Barlee

Dongara

L. Moore

Le Rebecca

D

Wubin

Le Lefroy

Kalgoorlie-Boulder

Rawlinna

−30°

Southern Cross

Merredin

Kambalda

L. Cowan

Eucla

Cape Adieu

Norseman

INDIAN

Perth ⊛

Rockingham

L. Johnston

L. Dundas

Point Culver

GREAT

OCEAN

Cape Peron

Swa

L. Hope

AUSTRALIAN BIGI

Geographe Bay

Bunbury

Katanning

Esperance

Cape Arid

130°

Cape Naturaliste

Busselton

Hopetoun

Manjimup

Cape Knob

Wilsons
Promontory

King I.

Cape Leeuwin

Point D'Entrecasteaux

Albany

West Cape Howe

King George Sound

Bass Strait

Furneaux
Group

E

Same Scale
as Main Map

Burnie
Devonport

Launceston

Queenstown

TASMANIA

Hobart ⊛

Tasman
Peninsula

148

110°

1

120°

2

3

Torres Strait
Endeavour Strait Cape York Great
140° Barrier 150° PAPUA 10°
Wessel Is. Reef NEW GUINEA
Cape Wilberforce Temple Bay
Gove Nhulunbuy Weipa A
Pen. Albatross Bay Cape Weymouth PACIFIC
Alyangula Groote Aurukun OCEAN
Eylandt Coen
Ngukurr Limmen GULF Princess Charlotte Bay
Bight CARPENTARIA OF Cape Flattery
HERN Borroloola Mornington Cooktown CORAL SEA ISLANDS TERRITORY
Island Cape Tribulation
ewcastle Waters Cairns Magdelaine Cays
Lake Woods Burketown Normanton Innisfail B
TORY Gilbert Rockingham Bay
Lake Croydon Georgetown Hinchinbrook I.
ylvester Camooweal Townsville
ennant Camooweal Ayr Bowen
Creek Mount Isa Cloncurry Charters Mackay Repulse Bay
Barrow Creek Hughenden Towers Swain
QUEENSLAND Reefs 20°
Alice Winton Lake Galilee Capricorn Chan.
Springs Longreach Yeppoon Cape
Rockhampton Manifold C
Emerald Mount Morgan
Birdsville Gladstone
Bundaberg Hervey
Quilpie Charleville Hervey Bay Bay Fraser Island
Roma Maryborough (Great Sandy I.)
Oodnadatta Gympie Double Island Pt.
Cunnamulla Nambour Caloundra
Lake Goondiwindi Toowoomba Brisbane Bongaree
Eyre L. Eyre North Gold Coast
USTRALIA Marree L. Eyre South Collarenebri Tweed Heads
Lake Leigh Lake Frome Moree Lismore D
Gairdner Creek Darling Bourke Walgett Grafton
Ceduna Lake Tamworth Coffs Harbour 30°
Port Augusta Torrens Broken Hill NEW SOUTH WALES Armidale
Whyalla Port Pirie Burrendong Res. Port Macquarie
Port Dubbo Taree
Lincoln Wallaroo Mildura Lachlan Orange Maitland
. Carnot Gawler Murrumbidgee Bathurst Newcastle
Kangaroo I. Adelaide Murray Wagga Wagga Broken Bay
Wodonga Albury Sydney
Bendigo Shepparton Canberra Wollongong
Mount Gambier VICTORIA AUSTRALIAN CAPITAL TERR. JERVIS BAY TERR. TASMAN
Ballarat E
Discovery Bay Geelong Melbourne SEA
Cape Nelson Traralgon Cape Howe
Warrnambool 140° Port Phillip Bay Wilsons Promontory 150°
Bass Str.
4 5 6

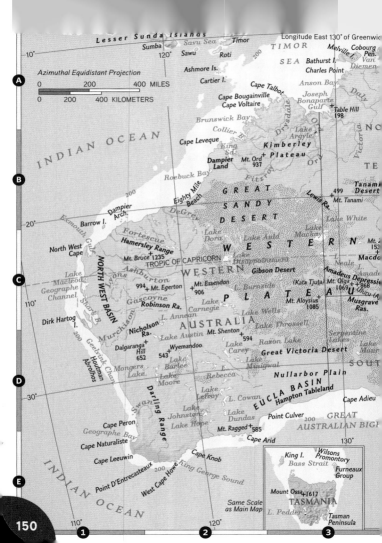

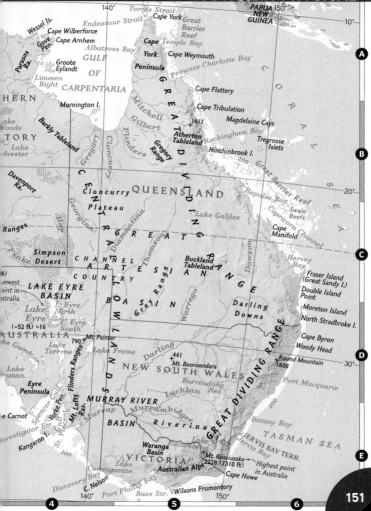

Torres Strait
Endeavour Strait
Cape York
Wessel Is.
Cape Wilberforce
Gove Pen.
Cape Arnhem
Parsons Ra.
Albatross Bay
GULF
Groote
Eylandt
OF
Limmen
Bight
CARPENTARIA
Mornington I.
Lake Woods
ake
TORY
Lake
lvester
Barkly Tableland
Davenport Ra.

PAPUA
NEW
GUINEA
Cape York
Great Barrier Reef
Temple Bay
Cape York
Cape Weymouth
Peninsula
Princess Charlotte Bay
Cape Flattery
Cape Tribulation
Magdelaine Cays
Atherton Tableland
1611
Rockingham Bay
Hinchinbrook I.
Tregrosse Islets
Gregory Range
Gilbert
Mitchell
Flinders
Cloncurry
Gregory
Cloncurry
Plateau
QUEENSLAND
Georgina
CENTRAL
Simpson Desert
Ranges
Finke
Diamantina
Thomson
Buckland Tableland
Lake Galilee
200
Great Barrier Reef
Repulse Bay
Swain Reefs
Capricorn Channel
Cape Manifold
Hervey Bay
Fraser Island
(Great Sandy I.)
Double Island Point
Moreton Island
North Stradbroke I.
Cape Byron
Woody Head
Round Mountain
1608
Port Macquarie
CHANNEL
CARTESIAN
COUNTRY
GREAT
ARTESIAN
BASIN
Warrego
Cooper
LOWLANDS
Darling Downs
Bulloo
Barcoo
LAKE EYRE
BASIN
Lake Eyre
(-52 ft) -16
L. Eyre North
L. Eyre South
Lake Gairdner
AUSTRALIA
owest
oint in
stralia
Lake Torrens
Lake Frome
790°
Mt Painter
Flinders Ranges
Lake Eyre
man
e Carnot
Eyre Peninsula
NEW SOUTH WALES
441
Mt Booroondara
Darling
MURRAY RIVER
BASIN
Lachlan
Murrumbidgee
Riverina
Burrendong Res.
Botany Bay
Spencer Gulf
Yorke Pen.
Mt. Lofty Ras.
St Vincent
Gulf
Kangaroo I.
Investigator Str.
200
Murray
Waranga Basin
VICTORIA
Lake Corangamite
Australian Alps
Mt. Kosciuszko
2228 (7310 ft)
Highest point in Australia
Cape Howe
C. Nelson
Discovery Bay
Port Phillip Bay
Bass Str.
Wilsons Promontory

CORAL SEA

TASMAN SEA

JERVIS BAY TERR.
Jervis Bay

GREAT DIVIDING RANGE

10°
A
B
20°
C
D
30°
E

151

140°   4   150°   5   6

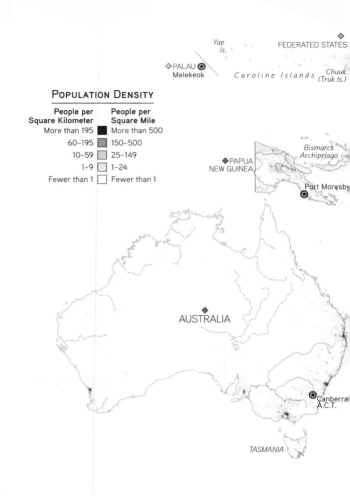

POPULATION DENSITY

People per Square Kilometer		People per Square Mile
More than 195	■	More than 500
60–195	■	150–500
10–59	□	25–149
1–9	□	1–24
Fewer than 1	□	Fewer than 1

Yap Is.

FEDERATED STATES

◇PALAU ✪
Melekeok

Caroline Islands

Chuuk
(Truk Is.)

Bismarck
Archipelago

◆PAPUA
NEW GUINEA

Port Moresby ✪

AUSTRALIA

Canberra ✪
A.C.T.

TASMANIA

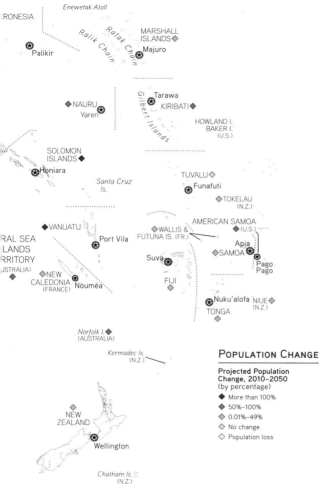

Enewetak Atoll

RONESIA

Palikir

Ralik Chain
Ratak Chain

MARSHALL
ISLANDS ◆
Majuro

◆NAURU
Yaren

Gilbert Islands

Tarawa
KIRIBATI ◆

HOWLAND I.
BAKER I.
(U.S.)

SOLOMON
ISLANDS ◆
Honiara

Santa Cruz
Is.

TUVALU ◇
Funafuti

◇TOKELAU
(N.Z.)

AMERICAN SAMOA
(U.S.)

◆VANUATU

◇WALLIS &
FUTUNA IS. (FR.)

Apia

RAL SEA
LANDS
RRITORY
(USTRALIA)

Port Vila

Suva

◇SAMOA

Pago
Pago

◆NEW
CALEDONIA
(FRANCE)
Nouméa

FIJI
◇

◉Nuku'alofa NIUE ◇
(N.Z.)
TONGA

Norfolk I. ◆
(AUSTRALIA)

Kermadec Is.
(N.Z.)

POPULATION CHANGE

**Projected Population
Change, 2010–2050**
(by percentage)

◆ More than 100%
◆ 50%–100%
◇ 0.01%–49%
◇ No change
◇ Population loss

NEW
ZEALAND

Wellington

Chatham Is.
(N.Z.)

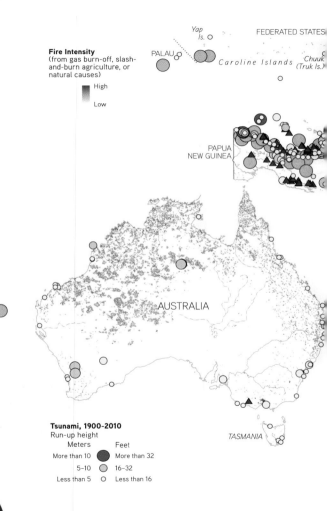

Fire Intensity
(from gas burn-off, slash-
and-burn agriculture, or
natural causes)

High

Low

Yap
Is. ○

FEDERATED STATES

PALAU ○

Caroline Islands

Chuuk
(Truk Is.)

○

PAPUA
NEW GUINEA

AUSTRALIA

TASMANIA

Tsunami, 1900-2010
Run-up height

Meters		Feet
More than 10	●	More than 32
5–10	○	16–32
Less than 5	○	Less than 16

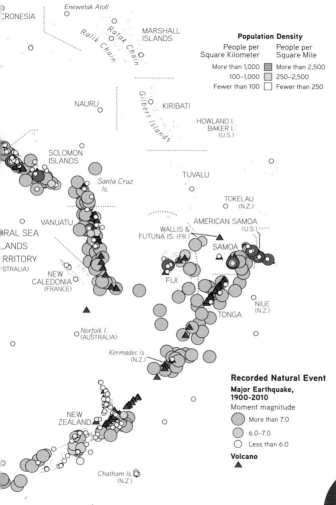

Population Density

People per Square Kilometer		People per Square Mile
More than 1,000		More than 2,500
100–1,000		250–2,500
Fewer than 100		Fewer than 250

CRONESIA

Enewetak Atoll

Ralik Chain
Ratak Chain

MARSHALL ISLANDS

NAURU

Gilbert Islands

KIRIBATI

HOWLAND I.
BAKER I.
(U.S.)

SOLOMON ISLANDS

Santa Cruz Is.

TUVALU

TOKELAU
(N.Z.)

VANUATU

WALLIS & FUTUNA IS. (FR.)

AMERICAN SAMOA
(U.S.)

RAL SEA
LANDS
RRITORY
(STRALIA)

NEW CALEDONIA
(FRANCE)

SAMOA

FIJI

NIUE
(N.Z.)

TONGA

Norfolk I.
(AUSTRALIA)

Kermadec Is.
(N.Z.)

NEW ZEALAND

Recorded Natural Event

Major Earthquake, 1900-2010

Moment magnitude

- More than 7.0
- 6.0–7.0
- Less than 6.0

▲ Volcano

Chatham Is.
(N.Z.)

155

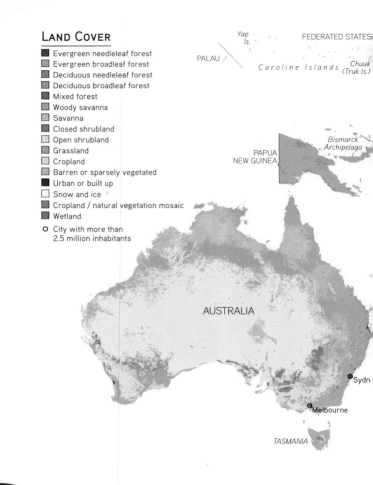

LAND COVER

- Evergreen needleleaf forest
- Evergreen broadleaf forest
- Deciduous needleleaf forest
- Deciduous broadleaf forest
- Mixed forest
- Woody savanna
- Savanna
- Closed shrubland
- Open shrubland
- Grassland
- Cropland
- Barren or sparsely vegetated
- Urban or built up
- Snow and ice
- Cropland / natural vegetation mosaic
- Wetland
- ○ City with more than 2.5 million inhabitants

Yap Is.

FEDERATED STATES

PALAU

Caroline Islands   Chuuk (Truk Is.)

Bismarck Archipelago

PAPUA NEW GUINEA

AUSTRALIA

Sydn

Melbourne

TASMANIA

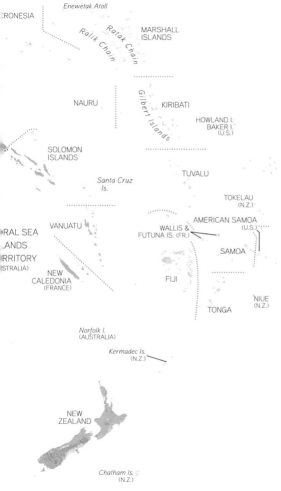

CRONESIA

Enewetak Atoll

Ratak Chain

Ralik Chain

MARSHALL
ISLANDS

NAURU

Gilbert Islands

KIRIBATI

HOWLAND I.
BAKER I.
(U.S.)

SOLOMON
ISLANDS

Santa Cruz
Is.

TUVALU

TOKELAU
(N.Z.)

AMERICAN SAMOA
(U.S.)

VANUATU

WALLIS &
FUTUNA IS. (FR.)

RAL SEA
ANDS
RRITORY
(STRALIA)

SAMOA

NEW
CALEDONIA
(FRANCE)

FIJI

NIUE
(N.Z.)

TONGA

Norfolk I.
(AUSTRALIA)

Kermadec Is.
(N.Z.)

NEW
ZEALAND

Chatham Is.
(N.Z.)

CLIMATE ZONES

(based on modified Köppen system)

Humid equatorial climate (A)
- No dry season (Af)
- Short dry season (Am)
- Dry winter (Aw)

Dry climate (B)
- Semiarid (BS) } h = hot
- Arid (BW) } k = cold

Humid temperate climate (C)
- No dry season (Cf)   a = hot summer
- Dry summer (Cs)   b = cool summer

Highland climate (H)
- Unclassified highlands

WATER AVAILABILITY

(in millimeters per-person per-year)

- ■ More than 750
- ■ 251–750
- ■ 26–250
- □ Less than 26
- □ No data available

CHINA
East China Sea
Nansei Shotō (Ryukyu Is.) Japan
Naha · Okinawa
Daitō Shotō Japan
Taiwan

Bonin Islands Japan
Volcano Islands Japan

TROPIC OF CANCER

N

Batan Is.
Babuyan Is.
Luzon
Quezon City
MANILA
PHILIPPINES
Cebu
Mindanao
Davao

PHILIPPINE
SEA

NORTHERN MARIANA ISLANDS U.S.
Capital Hill
Hagåtña (Agana)
Guam U.S.

MARSHALL ISLANDS

Ratak Chain

Sulu Sea

Yap Islands
PALAU ⊛ Melekeok

FEDERATED STATES OF MICRONESIA
CAROLINE ISLANDS
Sonsorol Is.

Chuuk (Truk Is.)
⊛ Palikir
Pohnpei (Ponape)
Mortlock Is.

Ralik Chain

Majuro
Tarawa (Bairiki)
Gilbert Islands

Celebes Sea
Manado
Sulawesi (Celebes)
Molucca Sea
Ambon
MOLUCCAS
Banda Sea
Ternate

Teluk Cenderawasih

Jayapura

Bismarck Archipelago

NAURU

K

TIMOR-LESTE (EAST TIMOR)
Dili
Timor
INDONESIA
NEW GUINEA
PAPUA NEW GUINEA
Huon Gulf
Port Moresby

Bismarck Sea
Bougainville

SOLOMON ISLANDS
⊛ Honiara
Santa Cruz Islands

Funafu
TUVAL

Dolak
Timor Sea
Arafura Sea
Torres Str.
Gulf of Papua
Cape York

Solomon Sea
Guadalcanal

MELANESIA

VANUATU
Vanua Le

Cape Talbot

Darwin

Gulf of Carpentaria

Cape York Pen.

CORAL SEA

Port Vila ⊛
New Caledonia France
Nouméa

FIJI
Viti Levu
Suva

Loyalty Is.

Derby
Newcastle Waters
Borroloola
Cairns
Townsville

Great Sandy Desert
Tennant Creek
Camooweal
Mackay

Alice Springs
Barrow Creek
Gladstone

Simpson Desert
Birdsville
AUSTRALIA
Great Victoria Desert
Lake Eyre
Oodnadatta
Cunnamulla
Brisbane

Kalgoorlie-Boulder
Nullarbor Plain
Darling
Newcastle

Esperance
Port Augusta
Sydney
Canberra, A.C.T.

Great Australian Bight
Adelaide
Murray
Kangaroo I.
Melbourne

Cape Pasley

Three Kings
North Cape
Auckland
Hamilton
North Island

Wellington
NEW ZEALAND

INDIAN OCEAN

Bass Strait
Tasmania
Hobart
Cape Pillar

TASMAN SEA

Cook Strait

Christchurch
South Island
Dunedin

Longitude East 165° of Greenwich

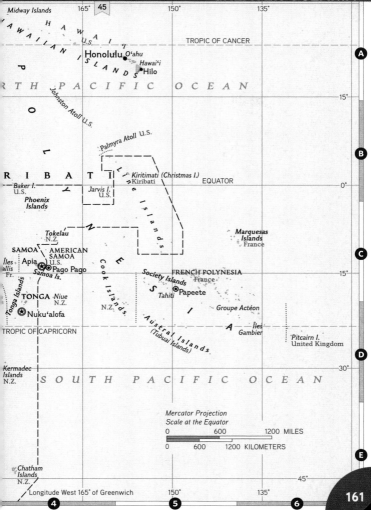

Midway Islands

165° | 45 | 150° | 135°

HAWAIIAN

H A W A I I A N

ISLANDS

U.S.

TROPIC OF CANCER

Honolulu O'ahu
Hawai'i
Hilo

NORTH PACIFIC OCEAN

Johnston Atoll U.S.

P O L Y N E S I A

Palmyra Atoll U.S.

KIRIBATI

Line Islands

Kiritimati (Christmas I.)
Kiribati

EQUATOR

Baker I.
U.S.

Jarvis I.
U.S.

Phoenix
Islands

Tokelau
N.Z.

Marquesas
Islands
France

SAMOA | AMERICAN
SAMOA
U.S.

Îles
Wallis
Fr.

Apia
Pago Pago
Samoa Is.

Cook Islands
N.Z.

Society Islands
France

FRENCH POLYNESIA
France

Papeete

Tonga Islands

TONGA
Nuku'alofa

Niue
N.Z.

Tahiti

Groupe Actéon

Austral Islands
(Tubuai Islands)

Îles
Gambier

Pitcairn I.
United Kingdom

TROPIC OF CAPRICORN

Kermadec
Islands
N.Z.

SOUTH PACIFIC OCEAN

Mercator Projection
Scale at the Equator

0 — 600 — 1200 MILES

0 — 600 — 1200 KILOMETERS

Chatham
Islands
N.Z.

Longitude West 165° of Greenwich

150° | 135°

15°

0°

15°

30°

45°

A

B

C

D

E

4 | 5 | 6

POLAR REGIONS

ARCTIC DATA

SURFACE AREA: 13,960,100 sq km (5,390,000 sq mi)

PERCENT OF EARTH'S WATER AREA: 4.0%

DEEPEST POINT: Molloy Deep -5,669 m (-18,599 ft)

AVERAGE WINTER SEA ICE EXTENT: 15,700,000 sq km (6,100,000 sq mi)

AVERAGE SUMMER SEA ICE EXTENT: 7,000,000 sq km (2,700,000 sq mi)

ANTARCTICA DATA

AREA: 13,209,000 sq km (5,100,000 sq mi)

HIGHEST POINT: Vinson Massif 4,897 m (16,066 ft)

LOWEST POINT: Bentley Subglacial Trench   -2,555 m (-8,383 ft)

LOWEST RECORDED TEMPERATURE: Vostok Research Station, Russia -89.2°C (-128.6°F) July 21, 1983

HIGHEST RECORDED TEMPERATURE: Vanda Station, New Zealand (currently closed)   15°C (59°F) January 5, 1974

COLDEST PLACE ON EARTH: Ridge A, annual average temperature -74°C (-94°F)

•Molloy Deep
-5,669 m (-18,599 ft)

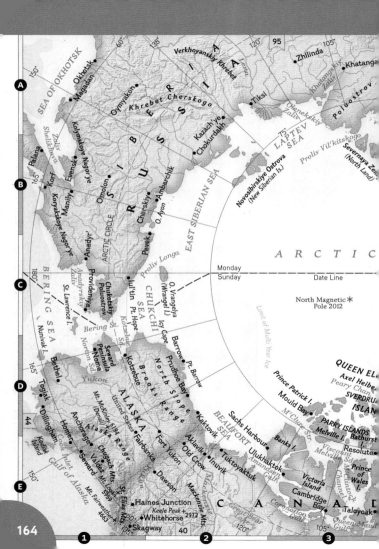

SEA OF OKHOTSK

Okhotsk
Magadan
Oymyakon
Zaliv
Shelikhova

Palana

Korf
Kolymskoye Nagor'ye
Evensk
Koryakskoye Nagor'ye
Manily
Anapar
Omolon
Oloy
Chenstiy
Anadyrskiy
Zaliv
Pevek

Providenija
St. Lawrence I.
Chukotskiy
Poluostrov
Nunivak I.

Verkhoyanskiy Khrebet

Khrebet Cherskogo

Kazač'ye
Chokurdakh
Ambarchik

O. Ayon

Proliv Longa

CHUKCHI
SEA

O. Vrangelya
(Wrangel I.)

Iul'tin
Pt. Hope
Icy Cape
Kotzebue Sd.
Barrow
Pt. Barrow
Prudhoe Bay

Zhilinda
Khatanga

Tiksi

Olenekskiy
Zaliv

LAPTEV
SEA

Proliv Vil'kitskogo

Severnaya Zemlya
(North Land)

Poluostrov

Novosibirskiye Ostrova
(New Siberian Is.)

EAST SIBERIAN SEA

S I B E R I A

R U S S I A

ARCTIC CIRCLE

BERING SEA

Bering St.
Norton Sd.
Kobuk
Seward
Peninsula
Nome

North Slope
Brooks Range
Kaktovik

ARCTIC

Date Line

Monday
Sunday

North Magnetic ✶
Pole 2012

Limit of Multi Year Ice

QUEEN EL

Axel Heibe
Peary Chan
Prince Patrick I.
Mould Bay
SVERDRU
ISLAN
Bathurst
Melville I.
Resolute
M'Clure Str.
Banks I.
Viscou
Melvill
Prince
of Wales
I.

Bethel
Toglak
Dillingham
Kodiak
Island
Homer
Anchorage
Seward
Valdez
Chugach Mts.
Fairbanks
Old Crow
Aklavik
Inuvik
Tuktoyaktuk
Ulukhaktok

Sachs Harbour

BEAUFORT
SEA

Amundsen

Amundsen

ALASKA
United States
Mt. McKinley 6194
(Denali)
Alaska Range
Mt. Logan 5951
Cook Inlet
Gulf of Alaska

Yukon

Fort Yukon
Dawson

Mackenzie Mts.

Victoria
Island

Cambridge
Bay

Coronation

Bear

Taloyoak

Queen Maud

Victoria

Mt. St. Elias 5489
Mt. Fairweather 4663
St. Elias Mts.
Haines Junction
Keele Peak 2972
Whitehorse
Skagway

C A N A D

44

150°

40

95

120°

105°

60°

135°

150°

165°

180°

165°

150°

75°

A

B

C

D

E

1

2

3

164

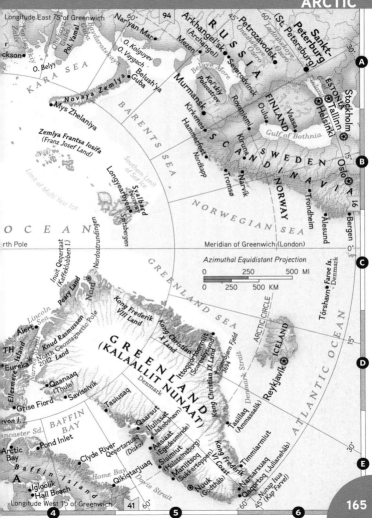

Longitude East 75° of Greenwich

Naryan Mar
60°
94
O. Belyy
ckson
Obskaya
Pol. Yamal
Gyd.
Baydaratskaya

O. Kolguyev
O. Vaygach
Belush'ya Guba
Mezen
Arkhangel'sk (Archangel)
Severodvinsk
RUSSIA
45°
Petrozavodsk
O. Ladozhskoye Ozero
Onezhskoye Ozero
Sankt-Peterburg (St. Petersburg)
30°

KARA SEA

Novaya Zemlya
Mys Zhelaniya

Zemlya Frantsa Iosifa
(Franz Josef Land)

Murmansk
Kol'skiy Poluostrov
Belaye More
Kirkenes
Rovaniemi
FINLAND
Oulu
Vaasa
ESTONIA
Tallinn
Stockholm
Helsinki
A

BARENTS SEA

Longyearbyen
Svalbard
Spitsbergen
Norway
Nordostrundingen

Southern Limit of Sea Ice
Limit of Multi Year Ice

Hammerfest
Nordkapp
Tromsø
Narvik
Kiruna
SCANDINAVIA
SWEDEN
Gulf of Bothnia
15°
B
16

O C E A N
rth Pole

NORWEGIAN SEA
Trondheim
NORWAY
Ålesund
Bergen
0°

Meridian of Greenwich (London)

GREENLAND SEA
Inuit Qeqertaat (Kaffeklubben I.)
Nord
Peary Land

Azimuthal Equidistant Projection
0   250   500 MI
0   250   500 KM

Tórshavn ● Faroe Is.
Denmark
C

Lincoln Sea
Alert
Knud Rasmussen Land
North Geomagnetic Pole
2012
Kong Frederik VIII Land
Kong Christian X Land
Ittoqqortoormiit (Scoresbysund)
Gunnbjørn Field
3694 m
ARCTIC CIRCLE
15°
D

TH
Eureka
Ellesmere Island
Axel Heiberg I.
Qaanaaq (Thule)
G R E E N L A N D
(KALAALLIT NUNAAT)
Denmark
Kong Christian IX Land
Denmark Strait
ICELAND
Reykjavík

ATLANTIC OCEAN

Grise Fiord
Savissivik
Tasiusaq

BAFFIN BAY
von I.
ncaster Sd.
Arctic Bay
Pond Inlet
Clyde River
Baffin Island
Home Bay
Qaarsut
Uummannaq
Qeqertarsuaq (Disko)
Ilulissat (Jakobshavn)
Aasiaat (Egedesminde)
Sisimiut (Holstensborg)
Maniitsoq (Sukkertoppen)
Nuuk (Godthåb)
Kong Frederik VI Coast
Tasiilaq (Ammassalik)
Timmiarmiut
30°
E

Igloolik
Hall Beach
Qikiqtarjuaq
Dixon Strait
Narsarsuaq
Qaqortoq (Julianehåb)
Nunap Isua (Kap Farvel)
45°

Longitude West 75° of Greenwich
41   60°
4   5   6

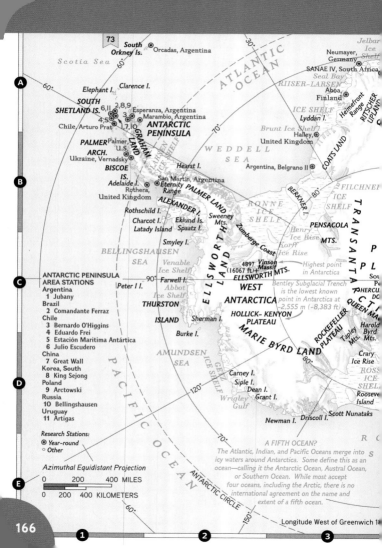

73

South Orkney Is. ◉ Orcadas, Argentina

Scotia Sea

ATLANTIC OCEAN

Jelbar Ice Shelf

Neumayer, Germany

SANAE IV, South Africa

Aboa, Finland

Heimefront Range

RIISER-LARSEN ICE SHELF

RITSCHER UPLANI

Clarence I.

Elephant I.

SOUTH SHETLAND IS.   6,11   2,8,9
4-5   3 ◉◉◉
Chile, Arturo Prat   1,7,10

Esperanza, Argentina
Marambio, Argentina

ANTARCTIC PENINSULA

PALMER ARCH.
Palmer, U.S.
Ukraine, Vernadsky ◉

BISCOE IS.

Adelaide I.
Rothera,
United Kingdom

Lyddan I.

Brunt Ice Shelf

Halley, ◉
United Kingdom

COATS LAND

WEDDELL SEA

Argentina, Belgrano II ◉

BERKNER I.

FILCHNEI ICE SHELF

Hearst I.

San Martín, Argentina

◉ Eternity Range

PALMER LAND

ALEXANDER I.

Rothschild I.

Charcot I.   Eklund Is.
Latady Island   Spaatz I.

Sweeney Mts.

Zumberge Coast

RONNE ICE SHELF

Henry Ice Rise

Korff Ice Rise

PENSACOLA MTS.

TRANSA

Smyley I.

BELLINGSHAUSEN SEA

Venable Ice Shelf

Peter I I.

4897 Vinson
(16067 ft) Massif
ELLSWORTH MTS.

Highest point in Antarctica

P
PL

TRANSA

Sou
P

ANTARCTIC PENINSULA AREA STATIONS

Argentina
1 Jubany

Brazil
2 Comandante Ferraz

Chile
3 Bernardo O'Higgins
4 Eduardo Frei
5 Estación Marítima Antártica
6 Julio Escudero

China
7 Great Wall

Korea, South
8 King Sejong

Poland
9 Arctowski

Russia
10 Bellingshausen

Uruguay
11 Artigas

Farwell I.

THURSTON ISLAND

Abbot Ice Shelf

Sherman I.

Burke I.

AMUNDSEN SEA

WEST ANTARCTICA

HOLLICK- KENYON PLATEAU

MARIE BYRD LAND

Bentley Subglacial Trench is the lowest known point in Antarctica at -2,555 m (-8,383 ft)

HERCU
DC

QUEEN MA

ROCKEFELLER PLATEAU

Harold Byrd Mts.

Tapley Mts.

Crary Ice Rise

ROSS ICE SHEL

Roosevel Island

PACIFIC OCEAN

Carney I.

Siple I.

Dean I.

Grant I.

Wrigley Gulf

Newman I.

Driscoll I.

Scott Nunataks

R

Research Stations:
◉ Year-round
○ Other

Azimuthal Equidistant Projection

0   200   400 MILES

0   200   400 KILOMETERS

A FIFTH OCEAN?
The Atlantic, Indian, and Pacific Oceans merge into icy waters around Antarctica. Some define this as an ocean—calling it the Antarctic Ocean, Austral Ocean, or Southern Ocean. While most accept four oceans, including the Arctic, there is no international agreement on the name and extent of a fifth ocean.

ANTARCTIC CIRCLE

ANTARCTIC OCEAN

Longitude West of Greenwich 1

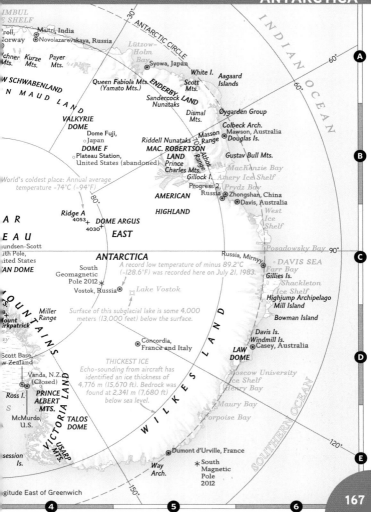

IMBUL
E SHELF

INDIAN OCEAN

roll,
lorway
Maitri, India
Novolazarevskaya, Russia

ANTARCTIC CIRCLE

60°
60°

A

chner Kurze Payer
Mts. Mts. Mts.

Lützow–
Holm
Bay

Syowa, Japan

W SCHWABENLAND

White I. Aagaard
Scott Islands
Mts.

Queen Fabiola Mts. ENDERBY
(Yamato Mts.) LAND
Sandercock
Nunataks

N MAUD LAND

Dismal
Mts.

Øygarden Group

VALKYRIE
DOME

Colbeck Arch.
Mawson, Australia
Douglas Is.

B

Dome Fuji,
Japan

DOME F

Riddell Nunataks Masson
Range

MAC. ROBERTSON

Gustav Bull Mts.

Plateau Station,
United States (abandoned)

LAND
Prince
Charles Mts.

Athos
Range

MacKenzie Bay

World's coldest place: Annual average
temperature –74°C (–94°F)

Gillock I. Amery Ice Shelf

Progress 2,
Russia

Prydz Bay

AMERICAN

Zhongshan, China
Davis, Australia

AR

Ridge A
4053

DOME ARGUS
4030

HIGHLAND

West
Ice
Shelf

EAU

EAST

undsen-Scott
th Pole,
ited States

AN DOME

ANTARCTICA

Posadowsky Bay
90°

Russia, Mirny

DAVIS SEA

C

South
Geomagnetic
Pole 2012

A record low temperature of minus 89.2°C
(–128.6°F) was recorded here on July 21, 1983.

Farr Bay
Gillies Is.

Shackleton

Vostok, Russia

Lake Vostok

Highjump Archipelago
Mill Island

OUNTAINS

Miller
Range

Surface of this subglacial lake is some 4,000
meters (13,000 feet) below the surface.

Bowman Island

Mount
rkpatrick

Concordia,
France and Italy

Davis Is.
Windmill Is.
Casey, Australia

LAW
DOME

D

Scott Base,
w Zealand

Ross I.

Vanda, N.Z.
(Closed)

THICKEST ICE
Echo-sounding from aircraft has
identified an ice thickness of
4,776 m (15,670 ft). Bedrock was
found at 2,341 m (7,680 ft)
below sea level.

Moscow University
Ice Shelf
Henry Ice

WILKES LAND

PRINCE
ALBERT
MTS.

Maury Bay

McMurdo,
U.S.

TALOS
DOME

Porpoise Bay

VICTORIA LAND

SOUTHERN OCEAN

120°

E

ssession
Is.

USARP
MTS.

Dumont d'Urville, France

Way
Arch.

South
Magnetic
Pole
2012

WORLD
FLAGS

Afghanistan

Albania

Algeria

Andorra

Angola

Antigua and Barbuda

Argentina

Armenia

Australia

Austria

Azerbaijan

Bahamas

Bahrain

Bangladesh

Barbados

Belarus

Belgium

Belize

Benin

Bhutan

Bolivia

Bosnia and Herzegovina

Botswana

Brazil

Brunei

Bulgaria

Burkina Faso

Burundi

Cambodia

Cameroon

Canada

Cape Verde

Central African Republic

Chad

Chile

China

Colombia

Comoros

Congo

Congo, Democratic Republic of the

Costa Rica

Côte d'Ivoire (Ivory Coast)

Croatia

Cuba

Cyprus

Czech Republic (Czechia)

Denmark

Djibouti

Dominica

Dominican Republic

Ecuador

Egypt

El Salvador

Equatorial Guinea

Eritrea

Estonia

Ethiopia

Fiji

Finland

France

Gabon

Gambia

Georgia

Germany

Ghana

Greece

Grenada

Guatemala

Guinea

Guinea-Bissau

Guyana

Haiti

Honduras

Hungary

Iceland

India

Indonesia

Iran

Iraq

Ireland

Israel

Italy

Jamaica

Japan

Jordan

Kazakhstan

Kenya

Kiribati

Korea, North

Korea, South

Kosovo

Kuwait

Kyrgyzstan

Laos

Latvia

Lebanon

Lesotho

Liberia

Libya

Liechtenstein

Lithuania

Luxembourg

Macedonia

Madagascar

Malawi

Malaysia

Maldives

Mali

Malta

Marshall Islands

Mauritania

Mauritius

Mexico

Micronesia

Moldova

Monaco

Mongolia

Montenegro

Morocco

Mozambique

Myanmar (Burma)

Namibia

Nauru

Nepal

Netherlands

New Zealand

Nicaragua

Niger

Nigeria

Norway

Oman

Pakistan

Palau

Panama

 Papua New Guinea

 Paraguay

 Peru

 Philippines

 Poland

 Portugal

 Qatar

 Romania

 Russia

 Rwanda

 Saint Kitts and Nevis

 Saint Lucia

 Saint Vincent and the Grenadines

 Samoa

 San Marino

 Sao Tome and Principe

 Saudi Arabia

 Senegal

 Serbia

 Seychelles

 Sierra Leone

 Singapore

 Slovakia

 Slovenia

 Solomon Islands

 Somalia

 South Africa

 South Sudan

 Spain

 Sri Lanka

 Sudan

Suriname

Swaziland

Sweden

Switzerland

Syria

Tajikistan

Tanzania

Thailand

Timor-Leste
(East Timor)

Togo

Tonga

Trinidad and
Tobago

Tunisia

Turkey

Turkmenistan

Tuvalu

Uganda

Ukraine

United Arab Emirates

United Kingdom

United States

Uruguay

Uzbekistan

Vanuatu

Vatican City

Venezuela

Vietnam

Yemen

Zambia

Zimbabwe

175

CONVERSION OF INTERNATIONAL UNITS *TO* U.S. UNITS

	SYMBOL	WHEN YOU KNOW	MULTIPLY BY	TO FIND	SYMBOL
LENGTH	cm	centimeters	0.393701	inches	in
	m	meters	3.280840	feet	ft
	m	meters	1.093613	yards	yd
	km	kilometers	0.621371	miles	mi
AREA	cm²	square centimeters	0.155000	square inches	in²
	m²	square meters	10.76391	square feet	ft²
	m²	square meters	1.195990	square yards	yd²
	km²	square kilometers	0.386102	square miles	mi²
	ha	hectares	2.471054	acres	--
MASS	g	grams	0.035274	ounces	oz
	kg	kilograms	2.204623	pounds	lb
	t	metric tons	1.102311	short tons	--
VOLUME	mL	milliliters	0.061024	cubic inches	in³
	mL	milliliters	0.033814	liquid ounces	liq oz
	L	liters	2.113376	pints	pt
	L	liters	1.056688	quarts	qt
	L	liters	0.264172	gallons	gal
	m³	cubic meters	35.31467	cubic feet	ft³
	m³	cubic meters	1.307951	cubic yards	yd³
TEMP.	°C	degrees Celsius (centigrade)	9/5 (1.8) then add 32	degrees Fahrenheit	°F

CONVERSION OF U.S. UNITS *TO* INTERNATIONAL UNITS

	SYMBOL	WHEN YOU KNOW	MULTIPLY BY	TO FIND	SYMBOL
LENGTH	in	inches	2.54	centimeters	cm
	ft	feet	0.3048	meters	m
	yd	yards	0.9144	meters	m
	mi	miles	1.609344	kilometers	km
AREA	in²	square inches	6.4516	square centimeters	cm²
	ft²	square feet	0.092903	square meters	m²
	yd²	square yards	0.836127	square meters	m²
	mi²	square miles	2.589988	square kilometers	km²
	--	acres	0.404686	hectares	ha
MASS	oz	ounces	28.349523	grams	g
	lb	pounds	0.453592	kilograms	kg
	--	short tons	0.907185	metric tons	t
VOLUME	in³	cubic inches	16.387064	milliliters	mL
	liq oz	liquid ounces	29.57353	milliliters	mL
	pt	pints	0.473176	liters	L
	qt	quarts	0.946353	liters	L
	gal	gallons	3.785412	liters	L
	ft³	cubic feet	0.028317	cubic meters	m³
	yd³	cubic yards	0.764555	cubic meters	m³
TEMP.	°F	degrees Fahrenheit	5/9 (.555) after subtracting 32	degrees Celsius (centigrade)	°C

1 METER — 1 FOOT — 1 FOOT = 12 INCHES — 1 METER = 100 CENTIMETERS

1 KILOMETER — 1 MILE — 1 KILOMETER = 1,000 METERS — 1 MILE = 5,280 FEET

Af. — African
Afghan. — Afgahnistan
Ala. — Alabama
Alban. — Albania
Arch. — Archipelago, Archipiélago
Ark. — Arkansas
Arm. — Armenia
Aust. — Austria
Azerb. — Azerbaijan

B. — Baai, Baía, Baie, Bahía, Bay, Bugt-en, Buḩayrat
Belg. — Belgium
Bosn. & Herzg. — Bosnia and Herzegovina

C. — Cabo, Cap, Cape, Capo
Cen. — Central
Chan. — Channel
Conn. — Connecticut
Croat. — Croatia

D.c. — District of Columbia
Dem. — Democratic
Den. — Denmark

E. — East-ern
Emb. — Embalse
Eq. — Equatorial
Est. — Estonia

G. — Golfe, Golfo, Gulf
Ga. — Georgia
Gl. — Glacier, Gletscher

Hung. — Hungary

I.-s. — Île-s, Ilha-s, Isla-s, Island-s, Isle, Isol-a, -e
Ill. — Illinois
Ind. — Indiana

Kaz. — Kazakhstan
Kep. — Kepulauan
Kos. — Kosovo
Kyrg. — Kyrgyzstan

L. — Lac, Lago, Lake
La. — Louisiana
Liech. — Liechtenstein
Lux. — Luxembourg

Maced. — Macedonia
Mass. — Massachusetts
Me. — Maine
Mich. — Michigan
Minn. — Minnesota
Miss. — Mississippi
Mo. — Missouri

Mold. — Moldova
Mt.-s. — Mont-s, Mount-ain-s

N. — North-ern
N.B. — New Brunswick
N.C. — North Carolina
N.H. — New Hampshire
N.J. — New Jersey
N.P. — National Park
N.S. — Nova Scotia
N.Y. — New York
N.Z. — New Zealand
Neth. — Netherlands

O. — Ostrov-a

P.R. — Puerto Rico
Pa. — Pennsylvania
Pak. — Pakistan
Pen. — Peninsula, Péninsula, Péninsule
Pol. — Poluostrov
Pres. — Preserve
Pt.-e. — Point-e
Pta. — Ponta, Punta

R.I. — Rhode Island
Ra.-s. — Range-s
Rep. — Republic
Res. — Reservoir, Reserve
Russ. — Russia

S. — South-ern
S.C. — South Carolina
Sa.-s. — Serra, Sierra-s
Sd. — Sound
Slov. — Slovenia
Sp. — Spain, Spanish
St.-e. — Saint-e, Sankt, Sint
Str.-s. — Strait-s
Switz. — Switzerland

Taj. — Tajikistan
Terr. — Territory
Turkm. — Turkmenistan

U.A.E. — United Arab Emirates
U.K. — United Kingdom
U.S. — United States
Uzb. — Uzbekistan

Va. — Virginia
Vdkhr. — Vodokhranilishche
Vdskh. — Vodoskhovyshche
Vt. — Vermont

W. — West-ern
W. Va. — West Virginia
Wash. — Washington
Wis. — Wisconsin

Adrar _____ mountain-s, plateau
Archipiélago _____ archipelago
Arquipélago _____ archipelago
Aylagy _____ gulf

Bāb _____ gate, strait
Bahía _____ bay
Bahr, Baḥr _____ bay, lake, river, sea
Baía, Baie _____ bay
Boğazı _____ strait
Boca _____ channel, mouth, river
Bögeni _____ reservoir
Bucht _____ bay
Burnu _____ cape, point

Cabo _____ cape
Canal _____ canal, channel, strait
Cap, Capo _____ cape
Catarata-s _____ cataract-s, waterfall-s
Cay-s, Cayo-s _____ island-s, key-s, shoal-s
Cerro-s _____ hill-s, peak-s
Cordillera _____ mountain chain

Dağı _____ mountain
Dağları _____ mountains
Dao _____ island
Daryācheh _____ lake, marshy lake
Dasht _____ desert, plain
Deniz, -i _____ sea
Desierto _____ desert
Do _____ island-s, rock-s
Doi _____ hill, mountain

Embalse _____ lake, reservoir
Emi _____ mountain, rock
Ensenada _____ bay, cove
Erg _____ sand dune region
Estrecho _____ strait

Feng _____ mount, peak
Fjeld _____ mountain, nunatak
Fjord-en _____ inlet, fjord

Gaoyuan _____ plateau
Gebel _____ mountain-s, range
Gezâir _____ islands
Gezīra-t, Gezîret _____ island, peninsula
Ghubb-at _____ bay, gulf
Gobi _____ desert
Gölü _____ lake

Golf-e, -o _____ gulf
Gora _____ mountain,-s
Got _____ point
Guba _____ bay, gulf

Hai _____ lake, sea
Haixia _____ channel, strait
Hamada, Ḥammādah _____ rocky desert
Hāyk` _____ lake, reservoir
He _____ canal, lake, river
Hu _____ lake, reservoir

Île-s, Ilha-s, Illa-s _____ island-s, islet-s
Isla-s _____ island-s
Isol-a, -e _____ island, -s
Istmo _____ isthmus

Jabal, Jebel _____ mountain-s, range
Jazā'ir, Jazīrat _____ island-s
Jezero _____ lake
Jiang _____ river, stream
Jibāl _____ hill, mountain, ridge
Jima _____ island-s, rock-s

Kap, Kapp _____ cape
Kaikyō _____ channel, strait
Kangri _____ mountain, peak
Kavīr _____ salt desert
Kepulauan _____ archipelago, islands
Khalīg, Khalīj _____ bay, gulf
Khrebet _____ mountain range
Ko _____ island, peak
Köli _____ lake
Kong _____ king, mountain
Körfezi _____ bay, gulf
Kūh, Kūhhā _____ mountain-s, range

Lac, Lac-ul _____ lake
Lae _____ cape, point
Lago, -a _____ lagoon, lake
Laguna-s _____ lagoon-s, lake-s
Laht _____ bay, gulf, harbor
Liedao _____ archipelago, islands
Ling _____ mountain-s, range

Man _____ bay
Mar, Mare _____ large lake, sea
Massif _____ mountain-s
Mesa, Meseta _____ plateau, tableland
Misaki _____ cape, peninsula, point
Mont-e, -s _____ mount, -ain, -s
Montagne-s _____ mount, -ain, -s

More — sea
Morro — bluff, headland, hill
Munkhafad — depression
Mys — cape

Nada — gulf, sea
Nafūd — area of dunes, desert
Nagor'ye — mountain range, plateau
Nevado-s — snow-capped mountain-s
Nord-re — north-ern
Nosy — island, reef, rock
Nunatak-s — peak-s surrounded by ice cap
Nur — lake, salt lake
Nuruu — mountain range, ridge
Nuur — lake

Ostrov,-a — island, -s
Ozer-o — lake, -s

Pampa-s — grassy plain-s
Pantanal — marsh, swamp
Pendi — basin
Península, Péninsule — peninsula
Phu — mountain
Pic, Pik — peak
Pico-s — peak-s
Playa — beach, inlet, shore
Planalto, Plato — plateau
Pointe — point
Poluostrov — peninsula
Ponta — cape, point
Proliv — strait
Puerto — bay, pass, port
Pulau — island
Punta — point

Qum — desert, sand
Qundao — archipelago, islands

Raas — cape, point
Ras, Râs, Ra's — cape
Represa — reservoir
Rettō — chain of islands
Rio, Río — river
Rocas — rocks

Sahara, Şaḩrā' — desert
Salar — salt flat
Salina — salt pan
Salin-as, -es — salt flat-s, salt marsh-es
Sankt — saint

Sanmaek — mountain range
São — saint
Sarīr — gravel desert
Selat — strait
Semenanjung — peninsula
Serra — range of hills or mountains
Shamo — desert
Shan — island-s, mountain-s, range
Shatt, Shaţţ — large river
Shima — island-s, rock-s
Shotō — archipelago
Shott — intermittent salt lake
Shyghanaghy — bay, gulf
Sierra-s — mountain range-s
Stretto — strait
Sud — south
Suidō — channel, strait
Sund — sound, strait

Tanjung — cape, point
Tassili — plateau, upland
Taüy — hills, mountains
Teluk — bay
Tierra — land, region
Tō — islands, rocks

Uul — mountain, range

Vodokhranilishche — reservoir
Volcan, Volcán — volcano
Vostochn-yy, -aya, -oye — eastern

Wadī — valley, watercourse
Wan — bay, gulf

Xia — gorge, strait
Xiao — lesser, little

Yoma — mountain range
Yuzhn-yy, -aya, -oye — southern

Zaki — cape, point
Zaliv — bay, gulf
Zapadn-yy, -aya, -oye — western
Zatoka — bay, gulf
Zemlya — land
Zhotasy — mountains

PLACE-NAME INDEX

Using the Index

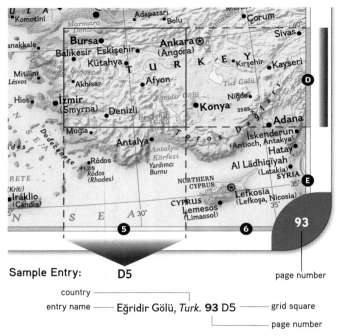

Sample Entry: **D5**

country ⎯⎯
entry name ⎯⎯ Eğridir Gölü, *Turk*. **93** D5 ⎯⎯ grid square
⎯⎯ page number

page number

The following system is used to locate a place on a map in this atlas. The bold-face type after an entry refers to the page on which the place name is found. The letter-number combination refers to the grid on which the place name is located. The edge of each map is marked with numbers and letters, dividing the map into a grid of squares. A name may appear on several maps, but the index lists only the best presentation. Some entries include a description, as in "Apure, *river, Venez*. **68** B3." In languages other than English, the description of a physical fea-ture may be part of the name: For instance, "Shotō" in "Izu Shotō, *Japan* **121** D6" means "islands." When a feature or place can be referred to by more than one name, both may appear in the index with cross-references. For example, the entry for Cairo, Egypt reads "Cairo *see* El Qâhira, *Egypt* **140** A2." That entry is: "El Qâhira (Cairo), *Egypt* **140** A2."

Ist Cataract, *Egypt*
140 B2
2nd Cataract, *Sudan*
140 C2
3rd Cataract, *Sudan*
140 C2

A

Aagaard Islands, *Antarctica*
167 A5
Aasiaat (Egedesminde),
Greenland, Den. **165** E5
Aba, *Nigeria* **139** E4
Abaco Island, *Bahamas*
50 A3
Ābādān, *Iran* **III** D5
Ābādeh, *Iran* **III** D5
Abaetetuba, *Braz.* **71** A5
Abancay, *Peru* **70** CI
Abashiri Wan, *Japan*
121 B6
Ābay *see* Blue Nile, *river,*
Eth. **141** D3
Ābaya Häyk', *Eth.* **141** E3
Abbot Ice Shelf, *Antarctica*
166 C2
'Abd al Kūrī, *island, Yemen*
113 E4
Abéché, *Chad* **139** D6
Abercorn *see* Mbala,
Zambia **143** C4
Aberdeen, *S. Dak., U.S.*
42 B3
Aberdeen, *U.K.* **88** A3
Abhā, *Saudi Arabia*
112 D2
Abidjan, *Côte d'Ivoire*
138 E3
Abilene, *Tex., U.S.* **48** A3
Abkhazia, *region, Rep. of Ga.*
110 A2
Åbo *see* Turku, *Fin.* **90** C3
Aboa, *research station,*
Antarctica **166** A3
Absaroka Range, *Wyo., U.S.*
42 B2
Abu Deleiq, *Sudan* **112** DI
Abu Dhabi, *U.A.E.* **113** C5
Abu Hamed, *Sudan*
140 C2
Abuja, *Nigeria* **139** E4

Abū Madd, Ra's, *Saudi*
Arabia **112** BI
Abu Shagara, Ras, *Sudan*
140 C3
Abyad, El Bahr el (White
Nile), *S. Sudan, Sudan*
141 D2
Abyei, *region, Sudan*
141 D2
Acadia National Park, *U.S.*
47 A6
Acapulco, *Mex.* **48** D3
Accra, *Ghana* **138** E3
Acklins Island, *Bahamas*
51 C4
Aconcagua, Cerro, *Arg.*
72 C3
Açores *see* Azores, *Port.*
126 AI
A Coruña, *Sp.* **89** D2
Acraman, Lake, *S. Austral.,*
Austral. **151** D4
Acre, *river, Bol., Braz., Peru*
70 C2
Actéon, Groupe, *Fr.*
Polynesia, Fr. **161** D5
Adak Island, *Alas., U.S.*
44 C4
Adam, *Oman* **113** C5
Adamawa, *mountains,*
Cameroon, Nigeria
128 C3
'Adan (Aden), *Yemen*
112 E3
Adana, *Turk.* **110** B2
Adapazarı, *Turk.* **93** C5
Ad Dahnā', *region, Saudi*
Arabia **112** B3
Ad Dakhla, *W. Sahara, Mor.*
138 BI
Ad Damer, *Sudan* **140** C3
Ad Dammām, *Saudi Arabia*
113 B4
Ad Dawḥah (Doha), *Qatar*
113 B4
Aḍ Ḍiffah *see* Libyan
Plateau, *Egypt, Lib.*
140 AI
Addis Ababa *see* Ādīs
Ābeba, *Eth.* **141** D3
Adelaide, *S. Austral., Austral.*
149 D3

Adelaide Island, *Antarctica*
166 B2
Aden *see* 'Adan, *Yemen*
112 E3
Aden, Gulf of, *Af., Asia*
100 DI
Adieu, Cape, *S. Austral.,*
Austral. **150** D3
Ādīs Ābeba (Addis Ababa),
Eth. **141** D3
Admiralty Island, *Alas., U.S.*
44 C5
Adrar, *region, Mauritania*
138 C2
Adrar des Ifôghas, *region,*
Mali **138** C3
Adrianople *see* Edirne,
Turk. **110** AI
Adriatic Sea, *Eur.* **78** D3
Ādwa, *Eth.* **141** D3
Aegean Sea, *Asia, Eur.*
79 E4
Afar, *region, Eth.* **141** D4
Afghanistan, *Asia* **98** C3
'Afīf, *Saudi Arabia* **112** C3
Afognak Island, *Alas., U.S.*
44 C3
Afyon, *Turk.* **110** BI
Agadez, *Niger* **139** D4
Agadir, *Mor.* **138** B2
Agana *see* Hagåtña, *Guam,*
U.S. **160** B2
Agattu Island, *Alas., U.S.*
44 C3
Agra, *India* **116** B3
Ağrı Dağı (Mount Ararat),
Turk. **III** B4
Agrigento, *It.* **92** D2
Agrínio, *Gr.* **92** D3
Agua Prieta, *Mex.* **48** A2
Aguascalientes, *Mex.*
48 C3
Aguja, Punta, *Peru* **68** EI
Agulhas, Cape, *S. Af.*
144 E2
Ahaggar (Hoggar),
mountains, Alg. **139** C4
Ahaggar Mountains, *Alg.*
128 B2
Ahmadabad, *India* **116** C3
Ahvāz, *Iran* **III** D5
Ahvenanmaa *see* Åland,
islands, Fin. **90** C3

Al Khurmah, *Saudi Arabia* 112 C2

Al Kuwayt (Kuwait City), *Kuwait* 111 D4

Al Lādhiqīyah (Latakia), *Syr.* 110 C2

Allahabad, *India* 117 B4

Al Lidām, *Saudi Arabia* 112 C3

Al Līth, *Saudi Arabia* 112 C2

Al Luḥayyah, *Yemen* 112 E2

Al Madīnah (Medina), *Saudi Arabia* 112 B2

Al Majma'ah, *Saudi Arabia* 112 B3

Al Manāmah (Manama), *Bahrain* 113 B4

Almaty, *Kaz.* 115 C5

Al Mawṣil (Mosul), *Iraq* 111 B4

Almería, *Sp.* 89 F3

Al Mukallā, *Yemen* 113 E4

Al Mukhā, *Yemen* 112 E3

Al Muwayliḥ, *Saudi Arabia* 112 B1

Alor, *island, Indonesia* 123 E4

Aloysius, Mount, *W. Austral., Austral.* 150 C3

Alps, *mountains, Eur.* 76 D3

Al Quds see Jerusalem, *Israel* 110 C2

Al Qunfudhah, *Saudi Arabia* 112 D2

Alta, *Nor.* 90 A3

Altay, *China* 118 A2

Altay, *Mongolia* 118 B3

Altay Mountains, *Asia* 118 A2

Altiplano, *plateau, Bol.* 70 D2

Alto Purus, *river, Braz., Peru* 70 B2

Altun Shan, *China* 118 C2

Alturas, *Calif., U.S.* 42 B1

Al 'Ubaylah, *Saudi Arabia* 113 C4

Al 'Ulā, *Saudi Arabia* 112 B2

Al 'Uwaynat see 'Uweinat, Jebel, *Lib., Sudan* 140 C1

Al Wajh, *Saudi Arabia* 112 B1

Alyangula, *N. Terr., Austral.* 149 A4

Amadeus, Lake, *N. Terr., Austral.* 150 C3

Amadeus Depression, *N. Terr., Austral.* 150 C3

Amami Ō Shima, *Japan* 119 D6

Amangeldi, *Kaz.* 114 B3

Amapá, *Braz.* 69 C6

Amarillo, *Tex., U.S.* 42 C3

Amazon (Amazonas, Solimões), *river, Braz.* 58 B2

Amazon, Mouths of the, *Braz.* 58 B4

Amazonas see Amazon, *river, Braz.* 56 B3

Amazon Basin, *S. Amer.* 58 B2

Ambanja, *Madagascar* 145 B6

Ambarchik, *Russ.* 164 B2

Ambargasta, Salinas de, *Arg.* 72 A3

Ambatondrazaka, *Madagascar* 145 B6

Ambergris Cays, *Turks & Caicos Is., U.K.* 51 C4

Ambilobe, *Madagascar* 145 A6

Ambon, *Indonesia* 123 D5

Amboseli, Lake, *Tanzania* 143 B5

Ambovombe, *Madagascar* 145 D6

Ambre, Cap d', *Madagascar* 145 A6

Amchitka Island, *Alas., U.S.* 44 C4

Amdo (Pagnag), *China* 118 C2

American Highland, *Antarctica* 167 B5

American Samoa, *possession, U.S.* 161 C4

Amery Ice Shelf, *Antarctica* 167 B5

Amgu, *Russ.* 121 A5

Amiens, *Fr.* 88 C4

Amisus see Samsun, *Turk.* 110 A3

Amlia Island, *Alas., U.S.* 44 C5

'Ammān (Philadelphia), *Jordan* 110 C2

Ammassalik see Tasiilaq, *Greenland, Den.* 165 E5

'Amrān, *Yemen* 112 E3

Amravati, *India* 116 C3

Amritsar, *India* 116 A3

Amsterdam, *Neth.* 88 B4

Am Timan, *Chad* 139 D5

Amu Darya, *river, Asia* 114 D3

Amundsen Gulf, *N.W.T., Can.* 40 C2

Amundsen-Scott South Pole, *research station, Antarctica* 167 C4

Amundsen Sea, *Antarctica* 166 D2

Amur see Heilong Jiang, *river, China, Russ.* 119 A6

Anadyr', *Russ.* 95 A6

Anadyr, Gulf of, *Russ.* 101 A5

Anadyrskiy Zaliv, *Russ.* 164 C1

Anak, *N. Kor.* 120 C1

Ana María, Golfo de, *Cuba* 50 C2

Anambas, Kepulauan, *Indonesia* 122 C2

Anápolis, *Braz.* 71 C4

Anār, *Iran* 111 D6

Anatolia (Asia Minor), *region, Turk.* 110 B2

Anbyŏn, *N. Kor.* 120 C2

Anchorage, *Alas., U.S.* 44 B3

Ancón de Sardinas, Bahía de, *Col., Ecua.* 68 C1

Ancud, *Chile* 73 D1

Ancud, Golfo de, *Chile* 73 D1

Åndalsnes, *Nor.* 90 C1

Andaman Islands, *India* 117 D5

Arakan Yoma, *mountains, Myanmar* 117 C5

Aral, *Kaz.* 114 C3

Aral Mangy Qaraqumy, *Kaz.* 114 B3

Aral Sea, *Kaz., Uzb.* 114 C2

Aran Islands, *Ire.* 88 B2

Araouane, *Mali* 138 C3

Arapiraca, *Braz.* 71 B6

'Ar'ar, *Saudi Arabia* 112 A2

Ararat, Mount *see* Ağrı Dağı, *Turk.* 111 B4

Aras, *river, Asia* 111 B4

Arauca, *Col., Venez.* 68 B3

Arauco Gulf, *Chile* 59 E2

Araya, Península de, *Venez.* 53 F2

Ārba Minch', *Eth.* 141 E3

Arbīl (Irbil), *Iraq* 111 B4

Archangel *see* Arkhangel'sk, *Russ.* 94 C2

Arches National Park, *U.S.* 46 C2

Arctic Bay, *Nunavut, Can.* 41 A4

Arctowski, *research station, Antarctica* 166 A1

Ardabīl, *Iran* 111 B4

Åre, *Sw.* 90 C2

Arecibo, *P.R., U.S.* 51 D6

Arenas, Punta de, *Arg.* 73 F2

Arendal, *Nor.* 91 D1

Arequipa, *Peru* 70 C2

Argentina, *S. Amer.* 57 E2

Argun' *see* Ergun, *river, Russ.* 119 A5

Argus, Dome, *Antarctica* 167 C4

Argyle, Lake, *W. Austral., Austral.* 150 B3

Århus, *Den.* 91 D1

Arica, *Chile* 70 D2

Arid, Cape, *W. Austral., Austral.* 150 E2

Arima, *Trin. & Tobago* 53 F4

Arinos, *river, Braz.* 70 B3

Aripuanã, *river, Braz.* 70 B3

Arizona, *state, U.S.* 42 C2

Arkansas, *river, U.S.* 42 C3

Arkansas, *state, U.S.* 43 C4

Arkhangel'sk (Archangel), *Russ.* 94 C2

Arles, *Fr.* 89 D4

Arlit, *Niger* 139 C4

Armenia, *Asia* 98 C2

Armidale, *N.S.W., Austral.* 149 D6

Arnhem, Cape, *N. Terr., Austral.* 151 A4

Ar Ramādī (Ramadi), *Iraq* 111 C4

Ar Riyāḍ (Riyadh), *Saudi Arabia* 112 B3

Ar Riyān, *Yemen* 113 E4

Ar Rub' al Khālī (Empty Quarter), *desert, Saudi Arabia* 112 D4

Ar Ruṭbah, *Iraq* 110 C3

Artemisa, *Cuba* 50 C1

Artigas, *research station, Antarctica* 166 A1

Arturo Prat, *research station, Antarctica* 166 A1

Aru, Kepulauan, *Indonesia* 123 E5

Arua, *Dem. Rep. of the Congo* 141 E2

Arua, *Uganda* 143 A4

Aruba, *possession, Neth.* 53 D1

Arusha, *Tanzania* 143 B5

Aruwimi, *river, Dem. Rep. of the Congo* 143 A4

Arvayheer, *Mongolia* 119 B4

Arviat, *Nunavut, Can.* 40 C3

Arxan, *China* 119 A5

Ary, *Russ.* 95 B4

Aryqbayq, *Kaz.* 115 A4

Asahikawa, *Japan* 121 B6

Ascension, *island, U.K.* 129 D1

'Aseb, *Eritrea* 141 D4

Aşgabat (Ashgabat), *Turkm.* 114 E2

Ashburton, *river, W. Austral., Austral.* 150 C1

Ashgabat *see* Aşgabat, *Turkm.* 114 E2

Ashmore Islands, *W. Austral., Austral.* 150 A2

Ash Shiḥr, *Yemen* 113 E4

Asia Minor *see* Anatolia, *region, Turk.* 110 B2

Asmara (Asmera), *Eritrea* 140 C3

Asmera *see* Asmara, *Eritrea* 140 C3

Assal, Lake, *Djibouti* 128 C5

As Sanām, *Saudi Arabia* 113 C4

As Sīb, *Oman* 113 C5

As Sulaymānīyah, *Iraq* 111 C4

As Sulayyil, *Saudi Arabia* 112 D3

Astana, *Kaz.* 115 B4

Astrakhan', *Russ.* 114 B1

Asunción, *Parag.* 70 E3

Aswân (Syene), *Egypt* 140 B2

Asyûṭ, *Egypt* 140 B2

Atacama, Desierto de, *Chile* 70 D2

Atacama Desert, *Chile* 58 C2

Atamyrat (Kerki), *Turkm.* 114 E3

Atar, *Mauritania* 138 C2

Atbara, *river, Sudan* 140 C3

Atbara, *Sudan* 140 C3

Atbasar, *Kaz.* 115 A4

Athabasca, Lake, *Can.* 40 C2

Athens *see* Athína, *Gr.* 93 D4

Atherton Tableland, *Qnsld., Austral.* 151 B5

Athína (Athens), *Gr.* 93 D4

Athos Range, *Antarctica* 167 B5

Ati, *Chad* 139 D5

Atka Island, *Alas., U.S.* 44 C4

Atlanta, *Ga., U.S.* 43 D5

185

Bakwanga see Mbuji-Mayi,
Dem. Rep. of the Congo
142 C3
Balabac, island, Philippines
122 C3
Balabac Strait, Malaysia,
Philippines 122 C3
Balakovo, Russ. 77 C5
Balaton, lake, Hung. 92 B3
Balbina, Represa de, Braz.
69 D5
Balboa, Pan. 68 A1
Balearic Sea, Eur. 89 E4
Balearic Islands, Sp. 89 F4
Baleia, Ponta da, Braz.
56 C5
Baleia Point, Braz. 58 C5
Bali, island, Indonesia
122 C3
Balıkesir, Turk. 110 A1
Balikpapan, Indonesia
122 D3
Bali Sea, Indonesia
122 E3
Balkanabat (Nebitdag),
Turkm. 114 D2
Balkan Peninsula, Eur.
79 D4
Balkhash, Lake, Kaz.
100 C3
Ballarat, Vic., Austral.
149 E5
Ballenero, Canal, Chile
73 F1
Balmaceda, Chile 73 D2
Balqash, Kaz. 115 C5
Balqash Köli, Kaz. 115 C5
Bălți, Mold. 93 A4
Baltic Sea, Eur. 78 C3
Baltimore, Md., U.S. 43 C5
Bam, Iran 111 D6
Bamako, Mali 138 D2
Bambari, Cen. Af. Rep.
139 E6
Bamenda, Cameroon
139 E4
Bananal, Ilha do, Braz.
71 C4
Banaras see Varanasi, India
117 B4
Banâs, Râs, Egypt 140 B3
Banda, Pointe, Gabon
142 C1

Banda Aceh, Indonesia
122 C1
Bandar-e 'Abbās, Iran
111 E6
Bandar-e Anzalī, Iran
111 B5
Bandar-e Lengeh, Iran
111 E6
Bandar-e Torkaman, Iran
111 B5
Bandar Seri Begawan,
Brunei 122 C3
Banda Sea, Indonesia
123 E4
Bandeira, peak, Braz.
71 D5
Banderas Bay, Mex. 31 E2
Ban Don see Surat Thani,
Thai. 117 E4
Bandundu, Dem. Rep. of the
Congo 142 B2
Bandung, Indonesia
122 E2
Bangalore (Bengaluru),
India 116 D3
Bangassou, Cen. Af. Rep.
139 E6
Banggi, island, Malaysia
122 C3
Banghāzī (Benghazi), Lib.
139 A5
Bangka, island, Indonesia
122 D2
Bangkok see Krung Thep,
Thai. 122 B1
Bangladesh, Asia 99 D4
Bangor, Me., U.S. 43 B6
Bangui, Cen. Af. Rep.
139 E5
Bangweulu, Lake, Zambia
143 D4
Baní, Dom. Rep. 51 D5
Banja Luka, Bosn. & Herzg.
92 B2
Banjarmasin, Indonesia
122 D3
Banjul, Gambia 138 D1
Banks Island, N.W.T., Can.
40 A2
Banyak, Kepulauan,
Indonesia 122 D1
Banyuwangi, Indonesia
122 E3

Baochang see Taibus Qi,
China 119 B5
Baotou, China 119 B4
Baqên (Dartang), China
118 D3
Baraawe, Somalia 141 E4
Barahona, Dom. Rep.
51 D5
Baranavichy, Belarus
91 E4
Baranof Island, Alas., U.S.
44 C5
Barat Daya, Kepulauan,
Indonesia 123 E4
Barbados, N. Amer. 53 D5
Barbers Point see Kalaeloa,
Hawai'i, U.S. 45 E2
Barbuda, island, Antigua &
Barbuda 52 A4
Barcelona, Sp. 89 E4
Barcelona, Venez. 53 F1
Barcelos, Braz. 69 D4
Bareilly, India 117 B4
Barents Sea, Arctic Oc.
165 A5
Bari, It. 92 C2
Bârîs, Egypt 110 E1
Barkly Tableland, Austral.
151 B4
Barlee, Lake, W. Austral.,
Austral. 150 D2
Barnaul, Russ. 118 A2
Barquisimeto, Venez.
68 A3
Barra, Braz. 71 C5
Barra, Ponta da,
Mozambique 145 C4
Barra do São Manuel, Braz.
69 E5
Barranquilla, Col. 68 A2
Barra Point, Mozambique
129 E4
Barreiras, Braz. 71 C5
Barreirinhas, Braz. 71 A5
Barrow, Alas., U.S. 44 A3
Barrow, Point, Alas., U.S.
44 A3
Barrow Creek, N. Terr.,
Austral. 149 B4
Barrow Island, W. Austral.,
Austral. 150 B1
Bartolomeu Dias,
Mozambique 145 C4

Bengaluru *see* Bangalore, *India* **116** D3

Benghazi *see* Banghāzī, *Lib.* **139** A5

Bengkulu, *Indonesia* **122** D2

Bengo, Baía do, *Angola* **142** C1

Bengo Bay, *Angola* **129** D3

Bengoué, Mont, *Gabon* **142** A2

Benguela, *Angola* **142** D1

Beni, *river, Bol.* **70** C2

Beni Abbes, *Alg.* **138** B3

Beni Mazâr, *Egypt* **110** D1

Benin, *Af.* **126** C2

Benin, Bight of, *Af.* **128** C2

Benin City, *Nigeria* **139** E4

Beni Suef, *Egypt* **110** D1

Ben Nevis, *peak, U.K.* **76** B2

Benoni, *S. Af.* **144** D3

Bentley Subglacial Trench, *Antarctica* **166** C3

Benue, *river, Nigeria* **139** E4

Benxi, *China* **120** B1

Beograd (Belgrade), *Serb.* **92** B3

Bequia, *island, St. Vincent & the Grenadines* **53** D4

Berat, *Alban.* **92** D3

Berau, Teluk, *Indonesia* **123** D5

Berbera, *Somaliland* **141** D4

Berbérati, *Cen. Af. Rep.* **139** E5

Berdyans'k, *Ukr.* **93** A6

Berenice, *Egypt* **112** B1

Berezniki, *Russ.* **77** B6

Bergen, *Nor.* **90** C1

Beringovskiy, *Russ.* **95** A6

Bering Sea, *Pacific Oc.* **44** B1

Bering Strait, *Russ., U.S.* **164** C1

Berkner Island, *Antarctica* **166** B3

Berlin, *Ger.* **91** E2

Bermejo, *river, Arg.* **72** A2

Bermejo, *river, Arg.* **72** A4

Bermuda Islands, *possession, U.K.* **29** D5

Bern, *Switz.* **89** D5

Bernardo O'Higgins, *research station, Antarctica* **166** A1

Berry Islands, *Bahamas* **50** B3

Bertoua, *Cameroon* **142** A2

Bethanie, *Namibia* **144** D2

Bethel, *Alas., U.S.* **44** B2

Bethlehem, *S. Af.* **144** D3

Beyneu, *Kaz.* **114** C2

Beyoneisu Retsugan, *island, Japan* **121** E6

Beyrouth (Beirut), *Lebanon* **110** C2

Beyşehir Gölü, *Turk.* **93** D5

Bhamo, *Myanmar* **117** B6

Bhilai, *India* **117** C4

Bhisho, *S. Af.* **144** E3

Bhopal, *India* **116** C3

Bhubaneshwar, *India* **117** C4

Bhutan, *Asia* **99** D4

Biak, *island, Indonesia* **123** D6

Białystok, *Pol.* **91** E4

Biarritz, *Fr.* **89** D3

Bielefeld, *Ger.* **88** B5

Bien Hoa, *Vietnam* **122** B2

Big Bend National Park, *U.S.* **46** D3

Big Delta, *Alas., U.S.* **44** B4

Bighorn Mountains, *Wyo., U.S.* **42** B2

Big Wood Cay, *Bahamas* **50** B3

Bijagós, Arquipélago dos, *Guinea-Bissau* **138** D2

Bikaner, *India* **116** B3

Bikin, *Russ.* **121** A5

Bīkkū Bīttī, *peak, Lib.* **139** C5

Bila Tserkva, *Ukr.* **93** A5

Bilbao, *Sp.* **89** D3

Bilibino, *Russ.* **95** A5

Billings, *Mont., U.S.* **42** B2

Bilma, *Niger* **139** C5

Biloxi, *Miss., U.S.* **43** D4

Biltine, *Chad* **139** D6

Bimini Islands, *Bahamas* **50** B2

Bindura, *Zimb.* **145** B4

Binga, Monte, *Mozambique* **145** B4

Bintulu, *Malaysia* **122** C3

Bíobío, *river, Chile* **72** C1

Bioko, *Eq. Guinea* **142** A1

Birao, *Cen. Af. Rep.* **139** D6

Birdsville, *Qnsld., Austral.* **149** C4

Bīrjand, *Iran* **III** C6

Birmingham, *Ala., U.S.* **43** D5

Birmingham, *U.K.* **88** B3

Bir Mogreïn (Fort Trinquet), *Mauritania* **138** B2

Birni Nkonni, *Niger* **139** D4

Biscay, Bay of, *Eur.* **89** D3

Biscayne National Park, *U.S.* **47** E6

Biscoe Islands, *Antarctica* **166** B1

Bishkek, *Kyrg.* **115** D5

Biskra, *Alg.* **139** A4

Bismarck, *N. Dak., U.S.* **42** B3

Bismarck Archipelago, *P.N.G.* **160** C2

Bismarck Sea, *P.N.G.* **160** C2

Bissau, *Guinea-Bissau* **138** D1

Bitam, *Gabon* **142** A1

Bitlis, *Turk.* **110** B3

Bitola, *Maced.* **92** C3

Bitterfontein, *S. Af.* **144** E2

Bitterroot Range, *U.S.* **42** A2

Bizerte, *Tun.* **139** A4

Blackburn, Mount, *Alas., U.S.* **44** B4

Bla-Boy

Black Canyon of the Gunnison National Park, *U.S.* **46** C2
Black Hills, *U.S.* **42** B3
Black Rock, *Falkland Is.* **59** F4
Black Sea, *Asia, Eur.* **79** D4
Blagoveshchensk, *Russ.* **119** A5
Blanc, Cap, *Mauritania, W. Sahara* **138** C1
Blanc, Cape, *Mauritania, W. Sahara* **128** B1
Blanc, Mont, *Fr., It.* **89** D4
Blanca, Bahía, *Arg.* **57** E3
Blanca Bay, *Arg.* **59** E3
Blanchisseuse, *Trin. & Tobago* **53** F4
Blanquilla, Isla, *Venez.* **53** E1
Blantyre, *Malawi* **143** E5
Blida, *Alg.* **89** F4
Bloemfontein, *S. Af.* **144** D3
Bluefields, *Nicar.* **49** E5
Blue Mountain Peak, *Jam.* **50** D3
Blue Nile *see* Azraq, El Bahr el, *Eth., Sudan* **141** D3
Bo, *Sa. Leone* **138** E2
Boa Vista, *Braz.* **69** C4
Bobo Dioulasso, *Burkina Faso* **138** D3
Boca del Guafo, *strait, Chile* **73** D1
Boca do Acre, *Braz.* **68** E3
Boca Grande, *Venez.* **69** A4
Bodaybo, *Russ.* **95** D4
Bodø, *Nor.* **90** B2
Boende, *Dem. Rep. of the Congo* **142** B3
Bogda Feng, *peak, China* **100** C3
Bogor, *Indonesia* **122** E2
Bogotá, *Col.* **68** B2
Bo Hai, *bay, China* **119** C5
Bohol, *island, Philippines* **123** C4
Bohol Sea, *Philippines* **123** C4

Boise, *Idaho, U.S.* **42** B2
Bojeador, Cape, *Philippines* **119** E5
Bojnūrd, *Iran* **111** B6
Boké, *Guinea* **138** D1
Boknafjorden, *bay, Nor.* **91** D1
Bolivia, *S. Amer.* **56** C2
Bologna, *It.* **92** B1
Bologoye, *Russ.* **91** D5
Bolu, *Turk.* **93** C5
Boma, *Dem. Rep. of the Congo* **142** C1
Bombay *see* Mumbai, *India* **116** C3
Bomu, *river, Cen. Af. Rep., Dem. Rep. of the Congo* **142** A3
Bonaire, *possession, Neth.* **53** D2
Bonasse, *Trin. & Tobago* **53** F4
Bonavista Bay, *Can.* **30** C5
Bondo, *Dem. Rep. of the Congo* **142** A3
Bône *see* Annaba, *Alg.* **139** A4
Bone, Teluk, *Indonesia* **123** E4
Bongaree, *Qnsld., Austral.* **149** D6
Bonin Islands, *Japan* **101** C6
Bonn, *Ger.* **88** C5
Bonny, Bight of, *Cameroon, Eq. Guinea* **142** A1
Bontang, *Indonesia* **122** D3
Boorama, *Somaliland* **141** D4
Booroondara, Mount, *N.S.W., Austral.* **151** D5
Boosaaso (Bender Cassim), *Somalia* **141** D5
Boothia, Gulf of, *Nunavut, Can.* **41** B4
Boothia Peninsula, *Nunavut, Can.* **40** B3
Bor, *S. Sudan* **141** E2
Borāzjān, *Iran* **111** D5
Borba, *Braz.* **69** D5

Borborema Plateau, *Braz.* **58** B5
Bordeaux, *Fr.* **89** D3
Borden Peninsula, *Can.* **30** B3
Borneo (Kalimantan), *island, Brunei, Indonesia, Malaysia* **122** D3
Bornholm, *island, Den.* **91** E2
Borovichi, *Russ.* **91** D5
Borroloola, *N. Terr., Austral.* **149** B4
Borūjerd, *Iran* **111** C5
Boseong, *S. Kor.* **120** E2
Bosnia and Herzegovina, *Eur.* **76** D3
Bosobolo, *Dem. Rep. of the Congo* **142** A3
Bosporus *see* İstanbul Boğazı, *strait, Turk.* **93** C5
Bossangoa, *Cen. Af. Rep.* **139** E5
Boston, *Mass., U.S.* **43** B6
Botany Bay, *N.S.W., Austral.* **151** E6
Bothnia, Gulf of, *Fin., Sw.* **90** C3
Botswana, *Af.* **127** D3
Bouaké, *Côte d'Ivoire* **138** E2
Bouar, *Cen. Af. Rep.* **139** E5
Bougainville, *island, P.N.G.* **160** C2
Bougainville, Cape, *W. Austral., Austral.* **150** A3
Bougie *see* Bejaïa, *Alg.* **89** F5
Bouira, *Alg.* **89** F4
Boujdour, *W. Sahara, Mor.* **138** B1
Boujdour, Cape, *W. Sahara, Mor.* **128** B1
Boulder, *Colo., U.S.* **42** C3
Bourke, *N.S.W., Austral.* **149** D5
Bowen, *Qnsld., Austral.* **149** B5
Bowman Island, *Antarctica* **167** D6
Boyarka, *Russ.* **95** C4

Bozashchy Tübegi, *Kaz.*
114 C1
Bozeman, *Mont., U.S.*
42 B2
Brades, *Montserrat, U.K.*
52 B3
Braga, *Port.* 89 E2
Brahmapur, *India* 117 C4
Brahmaputra *see* Yarlung
Zangbo, *river, Bangladesh,
China, India* 117 B5
Bräila, *Rom.* 93 B4
Branco, *river, Braz.* 69 C4
Brandberg, *peak, Namibia*
144 C1
Brandon, *Man., Can.*
40 D3
Brandvlei, *S. Af.* 144 D2
Brasília, *Braz.* 71 C5
Brasileiro, Planalto, *Braz.*
71 D5
Braşov, *Rom.* 93 B4
Bratislava (Pressburg),
Slovakia 92 A3
Bratsk, *Russ.* 99 B4
Braunschweig (Brunswick),
Ger. 88 B5
Bravo del Norte, Río
see Grande, Rio, *Mex.*
48 A2
Brazil, *S. Amer.* 56 C3
Brazilian Highlands, *Braz.*
58 C4
Brazzaville, *Congo* 142 B2
Brecknock, Península, *Chile*
73 F2
Bredy, *Russ.* 114 A3
Brejo, *Braz.* 71 A5
Bremen, *Ger.* 91 B4
Brenner Pass, *Aust., It.*
92 A1
Brest, *Belarus* 91 F4
Brest, *Fr.* 88 C3
Bria, *Cen. Af. Rep.* 139 E6
Bridgetown, *Barbados*
53 D5
Brighton, *U.K.* 88 C3
Brindisi, *It.* 92 D3
Brisbane, *Qnsld., Austral.*
149 D6
Bristol, *U.K.* 88 B3
Bristol Bay, *Alas., U.S.*
44 C2

British Columbia, *province,
Can.* 40 C1
British Isles, *Ire., U.K.*
78 B2
British Virgin Islands,
possession, U.K. 52 A1
Britstown, *S. Af.* 144 D2
Brive, *Fr.* 89 D4
Brno, *Czech Rep.* 92 A2
Broken Bay, *N.S.W., Austral.*
149 E6
Broken Hill, *N.S.W., Austral.*
149 D4
Broken Hill *see* Kabwe,
Zambia 143 E4
Brønnøysund, *Nor.* 90 B2
Brooks Range, *Alas., U.S.*
44 A3
Broome, *W. Austral., Austral.*
148 B2
Broughton Island *see*
Qikiqtarjuaq, *Nunavut,
Can.* 41 B5
Brownsville, *Tex., U.S.*
42 E3
Bruce, Mount, *W. Austral.,
Austral.* 150 C2
Brunei, *Asia* 99 E5
Brunswick *see*
Braunschweig, *Ger.*
88 B5
Brunswick Bay, *W. Austral.,
Austral.* 150 A2
Brunt Ice Shelf, *Antarctica*
166 A3
Brussels *see* Bruxelles,
Belg. 76 C2
Bruxelles (Brussels), *Belg.*
76 C2
Bryce Canyon National
Park, *U.S.* 46 C2
Bucaramanga, *Col.* 68 B2
Buchanan, *Liberia* 138 E2
Bucharest *see* Bucureşti,
Rom. 93 B4
Buckland Tableland, *Qnsld.,
Austral.* 151 C5
Bucureşti (Bucharest),
Rom. 93 B4
Budapest, *Hung.* 92 A3
Buenaventura, *Col.* 68 B1
Buenaventura, Bahía de,
Col. 56 A1

Buenaventura Bay, *Col.*
58 B1
Buenos Aires, *Arg.* 72 B4
Buenos Aires, Lago, *Arg.*
73 E2
Buffalo, *N.Y., U.S.* 43 B5
Bug, *river, Eur.* 91 F4
Bügür *see* Luntai, *China*
115 C6
Bujumbura, *Burundi*
143 B4
Bukama, *Dem. Rep. of the
Congo* 143 D4
Bukavu, *Dem. Rep. of the
Congo* 143 B4
Bukhara *see* Buxoro, *Uzb.*
114 D3
Bulawayo, *Zimb.* 144 C3
Bulgan, *Mongolia* 119 A4
Bulgaria, *Eur.* 77 D4
Bumba, *Dem. Rep. of the
Congo* 142 A3
Bunbury, *W. Austral.,
Austral.* 148 E1
Bundaberg, *Qnsld., Austral.*
149 C6
Bungo Suidō, *Japan*
121 D4
Bunia, *Dem. Rep. of the
Congo* 143 A4
Buon Me Thuot, *Vietnam*
122 B2
Burao *see* Burco,
Somaliland 141 D5
Buraydah, *Saudi Arabia*
112 B3
Burco (Burao), *Somaliland*
141 D5
Burgas, *Bulg.* 93 C4
Burgos, *Sp.* 89 E3
Burica, Punta, *Pan.* 49 E5
Burke Island, *Antarctica*
166 C2
Burketown, *Qnsld., Austral.*
149 B4
Burkina Faso, *Af.* 126 C2
Burma *see* Myanmar, *Asia*
99 D4
Burnie, *Tas., Austral.*
148 E3
Burnside, Lake, *W. Austral.,
Austral.* 150 C2

191

Bur-Can

Burrendong Reservoir,
N.S.W., Austral. 151 D5
Bursa, *Turk.* 110 Al
Bûr Safâga, *Egypt* 110 E2
Bûr Saʿîd, *Egypt* 140 A2
Buru, *island, Indonesia*
123 D4
Burultokay *see* Fuhai, *China*
115 B6
Burundi, *Af.* 127 D4
Busan (Pusan), *S. Kor.*
120 D3
Bûshehr, *Iran* 111 D5
Businga, *Dem. Rep. of the
Congo* 142 A3
Busselton, *W. Austral.,
Austral.* 148 El
Buta, *Dem. Rep. of the
Congo* 142 A3
Butembo, *Dem. Rep. of the
Congo* 143 B4
Buton, *island, Indonesia*
123 E4
Butte, *Mont., U.S.* 42 B2
Butuan, *Philippines*
123 C4
Buxoro (Bukhara), *Uzb.*
114 D3
Buyant-Uhaa *see*
Saynshand, *Mongolia*
119 B4
Bydgoszcz, *Pol.* 91 E3
Bylot Island, *Nunavut, Can.*
41 A4
Byron, Cape, *N.S.W.,
Austral.* 151 D6

C

Cabinda, *region, Angola*
142 Cl
Cabinda, *Angola* 142 Cl
Cabo San Lucas, *Mex.*
48 Bl
Cáceres, *Braz.* 70 C3
Cáceres, *Sp.* 89 E2
Cachimbo, *Braz.* 69 E5
Cadale, *Somalia* 141 E5
Cádiz, *Sp.* 89 F2
Cagayan de Oro,
Philippines 123 C4
Cagliari, *It.* 92 Dl

Cahora Bassa, Lago de,
Mozambique 143 E4
Caicos Islands, *Turks &
Caicos Is., U.K.* 51 C4
Caicos Passage, *Bahamas,
Turks & Caicos Is.* 51 C4
Cairns, *Qnsld., Austral.*
149 B5
Cairo *see* El Qâhira, *Egypt*
140 A2
Cajamarca, *Peru* 68 El
Calais, *Fr.* 88 C4
Calama, *Braz.* 69 E4
Calama, *Chile* 70 D2
Calamar, *Col.* 68 C2
Calamian Group, *Philippines*
123 B4
Călăraşi, *Rom.* 93 B4
Calbayog, *Philippines*
123 B4
Calcanhar, Point, *Braz.*
58 B5
Calcanhar, Ponta do, *Braz.*
56 B5
Calçoene, *Braz.* 69 C6
Calcutta *see* Kolkata, *India*
117 C5
Calgary, *Alberta, Can.*
40 D2
Cali, *Col.* 68 C2
California, *state, U.S.*
42 Cl
California, Golfo de, *Mex.*
48 Al
California, Gulf of, *Mex.*
31 Dl
Callao, *Peru* 70 Cl
Caloundra, *Qnsld., Austral.*
149 C6
Calulo, *Angola* 142 D2
Calvinia, *S. Af.* 144 E2
Camabatela, *Angola*
144 Al
Camacupa, *Angola*
144 A2
Camagüey, *Cuba* 50 C3
Camagüey, Archipiélago
de, *Cuba* 50 C3
Camarones, *Arg.* 73 D3
Cambodia, *Asia* 99 D4
Cambridge Bay, *Nunavut,
Can.* 40 B2

Cambundi-Catembo, *Angola*
144 A2
Camden Bay, *Alas., U.S.*
44 A4
Cameroon, *Af.* 126 C3
Cameroon Mountain,
Cameroon 142 Al
Camiri, *Bol.* 70 D3
Camocim, *Braz.* 71 A6
Camooweal, *Qnsld., Austral.*
149 B4
Campeche, *Mex.* 49 C4
Campina Grande, *Braz.*
71 B6
Campinas, *Braz.* 71 D5
Campo Grande, *Braz.*
71 D4
Campos, *Braz.* 71 D5
Cam Ranh, *Vietnam*
122 B2
Canaan, *Trin. & Tobago*
53 F4
Canada, *N. Amer.* 28 C2
Canadian Shield, *region,
Can.* 30 D2
Çanakkale, *Turk.* 93 D4
Çanakkale Boğazı
(Dardanelles), *Turk.*
93 D4
Cananea, *Mex.* 48 A2
Canarias, Islas *see* Canary
Islands, *Sp.* 138 Bl
Canarreos, Archipiélago de
los, *Cuba* 50 Cl
Canary Islands (Islas
Canarias), *Sp.* 138 Bl
Canaveral, Cape (Cape
Kennedy), *Fla., U.S.*
43 D5
Canavieiras, *Braz.* 71 C6
Canberra, *Australian Capital
Terr., Austral.* 149 E5
Cancún, *Mex.* 49 C5
Candia *see* Iráklio, *Gr.*
93 E4
Canea *see* Haniá, *Gr.*
93 E4
Cangamba, *Angola*
144 A2
Caniapiscau, Réservoir,
Que., Can. 41 D4
Canouan, *island, St. Vincent
& the Grenadines* 53 E4

Can-Cen

Can Tho, *Vietnam* 122 B2
Canutama, *Braz.* 69 E4
Canyonlands National
Park, *U.S.* 46 C2
Cap Barbas, *W. Sahara, Mor.*
138 CI
Cape Breton Island, *N.S.,
Can.* 41 D6
Cape Dorset, *Nunavut, Can.*
41 B4
Capenda-Camulemba,
Angola 142 D2
Cape Parry, *N.W.T., Can.*
40 A2
Cape Town, *S. Af.* 144 E2
Cape York Peninsula,
Qnsld., Austral. 151 A5
Cap-Haïtien, *Haiti* 51 D4
Capital Hill, *N. Mariana Is.,
U.S.* 160 A2
Capitol Reef National Park,
U.S. 46 C2
Capricorn Channel, *Qnsld.,
Austral.* 151 C6
Caprivi Strip, *region,
Namibia* 144 B2
Caquetá, *river, Col.* 68 C2
Caracaraí, *Braz.* 69 C4
Caracas, *Venez.* 68 A3
Carajás, Serra dos, *Braz.*
69 E6
Caratasca, Laguna de,
Hond. 50 EI
Caravelas, *Braz.* 71 D6
Carbón, Laguna del, *Arg.*
73 E2
Carbonara, Capo, *It.*
92 DI
Carcasse, Cap, *Haiti*
51 D4
Cardiff, *U.K.* 88 B3
Carey, Lake, *W. Austral.,
Austral.* 150 D2
Cariaco, *Venez.* 53 F2
Caribbean Sea, *Atl. Oc.*
31 E4
Carinhanha, *Braz.* 71 C5
Caripito, *Venez.* 53 F3
Carlsbad, *N. Mex., U.S.*
42 D3
Carlsbad Caverns National
Park, *U.S.* 46 D3

Carmacks, *Yukon, Can.*
40 BI
Carnarvon, *W. Austral.,
Austral.* 148 CI
Carnegie, Lake, *W. Austral.,
Austral.* 150 C2
Carney Island, *Antarctica*
166 D2
Carnot, *Cen. Af. Rep.*
139 E5
Carnot, Cape, *S. Austral.,
Austral.* 151 E4
Caroebé, *Braz.* 69 C5
Carolina, *Braz.* 71 B5
Caroline Islands, *F.S.M.,
Palau* 160 BI
Carpathian Mountains,
Eur. 79 D4
Carpathos *see* Kárpathos,
island, Gr. 110 BI
Carpentaria, Gulf of,
Austral. 151 A4
Carrauntoohill, *peak, Ire.*
88 B2
Carriacou, *island, Grenada*
53 E4
Carson City, *Nev., U.S.*
42 CI
Cartagena, *Col.* 68 A2
Cartagena, *Sp.* 89 F3
Cartago, *Costa Rica* 49 E5
Cartier Island, *W. Austral.,
Austral.* 150 A2
Cartwright, *Nfld. & Lab.,
Can.* 41 C6
Carúpano, *Venez.* 53 F2
Carvoeiro, *Braz.* 69 D4
Casablanca, *Mor.* 138 A2
Cascade Range, *U.S.*
42 BI
Casey, *research station,
Antarctica* 167 D6
Casper, *Wyo., U.S.* 42 B3
Caspian Depression, *Kaz.,
Russ.* 114 BI
Caspian Sea, *Asia, Eur.*
100 B2
Cassai *see* Kasai, *river,
Angola, Dem. Rep. of the
Congo* 144 A2
Cassiar Mountains, *Can.*
40 BI

Castelló de la Plana *see*
Castellón de la Plana, *Sp.*
89 E3
Castellón de la Plana
(Castelló de la Plana), *Sp.*
89 E3
Castries, *St. Lucia* 53 D4
Catalina, Punta, *Arg., Chile*
73 F2
Catamarca, *Arg.* 72 A2
Catanduanes, *island,
Philippines* 123 B4
Catania, *It.* 92 D2
Catanzaro, *It.* 92 D2
Catete, *Angola* 142 D2
Catingas, *region, Braz.*
58 B3
Cat Island, *Bahamas*
50 B3
Caubvick, Mount *see*
D'Iberville, Mont, *Can.*
41 C5
Cauca, *river, Col.* 68 B2
Caucasus Mountains,
Azerb., Rep. of Ga., Russ.
110 A3
Caura, *river, Venez.* 69 B4
Cauto, *river, Cuba* 50 C3
Caxias, *Braz.* 71 B5
Caxias do Sul, *Braz.* 71 E4
Caxito, *Angola* 144 AI
Cayenne, *Fr. Guiana, Fr.*
69 B6
Cayman Brac, *island,
Cayman Is., U.K.* 50 D2
Cayman Islands, *possession,
U.K.* 50 D2
Cazombo, *Angola* 144 A2
Cebu, *island, Philippines*
123 B4
Cebu, *Philippines* 123 B4
Ceduna, *S. Austral., Austral.*
149 D4
Celebes *see* Sulawesi,
island, Indonesia 123 D4
Celebes Sea, *Indonesia,
Philippines* 123 C4
Celtic Sea, *Eur.* 78 C2
Cenderawasih, Teluk,
Indonesia 123 D6
Central, Cordillera, *Col.*
68 C2

193

Cen-Chi

Central, Cordillera, *Dom. Rep.* 51 D5
Central, Massif, *Fr.* 78 D2
Central African Republic, *Af.* 126 C3
Central America, *region, N. Amer.* 31 E3
Central Lowland, *U.S.* 31 D3
Central Lowlands, *Austral.* 151 B4
Central Siberian Plateau, *Russ.* 101 B4
Ceram, *island, Indonesia* 123 D5
Ceram Sea, *Indonesia* 123 D5
Cerro de Pasco, *Peru* 70 C1
Ceuta, *Sp.* 89 F2
Chābahār, *Iran* 113 B6
Chacao, Canal de, *Chile* 73 D1
Chad, *Af.* 126 C3
Chad, Lake, *Af.* 139 D5
Chagda, *Russ.* 95 C5
Chagos Archipelago, *possession, U.K.* 98 E3
Chaman, *Pak.* 116 A2
Chambi, Jebel ech, *Tun.* 139 A4
Chañaral, *Chile* 72 A1
Chandigarh, *India* 116 B3
Chandrapur, *India* 117 C4
Changchun, *China* 119 B5
Chang Jiang (Yangtze), *China* 119 D4
Changjin Reservoir (Chosin Reservoir), *N. Kor.* 120 B2
Changsan-got, *cape, N. Kor.* 120 C1
Changsha, *China* 119 D5
Changwon, *S. Kor.* 120 D2
Changyŏn, *N. Kor.* 120 C1
Channel Islands, *U.K.* 88 C3
Channel Country, *Austral.* 151 C4
Channel Islands, *Calif., U.S.* 42 C1

Channel Islands National Park, *U.S.* 46 C1
Chany, Ozero, *Russ.* 115 A5
Chapayevsk, *Russ.* 114 A2
Chappal Waddi, *peak, Cameroon, Nigeria* 139 E4
Charcot Island, *Antarctica* 166 B2
Chari, *river, Chad* 139 D5
Chärjew *see* Türkmenabat, *Turkm.* 115 D3
Charles, Cape, *U.S.* 31 D4
Charles Point, *N. Terr., Austral.* 150 A3
Charleston, *S.C., U.S.* 43 D5
Charleston, *W. Va., U.S.* 43 C5
Charlestown, *St. Kitts & Nevis* 52 B3
Charleville, *Qnsld., Austral.* 149 C5
Charlotte, *N.C., U.S.* 43 C5
Charlotte Amalie, *U.S. Virgin Is., U.S.* 52 A1
Charlotte Harbor, *U.S.* 50 A1
Charlottetown, *P.E.I., Can.* 41 D6
Charlotteville, *Trin. & Tobago* 53 F5
Charters Towers, *Qnsld., Austral.* 149 B5
Chartres, *Fr.* 88 C4
Chasŏng, *N. Kor.* 120 A2
Chatham Islands, *N.Z.* 161 E4
Chaves, *Braz.* 69 C6
Chech, 'Erg, *Alg., Mali* 138 D3
Cheduba Island, *Myanmar* 117 C5
Cheekha Dar, *peak, Iran, Iraq* 111 B4
Chegutu, *Zimb.* 144 B3
Cheju *see* Jeju, *S. Kor.* 120 E2
Chełm, *Pol.* 91 F4
Chelyabinsk, *Russ.* 94 D2
Chemnitz, *Ger.* 91 F2

Chengchow *see* Zhengzhou, *China* 119 B5
Chengdu, *China* 119 D4
Chennai (Madras), *India* 117 D4
Cheonan, *S. Kor.* 120 D2
Cheongju, *S. Kor.* 120 D2
Cherbourg-Octeville, *Fr.* 88 C3
Cherlak, *Russ.* 115 A5
Chernihiv, *Ukr.* 91 F5
Chernivtsi, *Ukr.* 93 A4
Chernyakhovsk, *Russ.* 91 E3
Cherskiy, *Russ.* 95 B5
Cherskogo, Khrebet, *Russ.* 95 B5
Chesapeake Bay, *U.S.* 43 C6
Chesha Bay, *Russ.* 79 A5
Cheshskaya Guba, *Russ.* 77 A5
Chesterfield Inlet, *Can.* 30 B3
Chesterfield Inlet, *Nunavut, Can.* 40 C3
Chetumal, *Mex.* 49 C5
Ch'ew Bahir, *lake, Eth.* 143 A6
Cheyenne, *Wyo., U.S.* 42 C3
Chiang Mai, *Thai.* 122 A1
Chibemba, *Angola* 144 B1
Chibougamau, *Que., Can.* 41 D5
Chicago, *Ill., U.S.* 43 B4
Chichagof Island, *Alas., U.S.* 44 C5
Chiclayo, *Peru* 68 E1
Chico, *river, Arg.* 73 D2
Chigubo, *Mozambique* 145 C4
Chihuahua, *Mex.* 48 B2
Chile, *S. Amer.* 57 E2
Chillán, *Chile* 72 C1
Chiloé, Isla Grande de, *Chile* 73 D1
Chilpancingo, *Mex.* 48 D3
Chilwa, Lake, *Malawi, Mozambique* 143 E5
Chimborazo, *peak, Ecua.* 58 B1
Chimbote, *Peru* 68 E1

Chimboy, *Uzb.* 114 D3
Chimoio, *Mozambique*
145 B4
China, *Asia* 99 C4
Chinde, *Mozambique*
145 B4
Chindwin, *river, Myanmar*
117 C5
Chingola, *Zambia* 143 D4
Chinhoyi, *Zimb.* 144 B3
Chipata, *Zambia* 143 D5
Chirinda, *Russ.* 95 C4
Chisasibi, *Que., Can.*
41 D4
Chisimayu see Kismaayo,
Somalia 141 F4
Chişinău, *Mold.* 93 A5
Chita, *Russ.* 95 D5
Chitado, *Angola* 144 B1
Chitato (Dundo), *Angola*
142 C3
Chitré, *Pan.* 49 E6
Chittagong, *Bangladesh*
117 C5
Chitungwiza, *Zimb.*
145 B4
Chivilcoy, *Arg.* 72 B4
Chlef, *Alg.* 89 F4
Chokurdakh, *Russ.*
164 B2
Choma, *Zambia* 144 B3
Ch'ŏngjin, *N. Kor.* 120 A3
Chongqing, *China* 119 D4
Chonos, Archipiélago de
los, *Chile* 73 D1
Chonos Archipelago, *Chile*
59 E2
Chornobyl', *Ukr.* 91 F5
Ch'osan, *N. Kor.* 120 B2
Chosin Reservoir see
Changjin Reservoir, *N.
Kor.* 120 B2
Choybalsan, *Mongolia*
119 A4
Christchurch, *N.Z.*
160 E3
Christiansted, *U.S. Virgin
Is., U.S.* 52 A1
Christmas Island, *Austral.*
122 E2
Christmas Island see
Kiritimati, *Kiribati*
161 B5

Chubut, *river, Arg.* 73 D2
Chudovo, *Russ.* 91 D5
Chugach Mountains, *Alas.,
U.S.* 44 B3
Chukchi Peninsula, *Russ.*
101 A5
Chukchi Sea, *Arctic Oc.*
164 C1
Chukotskiy Poluostrov,
Russ. 164 C1
Chul'man, *Russ.* 95 C5
Chumikan, *Russ.* 95 C5
Chuncheon, *S. Kor.*
120 C2
Chur, *Switz.* 92 A1
Churchill, *Man., Can.*
40 C3
Churchill, Cape, *Can.*
30 B3
Chuuk (Truk Islands),
F.S.M. 160 B2
Ciego de Ávila, *Cuba*
50 C2
Cienfuegos, *Cuba* 50 C2
Cincinnati, *Ohio, U.S.*
43 C5
Cinto, Monte, *Fr.* 92 C1
Cistern Point, *Bahamas*
50 B3
Ciudad Acuña, *Mex.*
48 A3
Ciudad Bolívar, *Venez.*
69 B4
Ciudad del Carmen, *Mex.*
49 C4
Ciudad Guayana, *Venez.*
69 A4
Ciudad Juárez, *Mex.*
48 A2
Ciudad Madero, *Mex.*
48 C3
Ciudad Obregón, *Mex.*
48 B2
Ciudad Valles, *Mex.*
48 C3
Ciudad Victoria, *Mex.*
48 B3
Clarence Island, *Antarctica*
166 A1
Clarines, *Venez.* 53 F1
Cleveland, *Ohio, U.S.*
43 B5

Clipperton, *island, Pacific
Oc.* 48 E1
Cloncurry, *river, Qnsld.,
Austral.* 151 B4
Cloncurry, *Qnsld., Austral.*
149 B5
Cloncurry Plateau, *Qnsld.,
Austral.* 151 B4
Cluj-Napoca, *Rom.* 93 B4
Clyde River, *Nunavut, Can.*
41 A4
Coari, *river, Braz.* 69 D4
Coari, *Braz.* 69 D4
Coastal Plain, *U.S.* 31 D3
Coast Mountains, *Can.*
40 B1
Coast Ranges, *U.S.* 42 A1
Coats Island, *Nunavut, Can.*
41 C4
Coats Land, *Antarctica*
166 B3
Coatzacoalcos, *Mex.*
49 D4
Cobija, *Bol.* 70 C2
Cobourg Peninsula, *N.
Terr., Austral.* 150 A3
Cóbuè, *Mozambique*
145 A4
Coburg, *Ger.* 91 F1
Cochabamba, *Bol.* 70 D2
Cochin see Kochi, *India*
116 E3
Cockburn Town, *Turks &
Caicos Is., U.K.* 51 C5
Coco, *river, Hond., Nicar.*
49 D5
Coco, Isla del, *Costa Rica*
29 F3
Cocos Island, *Costa Rica*
31 F3
Cod, Cape, *Mass., U.S.*
43 B6
Codrington, *Antigua &
Barbuda* 52 A3
Coen, *Qnsld., Austral.*
149 A5
Coffs Harbour, *N.S.W.,
Austral.* 149 D6
Coiba Island, *Pan.* 31 F4
Coig, *river, Arg.* 73 E2
Coimbatore, *India* 116 E3
Coimbra, *Port.* 89 E2

Crary Ice Rise, *Antarctica* **166** D3

Crater Lake National Park, *U.S.* **46** B1

Crateús, *Braz.* **71** B6

Crete (Kríti), *island, Gr.* **93** E4

Crete, Sea of, *Gr.* **93** E4

Creus, Cap de, *Sp.* **89** E4

Crimea, *peninsula, Ukr.* **79** D5

Croatia, *Eur.* **76** D3

Crooked Island, *Bahamas* **51** C4

Crooked Island Passage, *Bahamas* **51** C4

Croydon, *Qnsld., Austral.* **149** B5

Cruz, Cabo, *Cuba* **50** D3

Cruzeiro do Sul, *Braz.* **68** E2

Crystal Mountains, *Af.* **142** B1

Cuamba, *Mozambique* **145** B4

Cuando, *river, Angola, Namibia, Zambia* **142** E3

Cuango, *river, Angola, Dem. Rep. of the Congo* **144** A1

Cuanza, *river, Angola* **142** D2

Cuba, *N. Amer.* **29** E4

Cúcuta, *Col.* **68** B2

Cuenca, *Ecua.* **68** D1

Cuenca, *Sp.* **89** E3

Cuiabá, *Braz.* **71** C4

Cuito, *river, Angola* **142** E3

Cuito Cuanavale, *Angola* **142** E2

Culebra, *island, P.R., U.S.* **52** A1

Culiacán, *Mex.* **48** B2

Culver, Point, *W. Austral., Austral.* **150** D3

Cumaná, *Venez.* **69** A4

Cumanacoa, *Venez.* **53** F2

Cumberland Peninsula, *Nunavut, Can.* **41** B5

Cumberland Sound, *Nunavut, Can.* **41** B5

Cuneo, *It.* **89** D5

Cunnamulla, *Qnsld., Austral.* **149** D5

Cupica, Golfo de, *Col.* **68** B1

Curaçao, *possession, Neth.* **53** D2

Curaray, *river, Ecua., Peru* **68** D2

Curicó, *Chile* **72** B1

Curitiba, *Braz.* **71** E4

Curralinho, *Braz.* **69** D6

Curvelo, *Braz.* **71** D5

Cusco, *Peru* **70** C2

Cuttack, *India* **117** C4

Cuyahoga Valley National Park, *U.S.* **47** B5

Cuyuni, *river, Guyana, Venez.* **69** B4

Cyclades see Kikládes, *islands, Gr.* **93** E4

Cyprus, *Eur.* **77** E4

Cyrenaica, *region, Lib.* **138** B5

Czechia see Czech Republic, *Eur.* **76** C3

Czech Republic (Czechia), *Eur.* **76** C3

D

Daegu (Taegu), *S. Kor.* **120** D2

Daejeon (Taejŏn), *S. Kor.* **120** D2

Dagelet see Ulleungdo, *island, S. Kor.* **120** C3

Dagö see Hiiumaa, *island, Est.* **91** D3

Da Hinggan Ling, *mountains, China* **119** B5

Dahlak Archipelago, *Eritrea* **140** C4

Dairen see Dalian, *China* **119** C5

Daitō Shotō, *Japan* **160** A1

Dakar, *Senegal* **138** D1

Dalandzadgad, *Mongolia* **119** B4

Da Lat, *Vietnam* **122** B2

Dalgaranga Hill, *W. Austral., Austral.* **150** D1

Dali, *China* **118** E3

Dalian (Dairen), *China* **119** C5

Dallas, *Tex., U.S.* **42** D3

Dall Island, *Alas., U.S.* **44** C5

Dal'negorsk, *Russ.* **95** D6

Dal'nerechensk, *Russ.* **121** A5

Daloa, *Côte d'Ivoire* **138** E2

Daly, *river, N. Terr., Austral.* **150** A3

Damar, *island, Indonesia* **123** E5

Damascus see Dimashq, *Syr.* **110** C2

Damāvand, Kūh-e, *Iran* **111** B3

Dampier Archipelago, *W. Austral., Austral.* **150** B1

Dampier Land, *W. Austral., Austral.* **150** B2

Danakil, *region, Eth.* **128** C5

Da Nang, *Vietnam* **122** B2

Dandong, *China* **119** B5

Danube, *river, Eur.* **79** D4

Dao Phu Quoc, *island, Vietnam* **122** B2

Da Qaidam, *China* **118** C3

Daqing, *China* **119** A5

Dardanelles see Çanakkale Boğazı, *strait, Turk.* **93** D4

Dar es Salaam, *Tanzania* **143** C6

Darfur, *region, Sudan* **141** D1

Darhan, *Mongolia* **119** A4

Darling, *river, N.S.W., Austral.* **151** D5

Darling Downs, *Qnsld., Austral.* **151** D5

Darling Range, *W. Austral., Austral.* **150** D2

Darnah (Derna), *Lib.* **139** A6

Dar Rounga, *hills, Cen. Af. Rep., Chad* **139** E6

Dartang see Baqên, *China* **118** D3

Darvel Bay, *Malaysia* 123 C4

Darwin, *N. Terr., Austral.* 148 A3

Daşoguz, *Turkm.* 114 D3

Datong, *China* 119 B4

Daugavpils, *Latv.* 91 D4

Dauphin, *Man., Can.* 40 D3

Davangere, *India* 116 D3

Davao, *Philippines* 123 C4

Davao Gulf, *Philippines* 123 C4

Davenport Range, *N. Terr., Austral.* 151 B4

David, *Pan.* 49 E5

Davis, *research station, Antarctica* 167 C6

Davis Islands, *Antarctica* 167 D6

Davis Sea, *Antarctica* 167 C6

Davis Strait, *Can., Greenland* 30 B4

Dawa, *river, Eth.* 143 A6

Dawei, *Myanmar* 122 B1

Dawmat al Jandal (Al Jawf), *Saudi Arabia* 112 A2

Dawson, *river, Qnsld., Austral.* 151 C6

Dawson, *Yukon, Can.* 40 A1

Dawson Creek, *B.C., Can.* 40 C2

Dayr az Zawr, *Syr.* 110 C3

Deadmans Cay, *Bahamas* 50 C3

Dead Sea, *Israel, Jordan* 110 D2

Dean Island, *Antarctica* 166 D2

Death Valley, *Calif., U.S.* 42 C1

Death Valley National Park, *U.S.* 46 C1

Débo, Lake, *Mali* 128 C2

Debrecen, *Hung.* 92 A3

Debre Mark'os, *Eth.* 141 D3

Deccan, *region, India* 116 D3

Deccan Plateau, *India* 100 D3

DeGrey, *river, W. Austral., Austral.* 150 B2

Deh Bīd, *Iran* 111 D5

Dejen, Ras, *Eth.* 141 D3

Delaware, *state, U.S.* 43 C6

Delgado, Cabo, *Mozambique* 145 A5

Delgado, Cape, *Mozambique, Tanzania* 129 D5

Delhi, *India* 116 B3

Delicias, *Mex.* 48 B2

Déline, *N.W.T., Can.* 40 B2

Dellys, *Alg.* 89 F4

De Long Mountains, *Alas., U.S.* 44 A2

Democratic Republic of the Congo, *Af.* 127 D3

Denakil, *region, Eth.* 141 D4

Denali *see* McKinley, Mount, *Alas., U.S.* 44 B3

Denali National Park and Preserve, *U.S.* 46 E2

Den Haag (The Hague), *Neth.* 88 B4

Denham, *W. Austral., Austral.* 148 C1

Denizli, *Turk.* 110 B1

Denmark, *Eur.* 76 C3

Denmark Strait, *Greenland, Ice.* 165 D6

Denpasar, *Indonesia* 122 E3

D'Entrecasteaux, Point, *W. Austral., Austral.* 150 E1

Denver, *Colo., U.S.* 42 C3

Deputatskiy, *Russ.* 95 B5

Derbent, *Russ.* 114 D1

Derby, *W. Austral., Austral.* 148 B2

Derna *see* Darnah, *Lib.* 139 A6

Dernberg, Cape, *Namibia* 144 D1

Derudeb, *Sudan* 140 C3

Derzhavīnsk, *Kaz.* 115 B4

Desē, *Eth.* 141 D4

Deseado, *river, Arg.* 73 E2

Desengaño, Punta, *Arg.* 73 E2

Des Moines, *Iowa, U.S.* 43 B4

Detroit, *Mich., U.S.* 43 B5

Devon Island, *Nunavut, Can.* 41 A4

Devonport, *Tas., Austral.* 148 E3

Deyang, *China* 119 D4

Dezfūl, *Iran* 111 C5

Dhaka, *Bangladesh* 117 C5

Dhamār, *Yemen* 112 E3

Dhofar *see* Ẓufār, *region, Oman* 113 D5

Diamante, *river, Arg.* 72 B2

Diamantina, *Braz.* 71 D5

Diamantina, *river, Qnsld., Austral.* 151 C5

Diamond Head, *Hawai‘i, U.S.* 45 E3

D'Iberville, Mont (Mount Caubvick), *Can.* 41 C5

Dibrugarh, *India* 117 B5

Dickson, *Russ.* 94 B3

Didao, *China* 119 A6

Diego de Almagro, *Chile* 72 A2

Diffa, *Niger* 139 D5

Dijon, *Fr.* 88 C4

Dika, Mys, *Russ.* 95 B4

Dili, *Timor-Leste* 123 E4

Dillingham, *Alas., U.S.* 44 C2

Dilolo, *Dem. Rep. of the Congo* 142 D3

Dimapur, *India* 117 B5

Dimashq (Damascus), *Syr.* 110 C2

Dimitrovgrad, *Russ.* 114 A2

Diourbel, *Senegal* 138 D1

Dirē Dawa, *Eth.* 141 D4

Dirico, *Angola* 142 E3

Dirk Hartog Island, *W. Austral., Austral.* 150 C1

Disappointment, Lake, *W. Austral., Austral.* 150 C2

Discovery Bay, *Austral.* 151 E4

D'Ur-Eng

D'Urville, Tanjung, *Indonesia* 123 D6
Dushanbe, *Taj.* 115 E4
Düsseldorf, *Ger.* 88 B5
Dvina Bay, *Russ.* 79 A4
Dvinskaya Guba, *Russ.* 77 A4
Dzaoudzi, *Mayotte, Fr.* 145 A6
Dzhankoy, *Ukr.* 93 B6
Dzungarian Basin *see* Junggar Pendi, *China* 118 B2
Dzungarian Gate, *China, Kaz.* 115 C6

E

East Antarctica, *Antarctica* 167 C4
East China Sea, *Asia* 119 D6
Eastern Desert, *Egypt* 140 B2
Eastern Ghats, *mountains, India* 116 D3
East Falkland, *island, Falkland Is.* 73 F4
East London, *S. Af.* 144 E3
East Sea *see* Japan, Sea of, *Asia* 101 C5
East Siberian Sea, *Arctic Oc.* 164 B2
East Timor *see* Timor-Leste, *Asia* 99 E5
Ebolowa, *Cameroon* 142 A1
Ebro, *river, Sp.* 89 E3
Ecbatana *see* Hamadān, *Iran* 111 C5
Echo Bay, *N.W.T., Can.* 40 B2
Ecuador, *S. Amer.* 56 B1
Ed Da'ein, *Sudan* 141 D1
Ed Damazin, *Sudan* 141 D3
Ed Damer, *Sudan* 112 D1
Ed Debba, *Sudan* 140 C2
Edinburgh, *U.K.* 88 A3
Edirne (Adrianople), *Turk.* 110 A1

Edmonton, *Alberta, Can.* 40 C2
Eduardo Frei, *research station, Antarctica* 166 A1
Edward, Lake, *Dem. Rep. of the Congo, Uganda* 143 B4
Edwards Plateau, *Tex., U.S.* 42 D3
Egedesminde *see* Aasiaat, *Greenland, Den.* 165 E5
Eger, *Hung.* 92 A3
Egerton, Mount, *W. Austral., Austral.* 150 C2
Eğridir Gölü, *Turk.* 93 D5
Egypt, *Af.* 126 B4
Eight Degree Channel, *Maldives* 116 E3
Eighty Mile Beach, *W. Austral., Austral.* 150 B2
Eindhoven, *Neth.* 88 B4
Éire *see* Ireland, *Eur.* 76 C2
Eirunepé, *Braz.* 68 E3
Ejin Qi, *China* 118 B3
Ekibastuz, *Kaz.* 115 A5
Eklund Islands, *Antarctica* 166 B2
El 'Alamein, *Egypt* 110 D1
Elat, *Israel* 110 D2
Elazığ, *Turk.* 110 B3
Elba, *island, It.* 92 C1
Elba, Cape *see* Hadarba, Râs, *Egypt* 140 C3
El Bauga, *Sudan* 140 C3
Elbe, *river, Ger.* 91 E1
El'brus, *peak, Russ.* 94 D1
Elburz Mountains *see* Alborz, Reshteh-ye, *Iran* 111 B5
El Calafate, *Arg.* 73 E2
El Djouf, *desert, Mali, Mauritania* 138 C2
El Djouf, *region, Mali, Mauritania* 128 B1
Eldoret, *Kenya* 143 B5
Elephant Island, *Antarctica* 166 A1
Eleuthera Island, *Bahamas* 50 B3
El Faiyûm, *Egypt* 140 B2
El Fasher, *Sudan* 141 D1

El Fuerte, *Mex.* 48 B2
El Gîza, *Egypt* 140 A2
El Golea, *Alg.* 138 B3
El Iskandarîya (Alexandria), *Egypt* 140 A2
El Khârga, *Egypt* 140 B2
Ellesmere Island, *Nunavut, Can.* 41 A6
Ellsworth Land, *Antarctica* 166 C2
Ellsworth Mountains, *Antarctica* 166 C2
El Manaqil, *Sudan* 141 D2
El Manşûra, *Egypt* 110 D1
El Minya, *Egypt* 140 B2
El Mreyyé, *region, Mali, Mauritania* 138 C2
El Obeid, *Sudan* 141 D2
El Oued, *Alg.* 139 A4
El Paso, *Tex., U.S.* 42 D2
El Pilar, *Venez.* 53 F3
El Qâhira (Cairo), *Egypt* 140 A2
El Qaşr, *Egypt* 110 E1
El Salvador, *N. Amer.* 29 E3
Ely, *Nev., U.S.* 42 C2
Embi, *Kaz.* 114 B2
Emerald, *Qnsld., Austral.* 149 C5
Emi Koussi, *peak, Chad* 139 C5
Empty Quarter *see* Ar Rub' al Khālī, *desert, Saudi Arabia* 112 D4
Ems, *river, Ger.* 91 E1
Endeavour Strait, *Qnsld., Austral.* 151 A5
Enderby Land, *Antarctica* 167 A5
Endicott Mountains, *Alas., U.S.* 44 A3
Enfer, Pointe d', *Martinique, Fr.* 52 C4
Engaño, Cabo, *Dom. Rep.* 51 D6
Engels, *Russ.* 114 A1
Enggano, *island, Indonesia* 122 E2
England, *region, U.K.* 88 B3

English Channel, *Eur.*
88 C3
Ennadai, *Nunavut, Can.*
40 C3
En Nahud, *Sudan* **141** D2
Ennedi, *region, Chad*
139 C6
Ensenada, *Mex.* **42** D1
Envira, *river, Braz.* **68** E2
Equatorial Guinea, *Af.*
127 D3
Erdenet, *Mongolia* **119** A4
Erenhot, *China* **119** B4
Erfurt, *Ger.* **88** B5
Ergun *see* Argun', *river,*
China **119** A5
Erie, Lake, *Can., U.S.*
43 B5
Erimo Misaki, *Japan*
121 B6
Eritrea, *Af.* **126** C5
Er Rif, *region, Mor.*
128 B2
Erris Head, *Ire.* **88** B2
Ertis, *river, Kaz.* **115** A5
Ertix, *river, China* **115** B6
Erzincan, *Turk.* **110** B3
Erzurum, *Turk.* **77** D5
Esbjerg, *Den.* **91** D1
Escocesa, Bahía, *Dom. Rep.*
51 D5
Escuinapa, *Mex.* **48** C2
Escuintla, *Guatemala*
49 D4
Esenguly, *Turkm.* **114** E2
Esfahan (Isfahan), *Iran*
111 C5
Eskişehir, *Turk.* **110** A2
Esmeraldas, *Ecua.* **68** C1
Esperance, *W. Austral.,*
Austral. **148** E2
Esperanza, *research station,*
Antarctica **166** A1
Espungabera, *Mozambique*
145 C4
Esquel, *Arg.* **73** D2
Essen, *Ger.* **88** B5
Essendon, Mount, *W.*
Austral., Austral. **150** C2
Essequibo, *river, Guyana*
69 B5
Estacado, Llano, *U.S.*
42 D3

Estación Maritima
Antártica, *research*
station, Antarctica
166 A1
Estados, Isla de los (Staten
Island), *Arg.* **73** F3
Estância, *Braz.* **71** C6
Este, Punta del, *Uru.*
59 E3
Estelí, *Nicar.* **49** D5
Estonia, *Eur.* **77** B4
Eternity Range, *Antarctica*
166 B2
Ethiopia, *Af.* **126** C4
Ethiopian Highlands, *Eth.*
128 C4
Etna, *peak, It.* **92** D2
Etosha Pan, *Namibia*
144 B1
Eucla, *W. Austral., Austral.*
148 D3
Eucla Basin, *W. Austral.,*
Austral. **150** D3
Eucumbene, Lake, *N.S.W.,*
Austral. **151** E5
Eugene, *Oreg., U.S.* **42** B1
Eugenia, Punta, *Mex.*
48 B1
Eugenia Point, *Mex.*
31 D1
Euphrates *see* Al Furāt,
river, Iraq, Turk., Syr.
110 C3
Eureka, *Calif., U.S.* **42** B1
Eureka, *Can.* **165** D4
Europa, Île, *island, Fr.*
145 C5
Evensk, *Russ.* **95** B6
Everest, Mount, *China,*
Nepal **117** B4
Everglades National Park,
U.S. **47** E5
Évia, *island, Gr.* **93** D4
Exeter, *U.K.* **88** C3
Exmouth, *W. Austral.,*
Austral. **148** C1
Exmouth Gulf, *W. Austral.,*
Austral. **150** C1
Exuma Sound, *Bahamas*
50 B3
Eyasi, Lake, *Tanzania*
143 B5
Eyl, *Somalia* **141** D5

Eyre, Lake, *S. Austral.,*
Austral. **151** D4
Eyre North, Lake, *S.*
Austral., Austral. **151** D4
Eyre Peninsula, *S. Austral.,*
Austral. **151** D4
Eyre South, Lake, *S.*
Austral., Austral. **151** D4
Ezequiel Ramos Mexia,
Embalse, *Arg.* **72** C2

F

F, Dome, *Antarctica*
167 B4
Fada, *Chad* **139** C6
Fairbanks, *Alas., U.S.*
44 B3
Fairweather, Mount, *Can.,*
U.S. **44** C4
Fais, *island, F.S.M.* **123** B6
Faisalabad, *Pak.* **116** A3
Fajardo, *P.R., U.S.* **52** A1
Fakfak, *Indonesia* **123** D5
Falkland Islands (Islas
Malvinas), *U.K.* **73** F3
Fallujah *see* Al Fallūjah,
Iraq **111** C4
Falmouth, *Antigua &*
Barbuda **52** B4
False Bay, *S. Af.* **144** E2
False Cape, *Mex.* **31** E2
Falso, Cabo, *Dom. Rep.*
51 E4
Falso, Cabo, *Hond.* **50** E1
Falso, Cabo, *Mex.* **29** E2
Falun, *Sw.* **90** C2
Fan Si Pan, *peak, Vietnam*
122 A2
Faradje, *Dem. Rep. of the*
Congo **143** A4
Farafangana, *Madagascar*
145 C6
Farah, *Afghan.* **116** A2
Farasān, Jazā'ir, *Saudi*
Arabia **112** D2
Farewell, Cape, *Greenland,*
Den. **30** B5
Fargo, *N. Dak., U.S.* **42** B3
Farg'ona, *Uzb.* **115** D4
Faro, *Port.* **89** F2
Faroe Islands, *Den.* **78** B2

Farr Bay, *Antarctica*
167 C6

Fartak, Ra's, *Yemen*
113 E4

Farvel, Kap *see* Nunap
Isua, *Greenland, Den.*
28 B5

Farwell Island, *Antarctica*
166 C2

Faxaflói, *bay, Ice.* **78** A2

Faya, *Chad* **139** C5

Fear, Cape, *U.S.* **31** D4

Federated States of
Micronesia, *Oceania*
160 B2

Feira de Santana, *Braz.*
71 C6

Fengcheng, *China* **120** B1

Feodosiya, *Ukr.* **93** B6

Fergana Valley, *Kyrg., Taj.,
Uzb.* **115** D4

Fès (Fez), *Mor.* **138** A3

Fez *see* Fès, *Mor.* **138** A3

Fezzan, *region, Lib.*
138 B4

Fianarantsoa, *Madagascar*
145 C6

Fiji, *Oceania* **160** C3

Filchner Ice Shelf,
Antarctica **166** B3

Filchner Mountains,
Antarctica **167** A4

Fimbul Ice Shelf, *Antarctica*
167 A4

Finisterre, Cape, *Sp.*
78 D1

Finke, *river, N. Terr.,
Austral.* **151** C4

Finland, *Eur.* **77** B4

Finland, Gulf of, *Eur.*
91 D4

Firenze (Florence), *It.*
92 B1

Fisterra, Cabo, *Sp.* **89** E1

Fitzgerald, *Alberta, Can.*
40 C2

Fitzroy, *river, W. Austral.,
Austral.* **150** B2

Fitzroy Crossing, *W.
Austral., Austral.* **148** B2

Flagstaff, *Ariz., U.S.* **42** C2

Flamingo, Teluk, *Indonesia*
123 E6

Flamingo Point, *Bahamas*
50 B3

Flattery, Cape, *Qnsld.,
Austral.* **151** A5

Flattery, Cape, *Wash., U.S.*
42 A1

Flekkefjord, *Nor.* **91** D1

Flinders, *river, Qnsld.,
Austral.* **151** B5

Flinders Ranges, *S. Austral.,
Austral.* **151** D4

Flin Flon, *Man., Can.*
40 D3

Florence *see* Firenze, *It.*
92 B1

Flores, *island, Indonesia*
123 E4

Flores Sea, *Indonesia*
123 E4

Florianópolis, *Braz.* **71** E4

Florida, *state, U.S.* **43** D5

Florida, Straits of,
Bahamas, Cuba, U.S.
50 B2

Florida Keys, *Fla., U.S.*
50 B2

Florø, *Nor.* **90** C1

Focşani, *Rom.* **93** B4

Foggia, *It.* **92** C2

Folda, *bay, Nor.* **90** B2

Fonte Boa, *Braz.* **68** D3

Formosa, *Arg.* **72** A4

Føroyar *see* Faroe Islands,
Den. **94** B2

Fort Albany, *Ont., Can.*
41 D4

Fortaleza, *Braz.* **71** A6

Fort-de-France,
Martinique, Fr. **52** C4

Fortescue, *river, W. Austral.,
Austral.* **150** C1

Fort Good Hope, *N.W.T.,
Can.* **40** A2

Forth, Firth of, *U.K.*
88 A3

Fort Laperrine *see*
Tamanrasset, *Alg.*
139 C4

Fort Lauderdale, *Fla., U.S.*
50 A2

Fort McMurray, *Alberta,
Can.* **40** C2

Fort Myers, *Fla., U.S.*
50 A2

Fort Nelson, *B.C., Can.*
40 C2

Fort Pierce, *Fla., U.S.*
50 A2

Fort Pierre Bordes *see*
Ti-n-Zaouâtene, *Alg.*
138 C3

Fort Saint John, *B.C., Can.*
40 C2

Fort Severn, *Ont., Can.*
41 D4

Fort Shevchenko, *Kaz.*
114 C1

Fort Simpson, *N.W.T., Can.*
40 B2

Fort Smith, *N.W.T., Can.*
40 C2

Fort Trinquet *see* Bir
Mogreïn, *Mauritania*
138 B2

Fort Worth, *Tex., U.S.*
42 D3

Fort Yukon, *Alas., U.S.*
44 A4

Foul Bay, *Egypt* **140** B3

Fouta Djallon, *mountains,
Guinea* **138** D1

Foux, Cap-à-, *Haiti* **51** D4

Foxe Basin, *Nunavut, Can.*
41 B4

Foxe Peninsula, *Nunavut,
Can.* **41** B4

Fox Islands, *Alas., U.S.*
44 C1

Foz do Cunene, *Angola*
142 E1

France, *Eur.* **76** D2

Francés, Cabo, *Cuba*
50 C1

Frances, Punta, *Cuba*
50 C1

Francés Viejo, Cabo, *Dom.
Rep.* **51** D5

Franceville, *Gabon*
142 B2

Francistown, *Botswana*
144 C3

Frankfort, *Ky., U.S.* **43** C5

Frankfurt, *Ger.* **91** F1

Franklin Mountains, *Can.*
30 B2

Frantsa Iosifa, Zemlya (Franz Josef Land), *Russ.* **94** B3

Franz Josef Land *see* Frantsa Iosifa, Zemlya, *Russ.* **94** B3

Fraser, *river, B.C., Can.* **40** D1

Fraserburg, *S. Af.* **144** E2

Fraser Island (Great Sandy Island), *Qnsld., Austral.* **151** C6

Frederikshåb *see* Paamiut, *Greenland, Den.* **41** B6

Fredericton, *N.B., Can.* **41** E5

Frederiksted, *U.S. Virgin Is., U.S.* **52** A1

Freeport, *Bahamas* **50** A2

Freetown, *Sa. Leone* **138** E1

Freiburg, *Ger.* **88** C5

French Guiana, *possession, Fr.* **56** A4

French Polynesia, *possession, Fr.* **161** C5

Fresnillo, *Mex.* **48** C3

Fresno, *Calif., U.S.* **42** C1

Fria, *Guinea* **138** D1

Frio, Cabo, *Braz.* **57** D5

Frio, Cape, *Braz.* **59** D5

Frisian Islands, *Neth.* **88** B4

Frobisher Bay, *Nunavut, Can.* **41** B5

Frolovo, *Russ.* **114** A1

Frome, Lake, *S. Austral., Austral.* **151** D4

Fuerteventura, *island, Sp.* **138** B1

Fuhai (Burultokay), *China* **115** B6

Fuji, *peak, Japan* **121** D5

Fujin, *China* **119** A6

Fukuoka, *Japan* **121** D4

Fukushima, *Japan* **121** C6

Funafuti, *Tuvalu* **160** C3

Funchal, *Port.* **138** A1

Fundy, Bay of, *Can.* **30** C4

Furneaux Group, *Tas., Austral.* **150** E3

Fushun, *China* **119** B5

Fuyun, *China* **118** B3

Fuzhou, *China* **119** D5

Fyn, *island, Den.* **91** E1

G

Gaalkacyo (Galcaio), *Somalia* **141** E5

Gabes, *Tun.* **139** A4

Gabes, Gulf of, *Tun.* **139** A4

Gabon, *Af.* **127** D3

Gaborone, *Botswana* **144** C3

Gabras, *Sudan* **141** D1

Gaillimh *see* Galway, *Ire.* **88** B2

Gairdner, Lake, *S. Austral., Austral.* **151** D4

Galana, *river, Kenya* **143** B6

Galápagos Islands, *Ecua.* **31** F3

Galcaio *see* Gaalkacyo, *Somalia* **141** E5

Galdhøpiggen, *peak, Nor.* **78** B3

Galegu, *Sudan* **112** E1

Galena, *Alas., U.S.* **44** B3

Galera, Punta, *Chile* **72** C1

Galera Point, *Ecua.* **58** B1

Galera Point, *Trin. & Tobago* **53** F4

Galilee, Lake, *Qnsld., Austral.* **151** C5

Gällivare, *Sw.* **90** B3

Galveston, *Tex., U.S.* **43** E4

Galway (Gaillimh), *Ire.* **88** B2

Gambell, *Alas., U.S.* **44** B1

Gambia, *Af.* **126** C1

Gambia, *river, Gambia, Guinea, Senegal* **128** C1

Gambier, Îles, *Fr. Polynesia, Fr.* **161** D6

Gamova, Mys, *Russ.* **120** A3

Gäncä, *Azerb.* **111** A4

Gandajika, *Dem. Rep. of the Congo* **142** C3

Gander, *Nfld. & Lab., Can.* **41** D6

Ganga (Ganges), *river, Bangladesh, India* **117** B4

Gangdisê Shan, *China* **118** C3

Ganges *see* Ganga, *river, Bangladesh, India* **117** B4

Ganges, Mouths of the, *Bangladesh* **117** C5

Ganggyeong, *S. Kor.* **120** D2

Gangjin, *S. Kor.* **120** E2

Gangneung, *S. Kor.* **120** C2

Ganta, *Liberia* **138** E2

Ganzhou, *China* **119** D5

Gao, *Mali* **138** D3

Garabogaz Aylagy, *Turkm.* **114** D2

Garabogaz Bay, *Turkm.* **79** D6

Garagum, *desert, Turkm.* **114** D2

Garanhuns, *Braz.* **71** B6

Garissa, *Kenya* **143** B6

Garonne, *river, Fr.* **89** D3

Garoowe, *Somalia* **141** D5

Garoua, *Cameroon* **139** E5

Gascoyne, *river, W. Austral., Austral.* **150** C1

Gaspé, *Que., Can.* **41** D5

Gaspé Peninsula, *Que., Can.* **41** D5

Gata, Cabo de, *Sp.* **89** F3

Gata, Cape, *Sp.* **78** E2

Gates of the Arctic National Park and Preserve, *U.S.* **46** D2

Gausta, *peak, Nor.* **90** C1

Gävle, *Sw.* **90** C3

Gawler, *S. Austral., Austral.* **149** E4

Gaya, *India* **117** C4

Gaya, *Niger* **138** D3

Gayny, *Russ.* **77** B5

Gaza City *see* Ghazzah, *Gaza Strip* **110** D2

Gaza Strip, *region, Asia* **110** D2

Gaziantep, *Turk.* **110** B3

Gbarnga, *Liberia* 138 E2
Gboko, *Nigeria* 139 E4
Gdańsk, *Pol.* 91 E3
Gdańsk, Gulf of, *Pol., Russ.* 91 E3
Gdynia, *Pol.* 91 E3
Gebeit, *Sudan* 140 C3
Gedaref, *Sudan* 141 D3
Geelong, *Vic., Austral.* 149 E5
Geelvink Channel, *W. Austral., Austral.* 150 D1
Gees Gwardafuy, *cape, Somalia* 141 D5
Gejiu, *China* 119 E4
Geladī, *Eth.* 141 E5
Gelasa, Selat, *Indonesia* 122 D2
Gemena, *Dem. Rep. of the Congo* 142 A3
Gemsa, *Egypt* 110 E2
Geneina, *Sudan* 139 D6
General Carrera, Lago, *Chile* 73 E2
General San Martín, *Arg.* 73 D2
General Santos, *Philippines* 123 C4
Genève, *Fr.* 89 D3
Genoa *see* Genova, *It.* 92 B1
Genova (Genoa), *It.* 92 B1
Geographe Bay, *W. Austral., Austral.* 150 E1
Geographe Channel, *W. Austral., Austral.* 150 C1
Geojedo, *island, S. Kor.* 120 E2
George, *S. Af.* 144 E2
George, Lake, *Uganda* 143 B4
George Town, *Cayman Is., U.K.* 50 D2
George Town, *Malaysia* 122 C1
Georgetown, *Guyana* 69 B5
Georgetown, *Qnsld., Austral.* 149 B6
Georgetown, *St. Vincent & the Grenadines* 53 D4
Georgia, *Asia, Eur.* 98 B2
Georgia, *state, U.S.* 43 D5

Georgia, Strait of, *Can.* 30 C1
Georgian Bay, *Ont., Can.* 41 E4
Georgina, *river, Austral.* 151 C4
Geraldton, *W. Austral., Austral.* 148 D1
Germany, *Eur.* 76 C3
Getz Ice Shelf, *Antarctica* 166 D2
Ghadames *see* Ghadāmis, *Lib.* 139 B4
Ghadāmis (Ghadames), *Lib.* 139 B4
Ghana, *Af.* 126 C2
Ghanzi, *Botswana* 144 C2
Ghardaïa, *Alg.* 138 A3
Ghāt, *Lib.* 139 B4
Ghazzah (Gaza City), *Gaza Strip* 110 C2
Gibraltar, *possession, U.K.* 76 E1
Gibraltar, Strait of, *Af., Eur.* 78 E1
Gibson Desert, *W. Austral., Austral.* 150 C2
Gijón, *Sp.* 89 D2
Gilbert, *river, Qnsld., Austral.* 151 B5
Gilbert Islands, *Kiribati* 160 B3
Gilgit, *Pak.* 115 E5
Gillam, *Man., Can.* 40 D3
Gillies Islands, *Antarctica* 167 C6
Gillock Island, *Antarctica* 167 B5
Gimhwa, *S. Kor.* 120 C2
Girga, *Egypt* 140 B2
Gjoa Haven, *Nunavut, Can.* 40 B3
Glacier Bay, *Alas., U.S.* 44 C5
Glacier Bay National Park and Preserve, *U.S.* 46 E2
Glacier National Park, *U.S.* 46 A2
Gladstone, *Qnsld., Austral.* 149 C6
Glåma, *river, Nor.* 90 C2
Glasgow, *U.K.* 88 A3

Goba, *Eth.* 141 E4
Gobi, *desert, China, Mongolia* 119 B4
Gochang, *S. Kor.* 120 D2
Godthåb *see* Nuuk, *Greenland, Den.* 165 E5
Godwin Austen *see* K2, *peak, China, Pak.* 100 C3
Goiânia, *Braz.* 71 C4
Gold Coast, *Ghana* 138 E3
Gold Coast, *Qnsld., Austral.* 149 D6
Golmud, *China* 118 C3
Goma, *Dem. Rep. of the Congo* 143 B4
Gómez Palacio, *Mex.* 48 B2
Gonābād, *Iran* 111 C6
Gonaïves, *Haiti* 51 D4
Gonâve, Golfe de la, *Haiti* 51 D4
Gonâve, Île de la, *Haiti* 51 D4
Gonder, *Eth.* 141 D3
Good Hope, Cape of, *S. Af.* 144 E2
Goondiwindi, *Qnsld., Austral.* 149 D6
Gorē, *Eth.* 141 D3
Gorontalo, *Indonesia* 123 D4
Gorzów Wielkopolski, *Pol.* 91 E2
Goseong, *S. Kor.* 120 E2
Göteborg, *Sw.* 91 D2
Gotland, *island, Sw.* 91 D3
Gotō Rettō, *Japan* 121 D4
Goulimine, *Mor.* 138 B2
Gove Peninsula, *N. Terr., Austral.* 151 A4
Governador Valadares, *Braz.* 71 D5
Goya, *Arg.* 72 A4
Goyang, *S. Kor.* 120 C2
Graaff-Reinet, *S. Af.* 144 E3
Gracias a Dios, Cabo, *Nicar.* 49 D5
Gracias a Dios, Cape, *Nicar.* 31 E4

Gra-Gua

Grafton, *N.S.W., Austral.*
149 D6

Graham Land, *Antarctica*
166 A1

Grahamstown, *S. Af.*
144 E3

Grain Coast, *Liberia*
138 E2

Granada, *Nicar.* **49** E5

Granada, *Sp.* **89** F3

Gran Canaria, *island, Sp.*
138 B1

Gran Chaco, *Arg., Bol.,
Parag.* **59** D3

Grand Bahama Island,
Bahamas **50** A2

Grand-Bourg, *Guadeloupe,
Fr.* **52** C4

Grand Canyon, *Ariz., U.S.*
42 C2

Grand Canyon National
Park, *U.S.* **46** C2

Grand Cayman, *island,
Cayman Is., U.K.* **50** D2

Grande, *river, Arg.* **72** B2

Grande, *river, Bol.* **70** C2

Grande, *river, Braz.* **71** C5

Grande, *river, Braz.* **71** D5

Grande, Bahía, *Arg.* **73** E2

Grande, Cuchilla, *Uru.*
72 B4

Grande, Rio *see* Bravo del
Norte, Río, *U.S.* **42** D2

Grande, Salina, *Arg.*
72 C2

Grande Comore *see*
Njazidja, *island, Comoros*
145 A5

Grande Prairie, *Alberta,
Can.* **40** C2

Grand Erg Occidental, *Alg.*
138 B3

Grand Erg Oriental, *Alg.,
Tun.* **139** B4

Grandes, Salinas, *Arg.*
72 A3

Grande-Terre, *island,
Guadeloupe, Fr.* **52** B4

Grand Teton National
Park, *U.S.* **46** B2

Grant Island, *Antarctica*
166 D2

Gravois, Pointe-à-, *Haiti*
51 D4

Graz, *Aust.* **92** A2

Great Artesian Basin,
Austral. **151** C4

Great Australian Bight,
Austral. **150** D3

Great Barrier Reef, *Austral.*
151 B6

Great Basin, *U.S.* **31** D1

Great Basin National Park,
U.S. **46** B2

Great Bear Lake, *N.W.T.,
Can.* **40** B2

Great Britain, *island, U.K.*
88 B3

Great Channel, *India,
Indonesia* **122** C1

Great Dividing Range,
Austral. **151** B5

Great Eastern Erg, *Alg.*
128 B2

Greater Antilles, *islands, N.
Amer.* **31** E4

Greater Sudbury, *Ont., Can.*
41 E4

Greater Sunda Islands,
Indonesia **122** D2

Great Exuma, *island,
Bahamas* **50** B3

Great Falls, *Mont., U.S.*
42 A2

Great Inagua Island,
Bahamas **51** C4

Great Indian Desert *see*
Thar Desert, *India, Pak.*
116 B3

Great Nicobar, *island, India*
117 E5

Great Pedro Bluff, *Jam.*
50 D3

Great Plains, *Can., U.S.*
30 C2

Great Rift Valley, *Af.*
129 D4

Great Salt Lake, *Utah, U.S.*
42 B2

Great Sand Dunes
National Park and
Preserve, *U.S.* **46** C3

Great Sandy Desert, *W.
Austral., Austral.* **150** B2

Great Sandy Island *see*
Fraser Island, *Qnsld.,
Austral.* **151** C6

Great Slave Lake, *N.W.T.,
Can.* **40** B2

Great Smoky Mountains
National Park, *U.S.*
47 C5

Great Victoria Desert,
Austral. **150** D3

Great Wall, *research
station, Antarctica*
166 A1

Great Western Erg, *Alg.*
128 B2

Greece, *Eur.* **77** E4

Green Bay, *Wis., U.S.*
43 B4

Greenland (Kalaallit
Nunaat), *possession, Den.*
28 A4

Greenland Sea, *Atl. Oc.*
165 C5

Greensboro, *N.C., U.S.*
43 C5

Greenville, *Liberia* **138** E2

Gregory, *river, Qnsld.,
Austral.* **151** B4

Gregory Range, *Qnsld.,
Austral.* **151** B5

Grenada, *island, Grenada*
53 E4

Grenada, *N. Amer.* **53** E4

Grenville, *Grenada* **53** E4

Grey Range, *Qnsld., Austral.*
151 D5

Grise Fiord, *Nunavut, Can.*
41 A4

Groningen, *Neth.* **88** B4

Groote Eylandt, *N. Terr.,
Austral.* **151** A4

Grootfontein, *Namibia*
144 C2

Groot Karasberge, *peak,
Namibia* **144** D2

Groznyy, *Russ.* **77** D6

Guacanayabo, Golfo de,
Cuba **50** D3

Guadalajara, *Mex.* **48** C2

Guadalcanal, *island,
Solomon Is.* **160** C3

Guadalquivir, *river, Sp.*
89 F2

205

Gua-Hai

Guadalupe, Isla, *Mex.*
29 DI

Guadalupe Island, *Mex.*
31 DI

Guadalupe Mountains
National Park, *U.S.*
46 D3

Guadeloupe, *possession, Fr.*
52 B3

Guadeloupe Passage,
Antigua & Barbuda,
Guadeloupe 52 B3

Guadiana, *river, Port., Sp.*
89 F2

Guadiana, Bahía, *Cuba*
50 CI

Guajará-Mirim, *Braz.*
70 B2

Guajira, Península de la,
Col., Venez. 68 A2

Guajira Peninsula, *Col.,*
Venez. 58 A2

Gualicho, Salina, *Arg.*
72 C3

Guam, *possession, U.S.*
160 B2

Guanal, Punta del, *Cuba*
50 CI

Guane, *Cuba* 50 CI

Guangyuan, *China* 119 D4

Guangzhou, *China* 119 E5

Guanta, *Venez.* 53 FI

Guantánamo, *Cuba* 50 D3

Guaporé *see* Iténez, *river,*
Braz. 70 C3

Guarico, Punta, *Cuba*
51 C4

Guasave, *Mex.* 48 B2

Guascama, Punta, *Col.*
68 CI

Guatemala, *N. Amer.*
29 E3

Guatemala City, *Guatemala*
49 D4

Guaviare, *river, Col.* 68 C2

Guayabal, *Cuba* 50 C3

Guayaguayare, *Trin. &*
Tobago 53 F4

Guayaquil, *Ecua.* 68 DI

Guayaquil, Golfo de, *Ecua.*
68 DI

Guayaquil, Gulf of, *Ecua.*
58 BI

Guaymas, *Mex.* 48 BI

Guban, *region, Somaliland*
141 D4

Guéckédo, *Guinea* 138 E2

Güeppí, *Peru* 68 C2

Guernsey, *island, U.K.*
88 C3

Guiana Highlands, *S. Amer.*
58 A2

Guider, *Cameroon* 139 E5

Guijá, *Mozambique*
145 C4

Guilin, *China* 119 D4

Guinea, *Af.* 126 CI

Guinea, Gulf of, *Af.*
129 D2

Guinea-Bissau, *Af.*
126 CI

Güines, *Cuba* 50 CI

Güiria, *Venez.* 53 F3

Guiyang, *China* 119 D4

Gujranwala, *Pak.* 116 A3

Gulja *see* Yining, *China*
118 B2

Gulu, *Uganda* 143 A5

Guma *see* Pishan, *China*
118 CI

Gumi, *S. Kor.* 120 D2

Gunnbjørn Fjeld, *peak,*
Greenland, Den. 30 A5

Gunsan, *S. Kor.* 120 D2

Guntur, *India* 117 D4

Gurupá, *Braz.* 69 D6

Gurupi, *river, Braz.* 71 A5

Gusau, *Nigeria* 139 D4

Guşgy, *river, Turkm.*
114 E3

Guşgy, *Turkm.* 114 E3

Gustav Bull Mountains,
Antarctica 167 B5

Gustavia, *St.-Barthélemy,*
Fr. 52 A3

Guwahati, *India* 117 B5

Guyana, *S. Amer.* 56 A3

Gwadar, *Pak.* 116 B2

Gwalior, *India* 116 B3

Gwangju (Kwangju), *S. Kor.*
120 D2

Gweru, *Zimb.* 144 B3

Gyangzê, *China* 117 B5

Gydanskiy Poluostrov,
Russ. 94 C3

Gyêgu *see* Yushu, *China*
118 C3

Gyeongju (Kyŏngju), *S. Kor.*
120 D3

Gympie, *Qnsld., Austral.*
149 C6

Gyumri, *Arm.* III A4

Gyzylarbat, *Turkm.*
114 D2

Gyzyletrek, *Turkm.*
114 E2

H

Hachijō Jima, *Japan*
121 D6

Hachinohe, *Japan* 121 B6

Hadabat el Gilf el Kebîr,
region, Egypt 140 BI

Hadarba, Râs (Cape Elba),
Egypt 140 C3

Ḥadd, Ra's al, *Oman*
113 C6

Haḏîboh, *Yemen* 113 E5

Haḏîyah, *Saudi Arabia*
112 B2

Ḥaḏramawt, *Yemen*
112 E4

Haedo, Cuchilla de, *Uru.*
72 B4

Haeju, *N. Kor.* 120 CI

Haeju-man, *N. Kor.*
120 CI

Haenam, *S. Kor.* 120 E2

Ḥafar al Bāṭin, *Saudi Arabia*
112 B3

Hagåtña (Agana), *Guam,*
U.S. 160 B2

Haida Gwaii (Queen
Charlotte Islands), *B.C.,*
Can. 40 CI

Haifa *see* Hefa, *Israel*
110 C2

Haikou, *China* 119 E4

Ḥā'il, *Saudi Arabia* 112 B2

Hailar, *China* 119 A5

Hailun, *China* 121 A4

Hainan, *island, China*
119 E4

Haines Junction, *Yukon,*
Can. 40 BI

Haiphong, *Vietnam*
122 A2

Haiti, *N. Amer.* **29** E4

Haiya, *Sudan* **140** C3

Hakodate, *Japan* **121** B6

Ḥalab (Aleppo), *Syr.*
110 B3

Hālawa, Cape, *Hawai'i, U.S.*
45 E4

Halayeb, *Egypt* **140** B3

Haleakala National Park,
U.S. **47** E4

Halifax, *N.S., Can.* **41** E6

Halkidikí, *peninsula, Gr.*
93 D4

Ḥallānīyāt, Jazāīr al (Kuria
Muria Islands), *Oman*
113 D5

Hallasan, *peak, S. Kor.*
120 E2

Hall Beach, *Nunavut, Can.*
41 B4

Halley, *research station,
Antarctica* **166** B3

Hallim, *S. Kor.* **120** E2

Hall Peninsula, *Nunavut,
Can.* **41** B5

Halls Creek, *W. Austral.,
Austral.* **148** B3

Halmahera, *island,
Indonesia* **123** D5

Halmahera Sea, *Indonesia*
123 D5

Halmstad, *Sw.* **91** D2

Hamadān (Ecbatana), *Iran*
111 C5

Ḥamāh (Hamath), *Syr.*
110 C2

Hamamatsu, *Japan*
121 D5

Hamamet, Gulf of, *Tun.*
92 E1

Hamar, *Nor.* **90** C2

Hamath *see* Ḥamāh, *Syr.*
110 C2

Hamburg, *Ger.* **91** E1

Hamersley Range, *W.
Austral., Austral.* **150** C1

Hamhŭng, *N. Kor.* **120** B2

Hami (Kumul), *China*
118 B3

Hamilton, *N.Z.* **160** E3

Hamilton, *Ont., Can.* **41** E4

Hammerfest, *Nor.* **90** A3

Hampton Tableland,
Austral. **150** D3

Hampyeong, *S. Kor.*
120 E2

Han, *river, China* **119** C4

Hāna, *Hawai'i, U.S.* **45** E4

Hanamalo Point, *Hawai'i,
U.S.* **45** F4

Handan, *China* **119** C5

Hangayn Nuruu,
mountains, Mongolia
118 A3

Hanggin Houqi, *China*
119 B4

Hangzhou, *China* **119** D5

Haniá (Canea), *Gr.* **93** E4

Hannover (Hanover), *Ger.*
91 E1

Hanoi, *Vietnam* **122** A2

Hanover *see* Hannover,
Ger. **91** E1

Hanzhong, *China* **119** C4

Haora, *India* **117** C5

Haparanda, *Sw.* **90** B3

Happy Valley-Goose Bay,
Nfld. & Lab., Can. **41** C5

Ḥaraḍ, *Saudi Arabia*
113 C4

Harare, *Zimb.* **145** B4

Harbin, *China* **119** B5

Hārer, *Eth.* **141** D4

Hargeysa, *Somaliland*
141 D4

Harirud, *river, Afghan.*
116 A2

Harold Byrd Mountains,
Antarctica **166** C3

Harper, *Liberia* **138** E2

Harrisburg, *Pa., U.S.*
43 B5

Harrison, Cape, *Nfld. &
Lab., Can.* **41** C6

Harrison Bay, *Alas., U.S.*
44 A3

Hartford, *Conn., U.S.*
43 B6

Har Us Nuur, *Mongolia*
118 A3

Hatay (Antioch), *Turk.*
110 B2

Ḥāṭibah, Ra's, *Saudi Arabia*
112 C2

Hatteras, Cape, *N.C., U.S.*
43 C6

Hat Yai, *Thai.* **122** C1

Haud, *region, Eth.* **141** D4

Haugesund, *Nor.* **90** C1

Hauta *see* Al Ḥillah, *Saudi
Arabia* **112** C3

Havana *see* La Habana,
Cuba **50** B1

Havre, *Mont., U.S.* **42** A2

Hawai'i, *island, Hawai'i, U.S.*
45 F5

Hawai'i, *U.S.* **161** A4

Hawaiian Islands, *Hawai'i,
U.S.* **161** A4

Hawai'i Volcanoes National
Park, *U.S.* **47** E4

Hāwī, *Hawai'i, U.S.* **45** E4

Hay, *river, N. Terr., Austral.*
151 C4

Hayes Peninsula,
Greenland, Den. **30** A3

Hay River, *N.W.T., Can.*
40 C2

Hearst Island, *Antarctica*
166 B2

Hebrides, *islands, U.K.*
78 B2

Hecate Strait, *Can.* **30** B1

Hefa (Haifa), *Israel*
110 C2

Hefei, *China* **119** D5

Hegang, *China* **121** A4

Heidelberg, *Ger.* **91** F1

Heidenheim, *Ger.* **88** C5

Heilong Jiang *see* Amur,
China, Russ. **119** A5

Heimefront Range,
Antarctica **166** A3

Hejaz *see* Al Ḥijāz, *region,
Saudi Arabia* **112** B1

Helagsfjället, *peak, Sw.*
90 C2

Helena, *Mont., U.S.* **42** B2

Helen Island, *Palau*
123 C5

Helgoländer Bucht, *Ger.*
91 E1

Hell-Ville *see* Andoany,
Madagascar **145** A6

Helmand, *river, Afghan.*
116 B2

Helong, *China* **120** A2

Hel-Hua

Helsingfors *see* Helsinki,
Fin. **90** C4
Helsinki (Helsingfors), *Fin.*
90 C4
Hengyang, *China* **119** D5
Henry Bay, *Antarctica*
167 D5
Henry Ice Rise, *Antarctica*
166 B3
Herat, *Afghan.* **116** A2
Hercules Dome, *Antarctica*
166 C3
Heredia, *Costa Rica* **49** E5
Hermosillo, *Mex.* **48** A1
Hervey Bay, *Qnsld., Austral.*
149 C6
Hervey Bay, *bay, Qnsld.,*
Austral. **151** C6
Hezuo, *China* **119** C4
Hicacos, Península de,
Cuba **50** B1
Hidalgo del Parral, *Mex.*
48 B2
Highjump Archipelago,
Antarctica **167** C6
High Plains, *U.S.* **31** D2
Hiiumaa (Dagö), *island, Est.*
91 D3
Hilalaye, *Somalia* **141** E5
Hillsborough, *Grenada*
53 E4
Hilo, *Hawai'i, U.S.* **45** F5
Hilo Bay, *Hawai'i, U.S.*
45 F5
Himalaya, *mountains, Asia*
116 A3
Ḥimş (Homs), *Syr.* **110** C3
Hinchinbrook Island,
Qnsld., Austral. **151** B5
Hindu Kush, *mountains,*
Afghan., Pak. **115** E4
Hinomi Saki, *cape, Japan*
121 D4
Hinthada, *Myanmar*
117 D6
Híos, *Gr.* **93** D4
Hirosaki, *Japan* **121** B6
Hiroshima, *Japan* **121** D4
Hispaniola, *island, Dom.*
Rep., Haiti **51** D5
Hitra, *island, Nor.* **90** B1
Hkakabo Razi, *peak, China,*
Myanmar **117** B6

Hobart, *Tas., Austral.*
148 E3
Hobbs, *N. Mex., U.S.*
42 D3
Ho Chi Minh City (Saigon),
Vietnam **122** B2
Hödrögö, *Mongolia*
118 A3
Höfn, *Ice.* **76** A2
Hofuf *see* Al Hufūf, *Saudi*
Arabia **113** B4
Hoggar *see* Ahaggar,
mountains, Alg. **139** C4
Hohhot, *China* **119** B4
Hoh Xil Shan, *China*
118 C2
Hokkaidō, *island, Japan*
121 B6
Holguín, *Cuba* **50** C3
Hollick-Kenyon Plateau,
Antarctica **166** C2
Hólmavík, *Ice.* **76** A2
Holsteinsborg *see* Sisimiut,
Greenland, Den. **165** E5
Hōlualoa, *Hawai'i, U.S.*
45 F4
Hombori, *Mali* **138** D3
Home Bay, *Nunavut, Can.*
41 D4
Homer, *Alas., U.S.* **44** C3
Homestead, *Fla., U.S.*
50 B2
Homs *see* Ḥimş, *Syr.*
110 C3
Homyel', *Belarus* **91** E5
Hōnaunau, *Hawai'i, U.S.*
45 F4
Honduras, *N. Amer.* **29** E3
Honduras, Golfo de, *N.*
Amer. **29** E3
Honduras, Gulf of, *N. Amer.*
31 E3
Hong Kong, *China* **119** E5
Honiara, *Solomon Is.*
160 C3
Honoka'a, *Hawai'i, U.S.*
45 E5
Honolulu, *Hawai'i, U.S.*
45 E3
Honomanū Bay, *Hawai'i,*
U.S. **45** E4
Honshū, *island, Japan*
121 D5

Hoonah, *Alas., U.S.* **40** B1
Hooper Bay, *Alas., U.S.*
44 B2
Hope, Lake, *W. Austral.,*
Austral. **150** D2
Hope, Point, *Alas., U.S.*
164 C1
Hopedale, *Nfld. & Lab., Can.*
41 C5
Hopetoun, *W. Austral.,*
Austral. **148** E2
Hormuz, Strait of, *Iran,*
Oman **113** B5
Horn (North Cape), *cape,*
Ice. **78** A2
Horn, Cape *see* Hornos,
Cabo de, *Chile* **73** F2
Hornos, Cabo de (Cape
Horn), *Chile* **73** F2
Hoste, Isla, *Chile* **73** F2
Hotan, *China* **118** C2
Hot Springs National Park,
U.S. **47** C4
Hotte, Massif de la, *Haiti*
51 D4
Hottentot Bay, *Namibia*
144 D1
Houston, *Tex., U.S.* **43** D4
Houtman Abrolhos, *W.*
Austral., Austral. **150** D1
Hövsgöl Nuur, *Mongolia*
118 A3
Howe, Cape, *Austral.*
151 E5
Høyanger, *Nor.* **90** C1
Hradec Králové, *Czech Rep.*
91 F2
Hrodna, *Belarus* **91** E4
Huadian, *China* **120** A2
Huainan, *China* **119** C5
Huallaga, *river, Peru*
68 E2
Huambo, *Angola* **142** D2
Huancayo, *Peru* **70** C1
Huang (Yellow), *China*
119 C5
Huangshi, *China* **119** D5
Huánuco, *Peru* **68** E2
Huaraz, *Peru* **68** E1
Huascarán, Nevado, *Peru*
70 B1
Huasco, *Chile* **72** A1

Hubli, *India* 116 D3
Hudson Bay, *Can.* 41 C4
Hudson Strait, *Can.* 41 B4
Hue, *Vietnam* 122 B2
Huelva, *Sp.* 89 F2
Hughenden, *Qnsld., Austral.* 149 B5
Hŭich'ŏn, *N. Kor.* 120 B2
Huinan, *China* 120 A2
Hulin, *China* 121 A5
Hulun Nur, *China* 119 A5
Humacao, *P.R., U.S.* 52 A1
Humaitá, *Braz.* 69 E4
Humbe, *Angola* 142 E2
Hŭn, *Lib.* 139 B5
Húnaflói, *bay, Ice.* 78 A2
Hungary, *Eur.* 78 D3
Hŭngnam, *N. Kor.* 120 B2
Huntsville, *Ala., U.S.* 43 D5
Huon Gulf, *P.N.G.* 160 C2
Hupo, *S. Kor.* 120 D3
Hurghada, *Egypt* 140 B3
Huron, Lake, *Can., U.S.* 43 B5
Ḩuşaybah, *Syr.* 110 C3
Hwange, *Zimb.* 144 B3
Hyargas Nuur, *Mongolia* 118 A3
Hyderabad, *India* 117 B5
Hyderabad, *Pak.* 116 B2
Hyères, Îles d', *Fr.* 89 D5
Hyesan, *N. Kor.* 120 A2

I

Iaşi, *Rom.* 93 A4
Ibadan, *Nigeria* 139 E4
Ibagué, *Col.* 68 B2
Ibb, *Yemen* 112 E3
Iberian Peninsula, *Eur.* 78 D1
Ibiza (Ivisa), *island, Sp.* 89 F4
Ibo, *Mozambique* 145 A5
Ica, *Peru* 70 C1
Içá, *river, Braz.* 68 D3
Içana, *river, Braz.* 68 C3
Iceland, *Eur.* 76 A2
Ichinoseki, *Japan* 121 C6
Ich'ŏn, *N. Kor.* 120 C2

Iconium *see* Konya, *Turk.* 110 B2
Icy Cape, *Alas., U.S.* 44 A2
Idaho, *state, U.S.* 42 B2
Idaho Falls, *Idaho, U.S.* 42 B2
Idfu, *Egypt* 140 B2
'Idī, *Eritrea* 141 D4
Iferouâne, *Niger* 139 C4
Igarka, *Russ.* 94 C3
Igloolik, *Nunavut, Can.* 41 B4
Iguaçu (Iguazú), *river, Arg., Braz.* 71 E4
Iguaçu, Cataratas do, *Arg., Braz.* 57 D3
Iguala, *Mex.* 48 C3
Iguape, *Braz.* 71 E5
Iguatu, *Braz.* 71 B6
Iguazú *see* Iguaçu, *river, Arg., Braz.* 71 E4
Iguazú Falls, *Arg., Braz.* 59 D3
Iguéla, *Gabon* 142 B1
Iguidi, 'Erg, *Alg., Mauritania* 138 B2
Ih Bogd Uul, *Mongolia* 118 B3
Iijoki, *river, Fin.* 90 B4
IJsselmeer, *lake, Neth.* 88 B4
Ikela, *Dem. Rep. of the Congo* 141 F1
Iksan, *S. Kor.* 120 D2
Ile, *river, Kaz.* 115 C5
Ilebo, *Dem. Rep. of the Congo* 142 C3
Ilemi Triangle, *region, Kenya, S. Sudan* 141 E3
Ilhéus, *Braz.* 71 C6
Iliamna Lake, *Alas., U.S.* 44 B3
Iligan, *Philippines* 123 C4
Illinois, *state, U.S.* 43 C4
Illizi, *Alg.* 139 B4
Iloilo, *Philippines* 123 B4
Ilorin, *Nigeria* 139 E4
Ilulissat (Jakobshavn), *Greenland, Den.* 165 E5
Imatra, *Fin.* 90 C4
Imbituba, *Braz.* 71 E4
Imperatriz, *Braz.* 71 B5
Impfondo, *Congo* 142 A2

Imphal, *India* 117 B5
I-n-Amenas, *Alg.* 139 B4
Inari, *lake, Fin.* 90 A4
Incheon (Inch'ŏn), *S. Kor.* 120 C2
Inch'ŏn *see* Incheon, *S. Kor.* 120 C2
India, *Asia* 98 D3
Indiana, *state, U.S.* 43 C4
Indianapolis, *Ind., U.S.* 43 C4
Indiga, *Russ.* 77 A5
Indochina Peninsula, *Asia* 101 D4
Indonesia, *Asia* 99 E4
Indore, *India* 116 C3
Indus, *river, Pak.* 116 B3
Ingal, *Niger* 139 D4
Inhambane, *Mozambique* 145 C4
Inharrime, *Mozambique* 145 C4
Inírida, *river, Col.* 68 C3
Inland Niger Delta, *Mali* 128 C2
Inner Hebrides, *islands, U.K.* 88 A2
Innisfail, *Qnsld., Austral.* 149 B5
Innsbruck, *Aust.* 92 A1
Inongo, *Dem. Rep. of the Congo* 142 B2
I-n-Salah, *Alg.* 138 B3
International Falls, *Minn., U.S.* 43 A4
Inuit Qeqertaat (Kaffeklubben Island), *Greenland, Den.* 165 C4
Inukjuak, *Que., Can.* 41 C4
Inuvik, *N.W.T., Can.* 40 A2
Inverness, *U.K.* 88 A3
Investigator Strait, *S. Austral., Austral.* 151 E4
Inyangani, *peak, Zimb.* 145 B4
Ioánina, *Gr.* 92 D3
Ionian Sea, *Eur.* 78 E3
Iowa, *state, U.S.* 43 C4
Ipoh, *Malaysia* 122 C1
Ipu, *Braz.* 71 B6
Iqaluit, *Nunavut, Can.* 41 B5
Iquique, *Chile* 70 D2

Iquitos, *Peru* **68** D2
Iráklio (Candia), *Gr.* **93** E4
Iran, *Asia* **98** C2
Īrānshahr, *Iran* **113** B6
Irapa, *Venez.* **53** F3
Irapuato, *Mex.* **48** C3
Iraq, *Asia* **98** C2
Irbil see Arbīl, *Iraq* **111** B4
Ireland, *island, Ireland, U.K.* **100** A2
Ireland (Éire), *Eur.* **76** C2
Iringa, *Tanzania* **143** C5
Iriomote Jima, *Japan* **119** D6
Iriri, *river, Braz.* **69** D6
Irish Sea, *Ire., U.K.* **88** B2
Irkutsk, *Russ.* **95** D4
Irrawaddy see Ayeyarwady, *river, Myanmar* **117** C6
Irtysh, *river, Russ.* **115** A4
Is, Jebel, *Sudan* **140** C3
Isère, Pointe, *Fr. Guiana, Fr.* **69** B6
Ise Wan, *Japan* **121** D5
Isfahan see Esfahan, *Iran* **111** C5
Ishigaki Shima, *Japan* **119** D6
Ishikari Wan, *Japan* **121** B6
Ishinomaki Wan, *Japan* **121** C6
Isiro (Paulis), *Dem. Rep. of the Congo* **143** A4
İskenderun, *Turk.* **110** B2
Islamabad, *Pak.* **116** A3
Isle Royale National Park, *U.S.* **47** A4
Ismāʻīlīya, *Egypt* **140** A2
Israel, *Asia* **98** C1
İstanbul (Constantinople), *Turk.* **110** A1
İstanbul Boğazı (Bosporus), *Turk.* **93** C5
Itabuna, *Braz.* **71** C6
Itacoatiara, *Braz.* **69** D5
Itaituba, *Braz.* **69** D5
Italy, *Eur.* **76** E3
Itapecuru, *river, Braz.* **71** B5
Iténez see Guaporé, *river, Bol.* **70** C3

Itezhi-Tezhi, Lake, *Zambia* **143** E4
Ittoqqortoormiit (Scoresbysund), *Greenland, Den.* **165** D5
Ituxi, *river, Braz.* **70** B2
Iul'tin, *Russ.* **164** C1
Ivalo, *Fin.* **90** A4
Ivisa see Ibiza, *island, Sp.* **89** F4
Ivory Coast see Côte d'Ivoire, *Af.* **126** C1
Ivory Coast, *Côte d'Ivoire* **138** E2
Ivujivik, *Que., Can.* **41** C4
Ixtapa, *Mex.* **48** D3
Izmayil, *Ukr.* **93** B5
İzmir (Smyrna), *Turk.* **110** B1
Izu Islands, *Japan* **101** C5
Izu Shotō, *Japan* **121** D6

J

Jabalpur, *India* **117** C4
Jabal Zuqar, Jazīrat, *Yemen* **112** E2
Jabiru, *N. Terr., Austral.* **148** A3
Jacareacanga, *Braz.* **69** E5
Jackson, *Miss., U.S.* **43** D4
Jacksonville, *Fla., U.S.* **43** D5
Jacmel, *Haiti* **51** D4
Jaffna, *Sri Lanka* **117** E4
Jagdaqi, *China* **119** A5
Jahrom, *Iran* **111** D6
Jaipur, *India* **116** B3
Jakarta, *Indonesia* **122** E2
Jakobshavn see Ilulissat, *Greenland, Den.* **165** E5
Jalālābād, *Afghan.* **116** A3
Jalingo, *Nigeria* **139** E4
Jalna, *India* **116** C3
Jamaame, *Somalia* **141** F4
Jamaica, *N. Amer.* **29** E4
Jambi, *Indonesia* **122** D2
James Bay, *Can.* **41** D4
Jan Mayen, *island, Nor.* **94** A2
Januária, *Braz.* **71** C5

Japan, *Asia* **99** C5
Japan, Sea of (East Sea), *Asia* **101** C5
Japurá, *river, Braz.* **68** D3
Japurá, *Braz.* **68** D3
Jardines de la Reina, *islands, Cuba* **50** C2
Jari, *river, Braz.* **69** C6
Jarvis Island, *possession, U.S.* **161** B4
Jāsk, *Iran* **111** E6
Jauaperi, *river, Braz.* **69** C4
Java (Jawa), *island, Indonesia* **122** E2
Javari see Yavarí, *river, Braz.* **68** D2
Java Sea, *Indonesia* **122** E2
Jawa see Java, *island, Indonesia* **122** E2
Jayapura, *Indonesia* **123** D6
Jecheon, *S. Kor.* **120** D2
Jeddah, *Saudi Arabia* **112** C2
Jefferson City, *Mo., U.S.* **43** C4
Jeju (Cheju), *S. Kor.* **120** E2
Jeju-Do, *island, S. Kor.* **120** E2
Jeju Strait, *S. Kor.* **120** E2
Jelbart Ice Shelf, *Antarctica* **166** A3
Jelgava (Mitau), *Latv.* **91** D4
Jengish Chokusu (Pobedy Peak, Victory Peak), *China, Kyrg.* **115** D6
Jeonju, *S. Kor.* **120** D2
Jequié, *Braz.* **71** C6
Jerba Island, *Tun.* **139** A4
Jerez de la Frontera, *Sp.* **89** F2
Jerid, Shott el, *Tanzania* **128** B2
Jersey, *island, U.K.* **88** C3
Jerusalem (Al Quds, Yerushalayim), *Israel* **110** C2

K

Kal-Kat

Kalemie, *Dem. Rep. of the Congo* 143 C4

Kalgoorlie-Boulder, *W. Austral., Austral.* 148 D2

Kalimantan *see* Borneo, *Indonesia* 122 D3

Kaliningrad, *Russ.* 91 E3

Kalohi Channel, *Hawai'i, U.S.* 45 E3

Kalyan, *India* 116 C3

Kama, *river, Russ.* 79 B5

Kamaishi, *Japan* 121 C6

Kamarān, *island, Yemen* 112 E2

Kama Reservoir, *Russ.* 79 B5

Kambalda, *W. Austral., Austral.* 148 D2

Kamchatka, Poluostrov (Kamchatka Peninsula), *Russ.* 95 B6

Kamchatka Peninsula, *Russ.* 101 B5

Kamina, *Dem. Rep. of the Congo* 142 C3

Kamino Shima, *Japan* 120 E3

Kamloops, *B.C., Can.* 40 D1

Kampala, *Uganda* 143 B5

Kamskoye Vodokhranilishche, *Russ.* 77 B3

Kamuela *see* Waimea, *Hawai'i, U.S.* 45 E5

Kamui Misaki, *Japan* 121 B6

Kamyshin, *Russ.* 114 A1

Kananga, *Dem. Rep. of the Congo* 142 C3

Kanazawa, *Japan* 121 C5

Kanchenjunga, *peak, India, Nepal* 117 B5

Kandahar, *Afghan.* 116 A2

Kandalaksha, *Russ.* 90 B4

Kandalakshskiy, Zaliv, *Russ.* 90 B5

Kandi, *Benin* 138 D3

Kāne'ohe, *Hawai'i, U.S.* 45 D3

Kangaroo Island, *S. Austral., Austral.* 151 E4

Kangean, Kepulauan, *Indonesia* 122 E3

Kangertittivaq, *bay, Greenland, Den.* 30 A4

Kanggye, *N. Kor.* 120 B2

Kangiqsujuaq, *Que., Can.* 41 C4

Kanin, Poluostrov, *Russ.* 94 B2

Kanin Peninsula, *Russ.* 79 A5

Kankan, *Guinea* 138 E2

Kano, *Nigeria* 139 D4

Kanoya, *Japan* 121 E4

Kanpur, *India* 116 C3

Kansas, *state, U.S.* 42 C3

Kansas City, *Mo., U.S.* 43 C4

Kanye, *Botswana* 144 C3

Kaohsiung, *Taiwan* 119 E5

Kaokoland, *region, Namibia* 144 B1

Kaolack, *Senegal* 138 D1

Kaoma, *Zambia* 144 B3

Kapa'a, *Hawai'i, U.S.* 45 D1

Kapuskasing, *Ont., Can.* 41 D4

Karachi, *Pak.* 116 B2

Karaginskiy Gulf, *Russ.* 31 F1

Karaginskiy Zaliv, *Russ.* 29 F1

Karakol, *Kyrg.* 115 D5

Karakoram Range, *China, Pak.* 115 E5

Karamay, *China* 118 B2

Karamken, *Russ.* 95 B6

Karasburg, *Namibia* 144 D2

Kara Sea, *Arctic Oc.* 165 A4

Karas Mountains, *Namibia* 129 E3

Karasuk, *Russ.* 115 A5

Karbalā', *Iraq* III C4

Kariba, *Zimb.* 144 B3

Kariba, Lake, *Zambia* 144 B3

Karima, *Sudan* 140 C2

Karimata, Kepulauan, *Indonesia* 122 D2

Karimata, Selat, *Indonesia* 122 D2

Karkinits'ka Zatoka, *Ukr.* 93 B5

Karkūk (Kirkuk), *Iraq* III C4

Karlskrona, *Sw.* 91 D2

Karlsruhe, *Ger.* 92 A1

Karonga, *Malawi* 143 D5

Kárpathos (Carpathos), *island, Gr.* 110 B1

Karratha, *W. Austral., Austral.* 148 B1

Kasai, *river, Dem. Rep. of the Congo* 142 B2

Kasama, *Zambia* 143 D5

Kasane, *Botswana* 144 B3

Kasar, Ras, *Eritrea* 140 C2

Kasempa, *Zambia* 144 A3

Kāshān, *Iran* III C5

Kashgar *see* Kashi, *China* 118 B1

Kashi (Kashgar), *China* 118 B1

Kāshmar, *Iran* III B6

Kashmir, *region, China, India, Pak.* 116 A3

Kasongo, *Dem. Rep. of the Congo* 143 C4

Kaspiyskiy, *Russ.* 114 C1

Kassala, *Sudan* 140 C3

Kastamonu, *Turk.* 110 A2

Kasulu, *Tanzania* 143 C4

Kasungu, *Malawi* 143 D5

Katal'ga, *Russ.* 94 D3

Katanga Plateau, *Dem. Rep. of the Congo, Zambia* 142 D3

Katanning, *W. Austral., Austral.* 148 E2

Kata Tjuta *see* Olga, Mount, *N. Terr., Austral.* 150 C3

Katherîna, Gebel, *Egypt* 140 B3

Katherine, *N. Terr., Austral.* 148 A3

Kathmandu, *Nepal* 117 B4

Katima Mulilo, *Namibia* 144 B3

Katmai National Park and Preserve, *U.S.* 46 E1

Katsina, *Nigeria* 139 D4

Kattegat, *strait, Den., Sw.*
91 D1

Kaua'i, *island, Hawai'i, U.S.*
45 D1

Kaua'i Channel, *Hawai'i,*
U.S. 45 D2

Kaukau Veld, *Botswana,*
Namibia 144 C2

Kaunā Point, *Hawai'i, U.S.*
45 F4

Kaunas, *Lith.* 91 E4

Kavīr, Dasht-e (Kavir
Desert), *Iran* 111 C6

Kavir Desert *see* Kavīr,
Dasht-e, *Iran* 111 C6

Kawaihae Bay, *Hawai'i, U.S.*
45 F4

Kawaihoa Point, *Hawai'i,*
U.S. 45 D1

Kawasaki, *Japan* 121 D6

Kawashiri Misaki, *Japan*
120 E3

Kayes, *Mali* 138 D2

Kayseri, *Turk.* 110 B2

Kazach'ye, *Russ.* 95 B5

Kazakhstan, *Asia, Eur.*
98 C3

Kazakh Uplands, *Kaz.*
115 B4

Kazan', *Russ.* 94 C2

Kāzerūn, *Iran* 113 A4

København (Copenhagen),
Den. 88 A5

Keāhole Point, *Hawai'i, U.S.*
45 F4

Kealaikahiki Channel,
Hawai'i, U.S. 45 E4

Kealakekua Bay, *Hawai'i,*
U.S. 45 F4

Kebnekaise, *peak, Sw.*
90 A3

Kédougou, *Senegal*
138 D2

Keele Peak, *Can.* 164 E2

Keetmanshoop, *Namibia*
144 D2

Kefaloniá, *island, Gr.*
92 D3

K'elafo, *Eth.* 141 E4

Kellett, Cape, *N.W.T., Can.*
40 A2

Kélo, *Chad* 139 E5

Kelowna, *B.C., Can.* 40 D1

Kem', *Russ.* 90 B5

Kemerovo, *Russ.* 94 D3

Kemi, *Fin.* 90 B4

Kemps Bay, *Bahamas*
50 B3

Kenai, *Alas., U.S.* 44 B3

Kenai Fjords National
Park, *U.S.* 46 E2

Kenai Peninsula, *Alas., U.S.*
44 B3

Kendari, *Indonesia*
123 D4

Kenema, *Sa. Leone*
138 E2

Kengtung, *Myanmar*
117 C6

Kenhardt, *S. Af.* 144 D2

Kenitra (Port Lyautey),
Mor. 138 A2

Kennedy, Cape *see*
Canaveral, Cape, *Fla., U.S.*
43 D5

Kenora, *Ont., Can.* 40 D3

Kentucky, *state, U.S.*
43 C5

Kenya, *Af.* 127 D4

Kenya, Mount, *Kenya*
143 B6

Kenya Highlands, *Kenya*
129 D4

Kepi, *Indonesia* 123 E6

Kerch, *Ukr.* 93 B6

Kerchenskiy Proliv, *Russ.,*
Ukr. 93 B6

Keren, *Eritrea* 112 D2

Keret', *Russ.* 77 A4

Kerinci, *peak, Indonesia*
122 D1

Keriya *see* Yutian, *China*
118 C2

Kerki *see* Atamyrat, *Turkm.*
114 E3

Kérkira (Corfu), *island, Gr.*
92 D3

Kerma, *Sudan* 140 C2

Kermadec Islands, *N.Z.*
161 D4

Kermān, *Iran* 111 D6

Kermānshāh, *Iran* 111 C4

Ketchikan, *Alas., U.S.*
44 C5

Key West, *Fla., U.S.* 43 E5

Khabarovsk, *Russ.* 95 D6

Khambhat, Gulf of, *India*
116 C3

Khamīs Mushayt, *Saudi*
Arabia 112 D2

Khanka, Ozero (Xingkai
Hu), *China, Russ.*
121 A4

Khan Tängiri, *peak, China,*
Kaz., Kyrg. 115 D6

Khanty-Mansiysk, *Russ.*
77 A6

Kharkiv, *Ukr.* 77 C5

Khartoum, *Sudan* 140 C2

Khartoum North, *Sudan*
140 C2

Khaşab, *Oman* 113 B5

Khāsh, *Iran* 113 A6

Khashm el Qirba, *Sudan*
112 E1

Khatanga, *Russ.* 95 B4

Khatangskiy Zaliv, *Russ.*
164 A3

Khiwa, *Uzb.* 114 D3

Khmel'nyts'kyy, *Ukr.*
93 A4

Kholmsk, *Russ.* 121 A6

Khon Kaen, *Thai.* 122 A2

Khor, *Russ.* 121 A5

Khorramshahr, *Iran*
111 D5

Khoy, *Iran* 111 B4

Khromtaū, *Kaz.* 114 B2

Khujand, *Taj.* 115 D4

Khujayli, *Uzb.* 114 D2

Khulna, *Bangladesh*
117 C5

Kibiti, *Tanzania* 143 C6

Kidal, *Mali* 138 C3

Kiel, *Ger.* 91 E1

Kielce, *Pol.* 91 F3

Kiev *see* Kyyiv, *Ukr.* 91 F5

Kiffa, *Mauritania* 138 D2

Kigali, *Rwanda* 143 B4

Kigoma, *Tanzania* 143 C4

Kīholo Bay, *Hawai'i, U.S.*
45 F4

Kii Suidō, *Japan* 121 D5

Kikládes (Cyclades),
islands, Gr. 93 E4

Kikwit, *Dem. Rep. of the*
Congo 142 C2

Kilimanjaro, *peak, Tanzania* **143** B6
Kilju, *N. Kor.* **120** B3
Kilwa Kivinje, *Tanzania* **143** C6
Kimberley, *S. Af.* **144** D3
Kimberley Plateau, *W. Austral., Austral.* **150** B2
Kimch'aek, *N. Kor.* **120** B3
Kimhyŏnggwŏn, *N. Kor.* **120** B2
Kimmirut, *Nunavut, Can.* **41** B5
Kimpese, *Dem. Rep. of the Congo* **142** C2
Kinabalu, *peak, Malaysia* **122** C3
Kindia, *Guinea* **138** D1
Kindu, *Dem. Rep. of the Congo* **143** B4
King George Sound, *W. Austral., Austral.* **150** E2
King Island, *Tas., Austral.* **150** E3
Kings Canyon National Park, *U.S.* **46** C1
King Sejong, *research station, Antarctica* **166** A1
King Sound, *W. Austral., Austral.* **150** B2
Kingston, *Jam.* **50** D3
Kingston upon Hull, *U.K.* **88** B3
Kingstown, *St. Vincent & the Grenadines* **53** D4
Kinshasa (Léopoldville), *Dem. Rep. of the Congo* **142** C2
Kinyeti, *peak, S. Sudan* **141** E2
Kiribati, *Oceania* **160** B3
Kiritimati (Christmas Island), *Kiribati* **161** B5
Kirkenes, *Nor.* **90** A4
Kirkpatrick, Mount, *Antarctica* **167** D4
Kirkuk *see* Karkūk, *Iraq* **111** C4
Kirov, *Russ.* **94** C2
Kirovohrad, *Ukr.* **93** A5
Kirovsk, *Russ.* **90** A5

Kırşehir, *Turk.* **93** D6
Kiruna, *Sw.* **90** B3
Kisangani, *Dem. Rep. of the Congo* **143** B4
Kiska Island, *Alas., U.S.* **44** C3
Kislokan, *Russ.* **95** C4
Kismaayo (Chisimayu), *Somalia* **141** F4
Kissidougou, *Guinea* **138** E2
Kissimmee, *river, U.S.* **50** A2
Kisumu, *Kenya* **143** B5
Kitale, *Kenya* **143** A5
Kitami, *Japan* **121** B6
Kitgum, *Uganda* **143** A5
Kitimat, *B.C., Can.* **40** C1
Kitwe, *Zambia* **143** D4
Kivu, Lac, *Dem. Rep. of the Congo, Rwanda* **143** B4
Kızılırmak, *river, Turk.* **93** D6
Kizlyar, *Russ.* **114** C1
Klagenfurt, *Aust.* **92** B2
Klaipėda, *Lith.* **91** E3
Klamath Falls, *Oreg., U.S.* **42** B1
Klarälven, *river, Sw.* **90** C2
Klerksdorp, *S. Af.* **144** D3
Klyuchi, *Russ.* **95** B6
Knob, Cape, *W. Austral., Austral.* **150** E2
Knud Rasmussen Land, *Greenland, Den.* **165** D4
Kōbe, *Japan* **121** D5
København (Copenhagen), *Den.* **91** E2
Kobroor, *island, Indonesia* **123** E5
Kobuk, *river, Alas., U.S.* **44** A3
Kobuk Valley National Park, *U.S.* **46** B1
Kōchi, *Japan* **121** D5
Kochi (Cochin), *India* **116** E3
Kodiak, *Alas., U.S.* **44** C3
Kodiak Island, *Alas., U.S.* **44** C3
Kodok, *S. Sudan* **141** D2
Kōfu, *Japan* **121** D5
Kohima, *India* **117** B5

Kokkola, *Fin.* **90** C3
Kökpekti, *Kaz.* **115** B6
Kökshetaū, *Kaz.* **115** A4
Kola, *river, Russ.* **90** A4
Kola, *Russ.* **90** A4
Kola Peninsula, *Russ.* **79** A4
Kolarovgrad *see* Shumen, *Bulg.* **93** C4
Kolguyev Island, *Russ.* **79** A5
Kolguyev, Ostrov, *island, Russ.* **77** A5
Kolhapur, *India* **116** D3
Kolkata (Calcutta), *India* **117** C5
Köln, *Ger.* **88** C5
Kołobrzeg, *Pol.* **91** E2
Kol'skiy Poluostrov, *Russ.* **94** B2
Kolwezi, *Dem. Rep. of the Congo* **143** D4
Kolymskoye Nagor'ye, *Russ.* **164** B1
Komandorskiye Ostrova, *Russ.* **95** B6
Komotiní, *Gr.* **93** C4
Komsomol'sk na Amure, *Russ.* **95** D6
Komusan, *N. Kor.* **120** A3
Kondoa, *Tanzania* **143** C5
Kondopoga, *Russ.* **90** C5
Kondoz (Kunduz), *Afghan.* **115** E4
Kong Christian IX Land, *Greenland, Den.* **165** E5
Kong Christian X Land, *Greenland, Den.* **165** D5
Kong Frederik VI Coast, *Greenland, Den.* **165** E5
Kong Frederik VIII Land, *Greenland, Den.* **165** D5
Kongur Shan, *China* **115** C5
Konosha, *Russ.* **77** B5
Konya (Iconium), *Turk.* **110** B2
Korba, *India* **117** C4
Korçë, *Alban.* **92** D3
Korea, *peninsula, Asia* **120** B2
Korea Bay, *China, N. Kor.* **120** B1

Korea Strait, *Japan, S. Kor.*
120 E2
Korem, *Eth.* 112 E2
Korf, *Russ.* 95 B6
Korff Ice Rise, *Antarctica*
166 C3
Korhogo, *Côte d'Ivoire*
138 E2
Korla, *China* 118 B2
Korosten', *Ukr.* 91 F5
Koro Toro, *Chad* 139 D5
Korsakov, *Russ.* 121 A6
Koryak Range, *Russ.*
31 F1
Koryakskoye Nagor'ye,
Russ. 164 B1
Kosciuszko, Mount, *N.S.W.,
Austral.* 151 E5
Košice, *Slovakia* 92 A3
Kosovo, *Eur.* 77 D4
Kosti, *Sudan* 141 D2
Kota, *India* 116 B3
Kota Baharu, *Malaysia*
122 C2
Kotabumi, *Indonesia*
122 E2
Kota Kinabalu, *Malaysia*
122 C3
Kotka, *Fin.* 90 C4
Kotlas, *Russ.* 77 B5
Kotzebue, *Alas., U.S.*
44 A2
Kotzebue Sound, *Alas., U.S.*
44 A2
Kouilou, *river, Congo*
142 C1
Koulikoro, *Mali* 138 D2
Koumra, *Chad* 139 E5
Kourou, *Fr. Guiana, Fr.*
69 B6
Koyukuk, *river, Alas., U.S.*
44 A3
Kra, Isthmus of, *Thai.*
122 B1
Kraków, *Pol.* 91 F3
Kralendijk, *Bonaire, Neth.*
53 D2
Krasnoarneysk see
Tayynsha, *Kaz.* 115 A4
Krasnodar, *Russ.* 94 D1
Krasnoyarsk, *Russ.* 95 D4
Krasnyy Kut, *Russ.*
114 A1

Krasnyy Yar, *Russ.* 114 B1
Kremenchuts'ke
Vodokhranilishche, *Ukr.*
93 A5
Kril'on, Mys, *Russ.*
121 A6
Kristiansand, *Nor.* 91 D1
Kristiansund, *Nor.* 90 C1
Kríti see Crete, *island, Gr.*
93 E4
Kroonstad, *S. Af.* 144 D3
Krui, *Indonesia* 122 E2
Krung Thep (Bangkok),
Thai. 122 B1
Krychaw, *Belarus* 91 E5
Kryvyy Rih, *Ukr.* 93 A5
Kuala Lumpur, *Malaysia*
122 C1
Kuala Terengganu,
Malaysia 122 C2
Kuantan, *Malaysia*
122 C2
Kuching, *Malaysia* 122 D3
Kugluktuk, *Nunavut, Can.*
40 B2
Kuito, *Angola* 142 D2
Kumamoto, *Japan* 121 D4
Kumano Nada, *Japan*
121 D5
Kumasi, *Ghana* 138 E3
Kumbo, *Cameroon* 139 E4
Kumul see Hami, *China*
118 B3
Kunashir (Kunashiri),
island, Russ. 121 A6
Kunashiri see Kunashir,
island, Russ. 121 A6
Kunduz see Kondoz, *Afghan.*
115 E4
Kunlun Mountains, *China*
100 C3
Kunlun Shan, *China*
118 C2
Kunming, *China* 119 E4
Kununurra, *W. Austral.,
Austral.* 148 A3
Kuopio, *Fin.* 90 C4
Kupang, *Indonesia* 123 E4
Kuqa, *China* 118 B2
Kuria Muria Islands see
Ḥallānīyāt, Jazāīr al,
Ōman 113 D5

Kuril Islands, *Russ.*
101 B5
Kurnool, *India* 116 D3
Kursk, *Russ.* 94 C1
Kurze Mountains,
Antarctica 167 A4
Kushiro, *Japan* 121 B6
Kuskokwim, *river, Alas., U.S.*
44 B2
Kuskokwim Mountains,
Alas., U.S. 44 B3
Kütahya, *Turk.* 110 A1
K'ut'aisi, *Rep. of Ga.*
110 A3
Kutch, Gulf of, *India*
116 C2
Kuujjuaq, *Que., Can.*
41 C5
Kuujjuarapik, *Que., Can.*
41 D4
Kuvango, *Angola* 142 E2
Kuwait, *Asia* 98 C2
Kuwait City see Al Kuwayt,
Kuwait 111 D4
Kuytun, *China* 115 C6
Kuzey Anadolu Dağları,
Turk. 110 A2
Kuz'movka, *Russ.* 94 C3
Kvænangen, *bay, Nor.*
90 A3
Kvaløy, *island, Nor.* 90 A3
Kwangju see Gwangju, *S.
Kor.* 120 D2
Kwango, *river, Angola,
Dem. Rep. of the Congo*
142 C2
Kyiv (Kiev), *Ukr.* 94 C1
Kyoga, Lake, *Uganda*
143 A5
Kyŏngju see Gyeongju, *S.
Kor.* 120 D3
Kyŏngsŏng, *N. Kor.*
120 A3
Kyōto, *Japan* 121 D5
Kyrgyzstan, *Asia* 98 C3
Kyūshū, *island, Japan*
121 D4
Kyustendil, *Bulg.* 93 C4
Kyyiv (Kiev), *Ukr.* 91 F5
Kyzyl, *Russ.* 118 A3

215

L

Le Maire, Estrecho de, *Arg.*
73 F3

Léman, Lac, *Switz.* **89** D5

Le Mans, *Fr.* **88** C3

Lemesos (Limassol), *Cyprus*
93 E6

Lemnos *see* Límnos, *island,*
Gr. **93** D4

Lena, *river, Russ.* **99** B4

Lenghu, *China* **118** D3

Lengua de Vaca Point,
Chile **59** D2

Leníñogorsk *see* Ridder,
Kaz. **115** A6

Lenin Peak, *Kyrg., Taj.*
115 D5

Leninsk *see* Bayqongyr,
Kaz. **114** C3

Leoben, *Aust.* **92** A2

León, *Mex.* **48** C3

León, *Nicar.* **49** D5

Leonora, *W. Austral.*
Austral. **148** D2

Léopoldville *see* Kinshasa,
Dem. Rep. of the Congo
142 C2

Lepsi, *Kaz.* **115** C5

Ler, *S. Sudan* **141** D2

Lerwick, *U.K.* **76** B2

Les Cayes, *Haiti* **51** D4

Lesotho, *Af.* **127** E4

Lesozavodsk, *Russ.*
121 A5

Les Saintes, *islands,*
Guadeloupe, Fr. **52** C4

Lesser Antilles, *islands, N.*
Amer. **52** B2

Lesser Sunda Islands,
Indonesia, Timor-Leste
122 E3

Lésvos (Mytilíni), *island,*
Gr. **93** D4

Leszno, *Pol.* **91** F2

Lethbridge, *Alberta, Can.*
40 D3

Lethem, *Guyana* **69** C5

Leticia, *Col.* **68** D3

Leveque, Cape, *W. Austral.,*
Austral. **150** B2

Lévrier, Baie du, *Mauritania*
138 C1

Lewis, Isle of, *U.K.* **78** B2

Lewis Range, *Austral.*
150 B3

Leyte, *island, Philippines*
123 B4

Lhasa, *China* **118** D2

Liancourt Rocks *see* Dokdo,
S. Kor. **121** C4

Liaoyang, *China* **120** A1

Liaoyuan, *China* **119** B5

Liard, *river, N.W.T., Can.*
40 B2

Liberia, *Af.* **126** C1

Liberia, *Costa Rica* **49** E5

Libreville, *Gabon* **142** B1

Libya, *Af.* **126** B3

Libyan Desert, *Egypt, Lib.,*
Sudan **140** B1

Libyan Plateau (Aḍ Diffah),
Egypt, Lib. **140** A1

Lichinga, *Mozambique*
145 A4

Licosa, Punta, *It.* **92** D2

Liechtenstein, *Eur.* **76** D3

Liège, *Belg.* **88** C4

Liepāja, *Latv.* **91** D3

Ligurian Sea, *Eur.* **89** D5

Līhu'e, *Hawai'i, U.S.*
45 D1

Likasi, *Dem. Rep. of the*
Congo **143** D4

Lillehammer, *Nor.* **76** B3

Lilongwe, *Malawi* **143** E5

Lima, *Peru* **70** C1

Limassol *see* Lemesos,
Cyprus **93** E6

Limerick, *Ire.* **88** B2

Limfjorden, *bay, Den.*
91 D1

Limmen Bight, *N. Terr.,*
Austral. **151** A4

Límnos (Lemnos), *island,*
Gr. **93** D4

Limoges, *Fr.* **89** D4

Limón, *Costa Rica* **49** E5

Limpopo, *river, Af.* **145** C4

Linares, *Sp.* **89** F3

Lincoln, *Nebr., U.S.* **42** C3

Lincoln Sea, *Can.,*
Greenland **165** D4

Lindesnes, *cape, Nor.*
91 D1

Lindi, *Tanzania* **143** D6

Line Islands, *Kiribati*
161 B5

Lingga, Kepulauan,
Indonesia **122** D2

Linz, *Aust.* **92** A2

Lion, Golfe du, *Fr.* **89** E4

Lions, Golf of, *Fr.* **78** D2

Lira, *Uganda* **143** A5

Lisala, *Dem. Rep. of the*
Congo **142** A3

Lisboa (Lisbon), *Port.*
89 F1

Lisbon *see* Lisboa, *Port.*
89 F1

Lismore, *N.S.W., Austral.*
149 D6

Lithuania, *Eur.* **77** C4

Little Abaco Island,
Bahamas **50** A3

Little Andaman, *island,*
India **117** E5

Little Cayman, *island,*
Cayman Is., U.K. **50** D2

Little Exuma, *island,*
Bahamas **50** B3

Little Inagua Island,
Bahamas **51** C4

Little Nicobar, *island, India*
117 E5

Little Rock, *Ark., U.S.*
43 D4

Liuhe, *China* **120** A2

Liuzhou, *China* **119** E4

Liverpool, *U.K.* **88** B3

Livingstone, *Zambia*
143 E4

Livorno, *It.* **92** B1

Ljubljana, *Slov.* **92** B2

Llanos, *region, Col., Venez.*
58 A2

Lleida, *Sp.* **89** E4

Llullaillaco, Volcán, *Arg.*
70 E2

Llullaillaco Volcano, *Arg.,*
Chile **59** D2

Lobamba, *Swaziland*
145 D4

Lobito, *Angola* **142** D2

Lodwar, *Kenya* **143** A5

Łódź, *Pol.* **91** F3

Lofoten, *islands, Nor.*
90 A2

Mackenzie, *river, N.W.T., Can.* 40 A2

MacKenzie Bay, *Antarctica* 167 B5

Mackenzie Bay, *Can.* 44 A4

Mackenzie Mountains, *Can.* 30 B2

Macleod, Lake, *W. Austral., Austral.* 150 C1

Macondo, *Angola* 144 A2

Macovane, *Mozambique* 145 C4

Macquarie, Port, *N.S.W., Austral.* 151 D6

Mac. Robertson Land, *Antarctica* 167 B5

Macurijes, Punta, *Cuba* 50 C2

Macuro, *Venez.* 53 F3

Madagascar, *Af.* 127 E5

Madeira, *river, Braz.* 70 B2

Madeira Islands, *Port.* 138 A1

Madeleine, Îles de la, *Que., Can.* 41 D6

Madison, *Wis., U.S.* 43 B4

Madoi, *China* 118 C3

Madrakah, Ra's al, *Oman* 113 D5

Madras *see* Chennai, *India* 117 D4

Madre de Dios, *river, Bol., Peru* 70 C2

Madre del Sur, Sierra, *Mex.* 48 D3

Madre Occidental, Sierra, *Mex.* 48 B2

Madre Oriental, Sierra, *Mex.* 48 B3

Madrid, *Sp.* 89 E3

Madura, *island, Indonesia* 122 E3

Madurai, *India* 116 E3

Maebashi, *Japan* 121 C5

Maestra, Sierra, *Cuba* 50 D3

Maevatanana, *Madagascar* 145 B6

Mafadi, *peak, Lesotho, S. Af.* 144 D3

Mafia Island, *Tanzania* 143 C6

Magadan, *Russ.* 95 B6

Magallanes, Estrecho de, *Chile* 73 F2

Magdalena, *river, Col.* 68 B2

Magdeburg, *Ger.* 91 E1

Magdelaine Cays, *Coral Sea Is. Terr., Austral.* 151 B6

Magellan, Strait of, *Chile* 59 F2

Magellanes, Estrecho de, *Chile* 57 F2

Magerøya, *island, Nor.* 90 A4

Magnitogorsk, *Russ.* 94 D2

Magotes Point, *Arg.* 59 E3

Mahajamba, Baie de la, *Madagascar* 145 B6

Mahajanga, *Madagascar* 145 B6

Mahalapye, *Botswana* 144 C3

Mahd adh Dhahab, *Saudi Arabia* 112 C2

Mahdia, *Tun.* 92 E1

Mahilyow, *Belarus* 91 E5

Mahón, *Sp.* 89 E4

Maiduguri, *Nigeria* 139 D5

Maigualida, Sierra, *Venez.* 69 B4

Main, *river, Ger.* 91 F1

Mai-Ndombe, Lac, *Dem. Rep. of the Congo* 142 B2

Maine, *state, U.S.* 43 A6

Maine, Gulf of, *Can., U.S.* 43 B6

Maintirano, *Madagascar* 145 B5

Maisí, Punta de, *Cuba* 51 D4

Maitland, *N.S.W., Austral.* 149 D6

Maitri, *research station, Antarctica* 167 A4

Maíz, Islas del, *Nicar.* 49 D5

Majorca *see* Mallorca, *island, Sp.* 89 E4

Majuro, *Marshall Is.* 160 B3

Makarikari *see* Makgadikgadi Pans, *Botswana* 144 C3

Makassar (Ujungpandang), *Indonesia* 123 E4

Makassar Strait, *Indonesia* 122 D3

Makgadikgadi Pans (Makarikari), *Botswana* 144 C3

Makhachkala, *Russ.* 114 C1

Makhado, *S. Af.* 144 C3

Makkah (Mecca), *Saudi Arabia* 112 C2

Makkovik, *Nfld. & Lab., Can.* 41 C5

Makokou, *Gabon* 142 B1

Mākole'ā Point, *Hawai'i, U.S.* 45 F4

Makurdi, *Nigeria* 139 E4

Malabo, *Eq. Guinea* 142 A1

Malacca, Strait of, *Indonesia, Malaysia* 122 C1

Maladzyechna, *Belarus* 91 E4

Málaga, *Sp.* 89 F2

Malakal, *S. Sudan* 141 D2

Malang, *Indonesia* 122 E3

Malanje, *Angola* 142 D2

Malaspina Glacier, *Alas., U.S.* 44 B4

Malatya, *Turk.* 110 B3

Malawi, *Af.* 127 D4

Malawi, Lake (Lake Nyasa), *Malawi, Mozambique, Tanzania* 143 D5

Malay Peninsula, *Malaysia, Thai.* 122 C1

Malaysia, *Asia* 99 E4

Maldive Islands, *Maldives* 100 E3

Maldives, *Asia* 98 E3

Male *see* Maale, *Maldives* 98 E3

Mali, *Af.* 126 C2

Malindi, *Kenya* **143** B6
Malin Head, *Ire.* **88** A2
Mallawi, *Egypt* **140** B2
Mallorca (Majorca), *island,
Sp.* **89** E4
Malmö, *Sw.* **91** E2
Malta, *Eur.* **76** E3
Malvinas, Islas *see* Falkland
Islands, *U.K.* **73** F3
Mammoth Cave National
Park, *U.S.* **47** C5
Mamoré, *river, Bol., Braz.*
70 C2
Man, *Côte d'Ivoire*
138 C4
Man, Isle of, *U.K.* **88** B3
Manado, *Indonesia*
123 D4
Managua, *Nicar.* **49** E5
Manakara, *Madagascar*
145 C6
Manama *see* Al Manāmah,
Bahrain **113** B4
Mananjary, *Madagascar*
145 C6
Manantiales, *Chile* **73** F2
Mānā Point, *Hawai'i, U.S.*
45 D1
Manaus, *Braz.* **69** D5
Manchester, *U.K.* **88** B3
Manchurian Plain, *China*
101 C5
Mand, *river, Iran* **111** D5
Mandalay, *Myanmar*
117 C6
Mandalgovĭ, *Mongolia*
119 B4
Mandimba, *Mozambique*
145 B4
Mangalore, *India* **116** D3
Mangnai, *China* **118** C3
Mangole, *island, Indonesia*
123 D4
Manicoré, *Braz.* **69** E4
Manicouagan, Réservoir,
Que., Can. **41** D5
Manīfah, *Saudi Arabia*
113 B4
Manifold, Cape, *Qnsld.,
Austral.* **151** C6
Maniitsoq (Sukkertoppen),
Greenland, Den. **165** E5

Manila, *Philippines*
123 B4
Manily, *Russ.* **95** B6
Manipa, Selat, *Indonesia*
123 D5
Manitoba, *province, Can.*
40 D3
Manitoba, Lake, *Man., Can.*
40 D3
Manizales, *Col.* **68** B2
Manja, *Madagascar*
145 C5
Manjimup, *W. Austral.,
Austral.* **148** E2
Mannar, Gulf of, *India, Sri
Lanka* **117** E4
Manono, *Dem. Rep. of the
Congo* **143** C4
Manp'o, *N. Kor.* **120** B2
Mansa, *Zambia* **143** D4
Mansel Island, *Nunavut,
Can.* **41** C4
Manta, *Ecua.* **68** C1
Manyara, Lake, *Tanzania*
143 B5
Manzanillo, *Cuba* **50** D3
Manzanillo, *Mex.* **48** C2
Mao, *Chad* **139** D5
Mapai, *Mozambique*
145 C4
Mapimí, Bolsón de, *Mex.*
31 D2
Mapuera, *river, Braz.*
69 C5
Maputo, *Mozambique*
145 D4
Maputo, Baía de,
Mozambique **145** D4
Maqat, *Kaz.* **114** B2
Marabá, *Braz.* **71** B4
Marāgheh, *Iran* **111** B4
Marahuaca, Cerro, *Venez.*
69 C4
Marajó, Baía de, *Braz.*
71 A5

Marajó, Ilha de, *Braz.*
71 A4
Marajó Island, *Braz.* **58** B4
Maralal, *Kenya* **143** A6
Marambio, *research station,
Antarctica* **166** A1
Marañón, *river, Peru*
68 D2
Marble Bar, *W. Austral.,
Austral.* **148** B2
Mar Chiquita, Laguna, *Arg.*
72 B3
Mar del Plata, *Arg.* **72** C4
Mardin, *Turk.* **110** B3
Margarita, Isla de, *Venez.*
69 A4
Margarita Island, *Venez.*
58 A4
Margherita Peak, *Dem.
Rep. of the Congo, Uganda*
143 B4
Mariana Islands, *U.S.*
101 C6
Marías, Islas, *Mex.* **48** C2
Marías Islands, *Mex.*
31 E2
Maribor, *Slov.* **92** B2
Maridi, *S. Sudan* **141** E2
Marie Byrd Land,
Antarctica **166** D3
Marie-Galante, *island,
Guadeloupe, Fr.* **52** B4
Mariental, *Namibia*
144 C2
Marigot, *St. Martin, Fr.*
52 A3
Marir, Gezâir (Mirear),
Egypt **112** C1
Mariscal Estigarribia,
Parag. **70** D3
Mariupol', *Ukr.* **93** A6
Marka (Merca), *Somalia*
141 E4
Markala, *Mali* **138** D2
Marmagao, *India* **116** D3
Marmara, Sea of, *Turk.*
79 E4
Marmara Denizi, *Turk.*
110 A1
Maroantsetra, *Madagascar*
145 B6
Maromokotro, *peak,
Madagascar* **145** B6

Maroua, *Cameroon*
139 D5

Marovoay, *Madagascar*
145 B6

Marquesas Islands, *Fr. Polynesia, Fr.* 161 C6

Marra, Jebel, *Sudan*
141 D1

Marrakech, *Mor.* 138 A2

Marree, *S. Austral., Austral.*
149 D4

Marromeu, *Mozambique*
145 B4

Marrupa, *Mozambique*
145 A4

Marsabit, *Kenya* 143 A6

Marseille, *Fr.* 89 D5

Marshall Islands, *Oceania*
160 B3

Martaban, Gulf of, *Myanmar* 117 D6

Martapura, *Indonesia*
122 D3

Martinique, *possession, Fr.*
52 C4

Martinique Passage, *Dominica, Martinique*
52 C4

Mary, *Turkm.* 114 E3

Maryborough, *Qnsld., Austral.* 149 C6

Maryland, *state, U.S.*
43 C6

Mary's Harbour, *Nfld. & Lab., Can.* 41 C6

Marzo, Cabo, *Col.* 68 B1

Marzūq, Şaḥrā', *Lib.*
139 B5

Masai Steppe, *Tanzania*
143 C6

Masan, *S. Kor.* 120 D2

Masasi, *Tanzania* 143 D6

Masbate, *island, Philippines*
123 B4

Masbate, *Philippines*
123 B4

Maseru, *Lesotho* 144 D3

Mashhad, *Iran* 111 B6

Masira see Maşīrah, Jazīrat, *Oman* 113 C6

Masira, Gulf of, *Oman*
100 D2

Maşīrah, Jazīrat (Masira), *Oman* 113 C6

Masjed Soleymān, *Iran*
111 C5

Masqaţ (Muscat), *Oman*
113 C6

Massachusetts, *state, U.S.*
43 B6

Massangena, *Mozambique*
145 C4

Massawa see Mits'iwa, *Eritrea* 140 C4

Massif Central, *mountains, Fr.* 89 D4

Masson Range, *Antarctica*
167 B5

Masvingo, *Zimb.* 144 C3

Matadi, *Dem. Rep. of the Congo* 142 C1

Matamoros, *Mex.* 48 B3

Matanzas, *Cuba* 50 C2

Matarani, *Peru* 70 D2

Matay, *Kaz.* 115 C5

Mathew Town, *Bahamas*
51 C4

Mato Grosso see Vila Bela da Santíssima Trindade, *Braz.* 70 C3

Mato Grosso, Planalto do, *Braz.* 70 C3

Mato Grosso Plateau, *Braz.*
58 C3

Mátra, *peak, Hung.* 92 A3

Maţraḥ, *Oman* 113 C5

Matsue, *Japan* 121 D4

Matsumoto, *Japan*
121 D5

Matsuyama, *Japan*
121 D4

Matterhorn, *peak, It., Switz.*
89 D5

Maturín, *Venez.* 69 A4

Mauá, *Mozambique*
145 A4

Maués, *river, Braz.* 70 B3

Maui, *island, Hawai'i, U.S.*
45 E4

Maun, *Botswana* 144 C2

Mauna Kea, *peak, Hawai'i, U.S.* 45 F5

Mauna Loa, *peak, Hawai'i, U.S.* 45 F5

Maunalua Bay, *Hawai'i, U.S.*
45 E3

Maurice, Lake, *S. Austral., Austral.* 150 D3

Mauritania, *Af.* 126 B1

Mauritania, *region, Mauritania, W. Sahara*
128 B2

Maury Bay, *Antarctica*
167 E5

Mavinga, *Angola* 144 B2

Mawlamyine, *Myanmar*
117 D6

Mawson, *research station, Antarctica* 167 B5

Maxixe, *Mozambique*
145 C4

Mayaguana Island, *Bahamas* 51 C4

Mayaguana Passage, *Bahamas* 51 C4

Maydī, *Yemen* 112 D2

Mayotte, *possession, Fr.*
145 A6

May Pen, *Jam.* 50 D3

Mayqayyn, *Kaz.* 115 A5

Mayumba, *Gabon* 142 B1

Mazabuka, *Zambia*
144 B3

Mazar-e Sharif, *Afghan.*
116 A2

Mazatlán, *Mex.* 48 B2

Mazyr, *Belarus* 91 E5

Mbabane, *Swaziland*
145 D4

Mbala (Abercorn), *Zambia*
143 C4

Mbandaka (Coquilhatville), *Dem. Rep. of the Congo*
142 B2

Mbanza-Ngungu, *Dem. Rep. of the Congo* 142 C2

Mbarara, *Uganda* 143 B4

Mbeya, *Tanzania* 143 C5

Mbour, *Senegal* 138 D1

Mbout, *Mauritania*
138 D2

Mbuji- Mayi (Bakwanga), *Dem. Rep. of the Congo*
142 C3

McAllen, *Tex., U.S.* 48 B3

McGrath, *Alas., U.S.*
44 B3

McK-Min

McKinley, Mount (Denali), *Alas., U.S.* **44** B3

M'Clintock Channel, *Can.* **164** E3

M'Clure Strait, *N.W.T., Can.* **40** A3

McMurdo, *research station, Antarctica* **167** D4

Mdennah, *region, Alg., Mali, Mauritania* **138** B2

Mecca *see* Makkah, *Saudi Arabia* **112** C2

Mecula, *Mozambique* **145** A4

Medan, *Indonesia* **122** CI

Médéa, *Alg.* **89** F4

Medellín, *Col.* **68** B2

Medford, *Oreg., U.S.* **42** BI

Medicine Hat, *Alberta, Can.* **40** D2

Medina *see* Al Madīnah, *Saudi Arabia* **112** B2

Mediterranean Sea, *Af., Asia, Eur.* **78** E2

Medvezh'yegorsk, *Russ.* **90** C5

Meekatharra, *W. Austral., Austral.* **148** C2

Mēga, *Eth.* **141** E3

Meihekou, *China* **120** AI

Mejillones, *Chile* **70** E2

Mejillones del Sur, Bahía de, *Chile* **70** D2

Mek'elē, *Eth.* **141** D3

Meknès, *Mor.* **138** A3

Mekong *see* Lancang, *river, Asia* **99** D4

Mekong River Delta, *Vietnam* **122** B2

Melanesia, *islands, Pacific Oc.* **160** B2

Melbourne, *Vic., Austral.* **149** E5

Melekeok, *Palau* **123** C5

Melfort, *Sask., Can.* **40** D3

Melilla, *Sp.* **89** F3

Melitopol', *Ukr.* **93** A6

Melut, *S. Sudan* **141** D2

Melville Island, *Can.* **40** A3

Melville Island, *N. Terr., Austral.* **150** A3

Melville Peninsula, *Nunavut, Can.* **41** B4

Memba, *Mozambique* **145** B5

Memphis, *Tenn., U.S.* **43** C4

Ménaka, *Mali* **138** D3

Mendocino, Cape, *U.S.* **30** CI

Mendoza, *Arg.* **72** B2

Menongue, *Angola* **142** E2

Menorca (Minorca), *island, Sp.* **89** E4

Mentawai, Kepulauan, *Indonesia* **122** DI

Merauke, *Indonesia* **123** E6

Merca *see* Marka, *Somalia* **141** E4

Mercedes, *Arg.* **72** A4

Meredith, Cape, *Falkland Is.* **73** F3

Mereeg, *Somalia* **141** E5

Mergui Archipelago, *Myanmar* **117** D6

Mérida, *Mex.* **49** C4

Mérida, *Venez.* **68** A2

Mérida, Cordillera de, *Venez.* **68** B2

Merir, *island, Palau* **123** C5

Merowe, *Sudan* **140** C2

Merredin, *W. Austral., Austral.* **148** D2

Merzifon, *Turk.* **93** C6

Mesa Verde National Park, *U.S.* **46** C2

Mesopotamia, *region, Iraq, Syr.* **100** C2

Messina, *It.* **92** D2

Messina, Stretto di, *It.* **92** D2

Meta, *river, Col.* **68** B3

Meta Incognita Peninsula, *Nunavut, Can.* **41** B5

Meuse, *river, Fr.* **88** C4

Mexicali, *Mex.* **48** AI

Mexico, *N. Amer.* **29** E2

Mexico, Gulf of, *N. Amer.* **31** E3

Mexico City, *Mex.* **48** C3

Meymaneh, *Afghan.* **114** E3

Mezen', *Russ.* **77** A5

Mezen' Bay, *Russ.* **79** A5

Miami, *Fla., U.S.* **43** E5

Miami Beach, *Fla., U.S.* **50** B2

Michigan, *state, U.S.* **43** B5

Michigan, Lake, *U.S.* **43** B4

Micronesia, *islands, Pacific Oc.* **160** D2

Middelburg, *S. Af.* **144** E3

Middle Andaman, *island, India* **117** D5

Middlesbrough, *U.K.* **88** B3

Midway Islands, *possession, U.S.* **161** A4

Miho Wan, *Japan* **121** D4

Mikhaiylovskiy, *Russ.* **115** A5

Mikhaylova, *Russ.* **94** B3

Milan *see* Milano, *It.* **92** BI

Milano (Milan), *It.* **92** BI

Mildura, *Vic., Austral.* **149** E4

Miles City, *Mont., U.S.* **42** B3

Mililani Town, *Hawai'i, U.S.* **45** D3

Miller Range, *Antarctica* **167** D4

Mill Island, *Antarctica* **167** D6

Milwaukee, *Wis., U.S.* **43** B4

Mīnāb, *Iran* **111** E6

Minatitlán, *Mex.* **49** D4

Mindanao, *island, Philippines* **123** C4

Mindoro, *island, Philippines* **123** B4

Minfeng (Niya), *China* **118** C2

Mingan, *Que., Can.* **41** D5

Minigwal, Lake, *W. Austral., Austral.* **150** D2

Minneapolis, *Minn., U.S.* **43** B4

Minnesota, *state, U.S.*
43 B4
Minorca *see* Menorca,
island, Sp. 89 E4
Minot, *N. Dak., U.S.* 42 A3
Minsk, *Belarus* 91 E4
Minxian, *China* 119 C4
Mirear *see* Marir, Gezâir,
Egypt 112 C1
Miri, *Malaysia* 122 C3
Mirik *see* Timiris, Cap,
Mauritania 138 C1
Mirim, Lagoa, *Braz.* 72 B5
Mīrjāveh, *Iran* 113 A6
Mirnyy, *research station,
Antarctica* 167 C6
Mirnyy, *Russ.* 95 C4
Miskitos, Cayos, *Nicar.*
49 D5
Misool, *island, Indonesia*
123 D5
Miṣrātah, *Lib.* 139 A5
Mississippi, *river, U.S.*
43 D4
Mississippi, *state, U.S.*
43 D4
Mississippi River Delta,
U.S. 31 D3
Missoula, *Mont., U.S.*
42 B2
Missouri, *river, U.S.* 43 C4
Missouri, *state, U.S.* 43 C4
Mitau *see* Jelgava, *Latv.*
91 D4
Mitchell, *river, Qnsld.,
Austral.* 151 B5
Mitilíni, *Gr.* 93 D4
Mito, *Japan* 121 C6
Mits'iwa (Massawa),
Eritrea 140 C4
Mitú, *Col.* 68 C3
Mitumba Mountains,
Dem. Rep. of the Congo
143 D4
Miyako Jima, *Japan*
119 D6
Miyazaki, *Japan* 121 E4
Moa, *island, Indonesia*
123 E5
Moanda, *Gabon* 142 B1
Mobile, *Ala., U.S.* 43 D4
Moçambique, *Mozambique*
145 B5

Mochudi, *Botswana*
144 C3
Mocuba, *Mozambique*
145 B4
Modica, *It.* 92 E2
Mogadishu *see* Muqdisho,
Somalia 141 E5
Mogok, *Myanmar* 117 C6
Mohéli *see* Mwali, *island,
Comoros* 145 A5
Mo i Rana, *Nor.* 90 B2
Mojave Desert, *Calif., U.S.*
42 C1
Mokpo, *S. Kor.* 120 E2
Moldova, *Eur.* 77 D4
Molepolole, *Botswana*
144 C3
Moloa'a Bay, *Hawai'i, U.S.*
45 D2
Moloka'i, *island, Hawai'i,
U.S.* 45 E3
Moluccas, *islands, Indonesia*
123 D5
Molucca Sea, *Indonesia*
123 D4
Moma, *Mozambique*
145 B5
Mombasa, *Kenya* 143 C6
Mona, Isla, *P.R., U.S.*
51 D6
Monaco, *Eur.* 76 D3
Mona Passage, *Dom. Rep.,
P.R.* 51 D6
Monchegorsk, *Russ.*
90 A4
Monclova, *Mex.* 48 B3
Mondah, Baie de, *Eq.
Guinea, Gabon* 142 B1
Mongers Lake, *W. Austral.,
Austral.* 150 D1
Mongo, *Chad* 139 D5
Mongolia, *Asia* 99 C4
Mongolian Plateau, *China,
Mongolia* 101 C4
Mongu, *Zambia* 142 E3
Monrovia, *Liberia* 138 E2
Montana, *state, U.S.*
42 B2
Monte Alegre, *Braz.*
71 A4
Monte Cristi, *Dom. Rep.*
51 D5
Montego Bay, *Jam.* 50 D3

Montego Bay, *Jam.* 50 D3
Monte Lindo, *river, Parag.*
70 D3
Montenegro, *Eur.* 76 D3
Monterey Bay, *U.S.* 31 D1
Montería, *Col.* 68 A2
Monterrey, *Mex.* 48 B3
Montes Claros, *Braz.*
71 C5
Montevideo, *Uru.* 72 B4
Montgomery, *Ala., U.S.*
43 D5
Montpelier, *Vt., U.S.*
43 B6
Montréal, *Que., Can.*
41 E5
Montserrat, *possession,
U.K.* 52 B3
Monywa, *Myanmar*
117 C6
Moore, Lake, *W. Austral.,
Austral.* 150 D2
Moose Jaw, *Sask., Can.*
40 D2
Moosonee, *Ont., Can.*
41 D4
Mopti, *Mali* 138 D3
Moquegua, *Peru* 70 D2
Moradabad, *India* 117 B4
Morant Point, *Jam.* 50 D3
Morawhanna, *Guyana*
69 B5
Moray Firth, *U.K.* 88 A3
Moree, *N.S.W., Austral.*
149 D6
Moreton Island, *Qnsld.,
Austral.* 151 D6
Morioka, *Japan* 121 C6
Mornington Island, *Qnsld.,
Austral.* 151 B4
Morocco, *Af.* 126 B1
Morogoro, *Tanzania*
143 C6
Moro Gulf, *Philippines*
123 C4
Morón, *Cuba* 50 C2
Mörön, *Mongolia* 118 A3
Morondava, *Madagascar*
145 C5
Moroni, *Comoros* 145 A5
Morotai, *island, Indonesia*
123 D5

223

Morris Jesup, Cape,
Greenland, Den. **30** A3
Morris Jesup, Kap,
Greenland, Den. **28** A3
Morro de Môco, *peak,*
Angola **142** D2
Mortlock Islands, *F.S.M.*
160 B2
Moruga, *Trin. & Tobago*
53 F4
Moscow *see* Moskva, *Russ.*
94 C1
Moscow University
Ice Shelf, *Antarctica*
167 D5
Moshi, *Tanzania* **143** B6
Mosjøen, *Nor.* **90** B2
Moskva (Moscow), *Russ.*
94 C1
Mosquito Coast, *Nicar.*
31 E4
Mosquitos, Gulf of, *Pan.*
31 F4
Mossaka, *Congo* **142** B2
Mosselbaai (Mossel Bay),
S. Af. **144** E2
Mossel Bay, *S. Af.* **129** F3
Mossel Bay *see* Mosselbaai,
S. Af. **144** E2
Mossendjo, *Congo*
142 B1
Mossoró, *Braz.* **71** B6
Mostaganem, *Alg.* **89** F3
Mostar, *Bosn. & Herzg.*
92 C2
Mosul *see* Al Mawşil, *Iraq*
111 B4
Motul, *Mex.* **49** C4
Mouchoir Passage, *Turks &
Caicos Is., U.K.* **51** C5
Mould Bay, *Can.* **164** D3
Moundou, *Chad* **139** E5
Mountain Nile, *river, S.
Sudan* **128** C4
Mount Gambier, *S. Austral.,
Austral.* **149** E4
Mount Isa, *Qnsld., Austral.*
149 B4
Mount Lofty Ranges, *S.
Austral., Austral.* **151** E4
Mount Magnet, *W. Austral.,
Austral.* **148** D2

Mount Morgan, *Qnsld.,
Austral.* **149** C6
Mount Rainier National
Park, *U.S.* **46** A1
Mowdok Mual, *peak,
Bangladesh, Myanmar*
117 C5
Moyynqum, *desert, Kaz.*
115 C4
Moyynqum, *Kaz.* **115** C4
Moyynty, *Kaz.* **115** C4
Mozambique, *Af.* **127** E4
Mozambique Channel,
Madagascar, Mozambique
145 C5
Mpanda, *Tanzania* **143** C5
Mpika, *Zambia* **143** D5
Mtwara, *Tanzania* **143** D6
Muchinga Mountains,
Zambia **143** D4
Muconda, *Angola* **144** A2
Mudanjiang, *China*
119 B6
Mueda, *Mozambique*
145 A5
Mufulira, *Zambia* **143** D4
Mughalzhar Taūy, *hills, Kaz.*
114 B2
Muğla, *Turk.* **110** B1
Muḩammad, Râs, *Egypt*
140 B3
Muhammad Qol, *Sudan*
140 C3
Muhembo, *Botswana*
144 B2
Mui Bai Bung, *cape,
Vietnam* **122** C2
Mulanje Mountains, *Malawi*
143 E5
Mulhacén, *peak, Sp.* **89** F3
Mullewa, *W. Austral.,
Austral.* **148** D1
Multan, *Pak.* **116** B3
Mumbai (Bombay), *India*
116 C3
Mumra, *Russ.* **114** C1
Muna, *island, Indonesia*
123 E4
München (Munich), *Ger.*
92 A2
Munich *see* München, *Ger.*
92 A2
Münster, *Ger.* **91** E1

Muonio, *Fin.* **90** A3
Muqdisho (Mogadishu),
Somalia **141** E5
Murchison, *river, W.
Austral., Austral.* **150** D1
Murcia, *Sp.* **89** F3
Mureş, *river, Rom.* **92** B3
Murgab, *Taj.* **115** E5
Murmansk, *Russ.* **94** B2
Murray, *river, Austral.*
151 E4
Murray River Basin,
Austral. **151** E5
Murrumbidgee, *river,
N.S.W., Austral.* **151** E5
Muş, *Turk.* **110** B3
Mûsa, Gebel (Mount
Sinai), *Egypt* **140** B3
Musan, *N. Kor.* **120** A3
Muscat *see* Masqaţ, *Oman*
113 C6
Musgrave Ranges, *S.
Austral., Austral.* **150** C3
Musina, *S. Af.* **144** C3
Mus Khaya, Gora, *Russ.*
95 C5
Musoma, *Tanzania*
143 B5
Mustique, *island, St.
Vincent & the Grenadines*
53 E4
Musudan, *cape, N. Kor.*
120 B3
Mûţ, *Egypt* **139** B6
Mutare, *Mozambique*
145 B4
Muting, *Indonesia* **123** E6
Mutoray, *Russ.* **95** C4
Mutsu Wan, *Japan*
121 B6
Mŭynoq, *Uzb.* **114** C2
Muztag, *peak, China*
117 A4
Muztag Feng, *peak, China*
118 C2
Mwali (Mohéli), *island,
Comoros* **145** A5
Mwanza, *Tanzania* **143** B5
Mweka, *Dem. Rep. of the
Congo* **142** C3
Mwene-Ditu, *Dem. Rep. of
the Congo* **142** C3

Mweru, Lake, *Dem. Rep.
   of the Congo, Zambia*
   143 D4
Mwinilunga, *Zambia*
   144 A3
Myanmar (Burma), *Asia*
   99 D4
Myeik, *Myanmar* **117** D6
Myitkyinā, *Myanmar*
   117 B6
Mysore, *India* **116** D3
Mys Zhelaniya, *Russ.*
   165 A4
Mytilíni *see Lésvos, island,
   Gr.* **93** D4
Mzuzu, *Malawi* **143** D5

N

Nā'ālehu, *Hawai'i, U.S.*
   45 F5
Nabeda, Mont, *Congo*
   142 A2
Nabeul, *Tun.* **92** E1
Nabī Shu'ayb, Jabal an,
   Yemen **112** E3
Nacala, *Mozambique*
   145 B5
Nafūd ad Daḥy, *region,
   Saudi Arabia* **112** C3
Nafūsah, Jabal, *Lib.*
   139 A4
Nagano, *Japan* **121** C5
Nagasaki, *Japan* **121** D4
Nagēlē, *Eth.* **141** E4
Nagorno-Karabakh, *region,
   Azerb.* **111** B4
Nagoya, *Japan* **121** D5
Nagpur, *India* **117** C4
Naha, *Japan* **119** D6
Nain, *Nfld. & Lab., Can.*
   41 C5
Nairobi, *Kenya* **143** B6
Najaf *see* An Najaf, *Iraq*
   111 D4
Najafābād, *Iran* **111** C5
Najin *see* Rajin, *N. Kor.*
   120 A3
Najrān, *region, Saudi Arabia*
   112 D3
Najrān, *Saudi Arabia*
   112 D3

Nakano Shima, *Japan*
   121 E4
Nakhodka, *Russ.* **121** B5
Nakhon Pathom, *Thai.*
   122 B1
Nakhon Ratchasima, *Thai.*
   122 B2
Nakhon Sawan, *Thai.*
   122 B1
Nakhon Si Thammarat,
   Thai. **122** C1
Nakuru, *Kenya* **143** B5
Namangan, *Uzb.* **115** D4
Nambour, *Qnsld., Austral.*
   149 C6
Nam Dinh, *Vietnam*
   122 A2
Namib Desert, *Namibia*
   144 C1
Namibe, *Angola* **142** E1
Namibia, *Af.* **127** E3
Namies, *S. Af.* **144** D2
Namp'o, *N. Kor.* **120** C1
Nampula, *Mozambique*
   145 B5
Namsos, *Nor.* **90** B2
Namuli, *peak, Mozambique*
   145 B4
Namutoni, *Namibia*
   144 B2
Namwon, *S. Kor.* **120** D2
Nanam, *N. Kor.* **120** A3
Nanchang, *China* **119** D5
Nancy, *Fr.* **88** C5
Nanded, *India* **116** C3
Nanga Parbat, *peak, Pak.*
   115 E5
Nangnim-sanmaek, *N. Kor.*
   120 B2
Nanjing, *China* **119** C5
Nanning, *China* **119** E4
Nanping, *China* **119** D5
Nansei Shotō (Ryukyu
   Islands), *Japan* **119** D6
Nansen Sound, *Nunavut,
   Can.* **41** A6
Nantes, *Fr.* **89** D3
Nantulo, *Mozambique*
   145 A5
Nānu'alele Point, *Hawai'i,
   U.S.* **45** E4
Nao, Cabo de la, *Sp.*
   89 F4

Nā Pali Coast, *Hawai'i, U.S.*
   45 D1
Naples *see* Napoli, *It.*
   92 C2
Napo, *river, Ecua., Peru*
   68 D2
Napoli (Naples), *It.* **92** C2
Napoli, Golfo di, *It.* **92** C2
Nara, *Mali* **138** D2
Narayanganj, *Bangladesh*
   117 C5
Narbonne, *Fr.* **89** E4
Nares Strait, *Can.,
   Greenland* **41** A6
Naricual, *Venez.* **53** F1
Narinda, Baie de,
   Madagascar **145** B6
Narodnaya, Gora, *Russ.*
   79 A5
Narsarsuaq, *Greenland,
   Den.* **165** E6
Narva, *Est.* **91** D4
Narvik, *Nor.* **90** A3
Nar'yan Mar, *Russ.*
   165 A5
Naryn, *Kyrg.* **115** D5
Nasca, *Peru* **70** C1
Nashville, *Tenn., U.S.*
   43 C5
Nasiriyah *see* An Nāşirīyah,
   Iraq **111** D4
Nassau, *Bahamas* **50** B3
Nasser, Lake, *Egypt*
   140 B2
Nata, *Botswana* **144** C3
Natal, *Braz.* **71** B6
Natara, *Russ.* **95** C4
Natuna Besar, Kepulauan,
   Indonesia **122** C2
Natuna Selatan,
   Kepulauan, *Indonesia*
   122 C2
Naturaliste, Cape, *W.
   Austral., Austral.* **150** E1
Nauru, *Oceania* **160** B3
Navarin, Mys, *Russ.*
   95 A6
Navarino, Isla, *Chile*
   73 F2
Navoiy, *Uzb.* **114** D3
Navojoa, *Mex.* **48** B2
Nāwiliwili Bay, *Hawai'i, U.S.*
   45 D1

Niger River Delta, *Nigeria*
128 C2

Niigata, *Japan* **121** C5

Ni'ihau, *island, Hawai'i, U.S.*
45 D1

Nikel', *Russ.* **90** A4

Nikšić, *Montenegro* **92** C3

Nîl, Bahr el (Nile), *Af.*
140 B2

Nile *see* Nîl, Bahr el, *Af.*
140 B2

Nile River Delta, *Egypt*
128 B4

Nîmes, *Fr.* **89** D4

Nine Degree Channel,
India **116** E2

Ninfas, Punta, *Arg.* **73** D3

Ningbo, *China* **119** D5

Nioro du Sahel, *Mali*
138 D2

Nipe, Bahía de, *Cuba*
50 C3

Nipigon, Lake, *Ont., Can.*
41 D4

Niš, *Serb.* **92** C3

Niterói, *Braz.* **71** D5

Niue, *possession, N.Z.*
161 C4

Niya *see* Minfeng, *China*
118 C2

Nizhnevartovsk, *Russ.*
94 C3

Nizhneyansk, *Russ.* **95** B5

Nizhniy Novgorod, *Russ.*
94 C1

Nizhyn, *Ukr.* **91** F5

Njazidja (Grande Comore),
island, Comoros **145** A5

Njombe, *Tanzania* **143** D5

Nkongsamba, *Cameroon*
142 A1

Noatak, *river, Alas., U.S.*
44 A3

Nogales, *Ariz., U.S.* **48** A1

Nogales, *Mex.* **48** A1

Noginsk, *Russ.* **94** C3

Nok Kundi, *Pak.* **116** B2

Nola, *Cen. Af. Rep.* **142** A2

Noma Misaki, *Japan*
121 E4

Nome, *Alas., U.S.* **44** B2

Nord, *research station,*
Greenland, Den. **165** C4

Nordfjord, *bay, Nor.*
90 C1

Nordkapp, *cape, Nor.*
90 A4

Nordostrundingen, *cape,*
Greenland, Den. **165** C4

Norfolk, *Va., U.S.* **43** C6

Noril'sk, *Russ.* **94** C3

Normanton, *Qnsld., Austral.*
149 B5

Norman Wells, *N.W.T., Can.*
40 B2

Norrköping, *Sw.* **91** D2

Norseman, *W. Austral.,*
Austral. **148** D2

Norte, Cabo, *Braz.* **69** C6

Norte, Canal do, *Braz.*
71 A4

Norte, Punta, *Arg.* **72** C4

North, Cape, *Braz.* **58** B4

North Andaman, *island,*
India **117** D5

North Aral Sea, *Kaz.*
114 C3

North Battleford, *Sask.,*
Can. **40** D2

North Bay, *Ont., Can.*
41 E4

North Cape *see* Horn, *Ice.*
78 A2

North Cape, *N.Z.* **160** E3

North Cape, *Nor.* **79** A4

North Carolina, *state, U.S.*
43 C5

North Cascades National
Park, *U.S.* **46** A1

North China Plain, *China*
101 C4

North Dakota, *state, U.S.*
42 B3

Northeast Point, *Jam.*
50 D3

Northern Cyprus, *Cyprus*
93 E6

Northern European Plain,
Eur. **78** C3

Northern Mariana Islands,
possession, U.S. **160** A2

Northern Territory,
Austral. **148** B3

North Geomagnetic Pole,
Can. **165** D4

North Ireland, *region, U.K.*
88 B2

North Island, *N.Z.* **160** E3

North Korea, *Asia* **99** C5

North Land, *Russ.* **101** A4

North Magnetic Pole,
Arctic Oc. **164** C3

North Negril Point, *Jam.*
50 D3

North Pole, *Arctic Oc.*
165 C4

North Saskatchewan, *river,*
Can. **40** D2

North Sea, *Eur.* **78** B2

North Slope, *Alas., U.S.*
44 A3

North Stradbroke Island,
Qnsld., Austral. **151** D6

North West Basin, *W.*
Austral., Austral. **150** C1

North West Cape, *W.*
Austral., Austral. **150** C1

Northwest Providence
Channel, *Bahamas*
50 A3

Northwest Territories,
Can. **40** B2

Norton, *Zimb.* **144** B3

Norton Sound, *Alas., U.S.*
44 B2

Norway, *Eur.* **76** B3

Norway House, *Man., Can.*
40 D3

Norwegian Sea, *Atl. Oc.*
165 C6

Norwich, *U.K.* **88** B4

Nouadhibou (Port
Étienne), *Mauritania*
138 C1

Nouakchott, *Mauritania*
138 C1

Nouméa, *New Caledonia, Fr.*
160 D3

Nova Friburgo, *Braz.*
71 D5

Nova Iguaçu, *Braz.* **71** D5

Nova Scotia, *province, Can.*
41 E6

Novaya Zemlya, *Russ.*
94 B3

Novaya Zemlya, *islands,*
Russ. **100** A3

Novi Sad, *Serb.* **92** B3

Novohrad-Volyns'kyy, *Ukr.*
91 F4
Novokuznetsk, *Russ.*
94 D3
Novolazarevskaya, *research*
station, Antarctica
167 A4
Novorossiysk, *Russ.* 93 B6
Novosibirsk, *Russ.* 94 D3
Novosibirskiye Ostrova
(New Siberian Islands),
Russ. 164 B2
Novozybkov, *Russ.* 91 E5
Novyy Uoyan, *Russ.*
95 D4
Novyy Urengoy, *Russ.*
94 C3
Nowshāk, *peak, Afghan.,*
Pak. 116 A3
Nowy Sącz, *Pol.* 91 F3
Nsanje (Port Herald),
Malawi 145 B4
Nu, *river, China* 118 D3
Nubia, Lake, *Sudan*
140 C2
Nubian Desert, *Sudan*
140 C2
Nuestra Señora, Bahía,
Chile 70 E2
Nueva Gerona, *Cuba*
50 C1
Nuevo, Golfo, *Arg.* 73 D3
Nuevo Casas Grandes,
Mex. 48 A2
Nuevo Laredo, *Mex.*
48 B3
Nuku'alofa, *Tonga*
161 D4
Nukus, *Uzb.* 114 D3
Nullarbor Plain, *Austral.*
150 D3
Nunap Isua (Kap Farvel),
Greenland, Den. 28 B5
Nunavut, *territory, Can.*
40 B3
Nunivak Island, *Alas., U.S.*
44 B2
Nuoro, *It.* 92 C1
Nürnberg, *Ger.* 91 F1
Nushagak Peninsula, *Alas.,*
U.S. 44 C2
Nuuk (Godthåb),
Greenland, Den. 165 E5

Nyagan', *Russ.* 77 A6
Nyainqêntanglha Shan,
China 118 D2
Nyala, *Sudan* 141 D1
Nyasa, Lake *see*
Malawi, Lake, *Malawi,*
Mozambique, Tanzania
143 D5
Nyima, *China* 118 C2
Nyong, *river, Cameroon*
142 A1
Nyūdō Zaki, *cape, Japan*
121 C6
Nzega, *Tanzania* 143 C5
Nzérékoré, *Guinea*
138 E2
N'zeto, *Angola* 142 C1
Nzwani (Anjouan), *island,*
Comoros 145 A5

O

Oahe, Lake, *U.S.* 30 C3
O'ahu, *island, Hawai'i, U.S.*
45 E2
Oakland, *Calif., U.S.* 42 C1
Oaxaca, *Mex.* 48 D3
Ob', *river, Russ.* 100 B3
Ob, Gulf of, *Russ.* 100 B3
Obi, *island, Indonesia*
123 D5
Óbidos, *Braz.* 69 D5
Obihiro, *Japan* 121 B6
Obo, *Cen. Af. Rep.* 139 E6
Obock, *Djibouti* 141 E3
Obskaya Guba, *Russ.*
94 C3
Occidental, Cordillera, *S.*
Amer. 68 C1
Ocoa, Bahía de, *Dom. Rep.*
51 D5
Odense, *Den.* 91 E1
Oder, *river, Ger., Pol.*
91 E2
Odesa, *Ukr.* 93 B5
Odessa, *Tex., U.S.* 42 D3
Odra, *river, Ger., Pol.*
91 F2
Ogadēn, *region, Eth.*
141 E4
Ogilvie Mountains, *Yukon,*
Can. 44 B4

Ogoki, *Ont., Can.* 41 D4
Ohio, *river, U.S.* 43 C5
Ohio, *state, U.S.* 43 C5
Ohridsko Jezero, *Alban.,*
Maced. 92 C3
Oiapoque *see* Oyapock,
river, Braz. 69 C6
Oiapoque, *Braz.* 69 B6
Ōita, *Japan* 121 D4
Okahandja, *Namibia*
144 C2
Okavango, *river, Angola,*
Botswana, Namibia
144 B2
Okavango Delta, *Botswana*
144 B2
Okeechobee, Lake, *Fla., U.S.*
43 E5
Okha, *Russ.* 95 C6
Okhotsk, *Russ.* 95 C5
Okhotsk, Sea of, *Japan,*
Russ. 101 B5
Okinawa, *island, Japan*
119 D6
Oki Shotō, *Japan* 121 D4
Oklahoma, *state, U.S.*
42 D3
Oklahoma City, *Okla., U.S.*
42 C3
Okp'yŏng, *N. Kor.* 120 B2
Oktyabr'sk, *Kaz.* 114 B2
Okushiri Tō, *Japan*
121 B5
Öland, *island, Sw.* 91 D2
Olavarría, *Arg.* 72 C4
Olbia, *It.* 92 C1
Old Bahama Channel, *Cuba*
50 C3
Old Crow, *Yukon, Can.*
40 A2
Olekminsk, *Russ.* 95 C5
Olenekskiy Zaliv, *Russ.*
164 A3
Olga, Mount (Kata Tjuṭa),
N. Terr., Austral. 150 C3
Ölgiy, *Mongolia* 118 A3
Ólimbos (Olympus), *peak,*
Gr. 92 D3
Olomouc, *Czech Rep.*
92 A3
Olsztyn, *Pol.* 91 E3
Olt, *river, Rom.* 93 B4

Olympia, *Wash., U.S.*
42 AI

Olympic National Park, *U.S.*
46 AI

Olympus *see* Ólimbos, *peak,
Gr.* **92** D3

Olyutorskiy, Mys, *Russ.*
95 A6

Omaha, *Nebr., U.S.* **42** C3

Oman, *Asia* **98** D2

Oman, Gulf of, *Iran, Oman,
U.A.E.* **113** B5

Omaruru, *Namibia*
144 CI

Omdurman, *Sudan*
140 C2

Ometepec, *Mex.* **48** D3

Omolon, *Russ.* **95** B5

Omsk, *Russ.* **94** D3

Ondjiva, *Angola* **142** E2

Onega, *Russ.* **90** B5

Onega, Lake, *Russ.* **79** B4

Onega Bay, *Russ.* **79** A4

Onezhskaya Guba, *Russ.*
90 B5

Onezhskoye Ozero, *Russ.*
90 C5

Ongjin, *N. Kor.* **120** CI

Onslow, *W. Austral., Austral.*
148 CI

Ontario, *province, Can.*
40 D4

Ontario, Lake, *Can., U.S.*
43 B5

Oodnadatta, *S. Austral.,
Austral.* **149** C4

'Ōpana Point, *Hawai'i, U.S.*
45 E4

Oporto *see* Porto, *Port.*
89 E2

Opuwo, *Namibia* **144** BI

Oradea, *Rom.* **92** B3

Oral, *Kaz.* **114** A2

Oran, *Alg.* **138** A3

Orange, *N.S.W., Austral.*
149 D5

Orange (Oranje), *river,
Lesotho, Namibia, S. Af.*
144 D2

Orange, Cabo, *Braz.*
69 B6

Orange Walk, *Belize*
49 C5

Oranje *see* Orange, *river,
Lesotho, Namibia, S. Af.*
144 D2

Oranjestad, *Aruba, Neth.*
53 DI

Oranjestad, *St. Eustatius,
Neth.* **52** A3

Orcadas, *research station,
Antarctica* **166** A2

Ord, *river, W. Austral.,
Austral.* **150** A3

Ord, Mount, *W. Austral.,
Austral.* **150** B2

Örebro, *Sw.* **91** D2

Oregon, *state, U.S.* **42** BI

Orel, *Russ.* **77** C5

Orenburg, *Russ.* **77** C6

Oriental, Cordillera, *S.
Amer.* **68** C3

Orinoco, *river, Col., Venez.*
69 B4

Orinoco River Delta, *Venez.*
58 A3

Oristano, *It.* **92** DI

Orizaba, Pico de, *Mex.*
31 E3

Orkney Islands, *U.K.*
88 A3

Orlando, *Fla., U.S.* **43** D5

Orléans, *Fr.* **88** C4

Örnsköldsvik, *Sw.* **76** B3

Orsha, *Belarus* **91** E5

Orsk, *Russ.* **77** B6

Orto Surt, *Russ.* **95** C5

Orūmīyeh (Urmia), *Iran*
111 B4

Orūmīyeh, Daryācheh-ye,
Iran **111** B4

Oruro, *Bol.* **70** D2

Ōsaka, *Japan* **121** D5

Ösel *see* Saaremaa, *island,
Est.* **91** D3

Osh, *Kyrg.* **115** D5

Oshakati, *Namibia*
144 BI

Osijek, *Croatia* **92** B3

Öskemen (Ust'
Kamenogorsk), *Kaz.*
115 B6

Oslo, *Nor.* **90** C2

Osorno, *Chile* **72** CI

Ossa, Mount, *Tas., Austral.*
150 E3

Östersund, *Sw.* **90** C2

Ōsumi Kaikyō (Van Diemen
Strait), *Japan* **121** E4

Ōsumi Shotō, *Japan*
121 E4

Otaru, *Japan* **121** B6

Otjiwarongo, *Namibia*
144 C2

Otranto, Strait of, *Alban.,
It.* **92** D3

Ottawa, *Ont., Can.* **41** E5

Otway, Bahía, *Chile* **73** FI

Ouachita Mountains, *U.S.*
31 D3

Ouadane, *Mauritania*
138 C2

Ouagadougou, *Burkina Faso*
138 D3

Ouargla, *Alg.* **139** A4

Ouesso, *Congo* **142** A2

Ouest, Pointe, *Haiti*
51 D4

Oujda, *Mor.* **138** A3

Oulu (Uleåborg), *Fin.*
90 B4

Oulujoki, *river, Fin.* **90** B4

Ounianga Kébir, *Chad*
139 C5

Ourense, *Sp.* **89** E2

Outer Hebrides, *islands,
U.K.* **88** A3

Outjo, *Namibia* **144** CI

Ovalle, *Chile* **72** BI

Oviedo, *Sp.* **89** E2

Owando, *Congo* **142** B2

Oyapock *see* Oiapoque,
river, Fr. Guiana, Fr.
69 C6

Oyem, *Gabon* **142** AI

Øygarden Group,
Antarctica **167** B5

Oymyakon, *Russ.* **95** B5

Ozark Plateau, *U.S.* **43** C4

Ozernoy, Mys, *Russ.*
95 B6

P

Paamiut (Frederikshåb),
Greenland, Den. **41** B6

Paarl, *S. Af.* **144** E2

Pacaraima, Sierra, *Braz.,
Venez.* 69 B4
Pacasmayo, *Peru* 68 El
Pachuca, *Mex.* 48 C3
Padang, *Indonesia* 122 DI
Padlei, *Nunavut, Can.*
40 C3
Paektu-san, *peak, N. Kor.*
120 A2
Pagadian, *Philippines*
123 C4
Pagai Selatan, *island,
Indonesia* 122 DI
Pagai Utara, *island,
Indonesia* 122 DI
Pagnag *see* Amdo, *China*
118 C2
Pago Pago, *Amer. Samoa,
U.S.* 161 C4
Pāhoa, *Hawai'i, U.S.* 45 F5
Pailolo Channel, *Hawai'i,
U.S.* 45 E4
Painter, Mount, *S. Austral.,
Austral.* 151 D4
Paistunturit, *peak, Fin.*
90 A4
Paita, *Peru* 68 DI
Pakaraima Mountains,
Guyana 69 B4
Pakistan, *Asia* 98 D3
Pakxé, *Laos* 122 B2
Pala, *Chad* 139 E5
Palana, *Russ.* 164 BI
Palangkaraya, *Indonesia*
122 D3
Palapye, *Botswana*
144 C3
Palau, *Oceania* 99 D6
Palawan, *island, Philippines*
122 C3
Palembang, *Indonesia*
122 D2
Palermo, *It.* 92 D2
Palikir, *F.S.M.* 160 B2
Palk Strait, *India, Sri Lanka*
117 E4
Palma de Mallorca, *Sp.*
89 E4
Palmas, Cape, *Côte d'Ivoire*
138 E2
Palmeirinhas, Ponta das,
Angola 142 DI

Palmeirinhas Point, *Angola*
129 D3
Palmer, *Alas., U.S.* 44 B3
Palmer, *research station,
Antarctica* 166 BI
Palmer Archipelago,
Antarctica 166 BI
Palmer Land, *Antarctica*
166 B2
Palmyra Atoll, *possession,
U.S.* 161 B4
Palu, *Indonesia* 123 D4
Pamirs, *mountains, Taj.*
115 E5
Pampas, *region, Arg.*
72 C3
Pamplona, *Sp.* 76 D2
Panama, *N. Amer.* 29 F3
Panamá, Golfo de, *Pan.*
29 F4
Panama, Gulf of, *Pan.*
31 F4
Panama, Isthmus of, *Pan.*
31 F4
Panama Canal, *Pan.* 49 E6
Panama City, *Pan.* 49 E6
Panay, *island, Philippines*
123 B4
Panevėžys, *Lith.* 91 E4
Pangani, *river, Tanzania*
143 C6
Pangnirtung, *Nunavut, Can.*
41 B5
Panj, *river, Afghan., Taj.*
115 E4
Panshi, *China* 120 A2
Pantanal, *wetland, Braz.*
70 D3
Pantar, *island, Indonesia*
123 E4
Panzhihua, *China* 118 D3
Papeete, *Fr. Polynesia, Fr.*
161 C5
Papua, Gulf of, *P.N.G.*
160 C2
Papua New Guinea,
Oceania 160 C2
Paracas, Península, *Peru*
56 CI
Paracas Peninsula, *Peru*
58 CI
Paracel Islands, *China*
122 B3

Paraguaná, Península de,
Venez. 68 A3
Paraguaná Peninsula,
Venez. 58 A2
Paraguay, *S. Amer.* 57 D3
Paraguay, *river, S. Amer.*
70 D3
Parakou, *Benin* 138 E3
Paramaribo, *Suriname*
69 B5
Paraná, *Arg.* 72 B4
Paraná, *river, Arg., Braz.,
Parag.* 57 D3
Paraná, *river, Braz.* 71 C5
Paranaguá, *Braz.* 71 E4
Paranaguá, Baía de, *Braz.*
71 E5
Pardo, *river, Braz.* 71 D4
Parepare, *Indonesia*
123 D4
Paria, Gulf of, *Trin. &
Tobago, Venez.* 53 F3
Paria, Península de, *Venez.*
53 F3
Pariñas, Punta, *Peru*
56 BI
Pariñas Point, *Peru* 58 BI
Parintins, *Braz.* 69 D5
Paris, *Fr.* 88 C4
Parnaíba, *river, Braz.*
71 B5
Parnaíba, *Braz.* 71 A6
Pärnu, *Est.* 91 D4
Parry Islands, *Can.* 40 A3
Parsons Range, *N. Terr.,
Austral.* 151 A4
Paru, *river, Braz.* 69 C6
Paryang, *China* 118 D2
Pasley, Cape, *Austral.*
160 DI
Pasni, *Pak.* 116 B2
Passau, *Ger.* 92 A2
Passero, Capo, *It.* 92 E2
Passo Fundo, *Braz.* 71 E4
Pastaza, *river, Peru* 68 D2
Pasto, *Col.* 68 CI
Patagonia, *region, Arg.*
73 E2
Pate Island, *Kenya*
143 B6
Pathein, *Myanmar* 122 AI
Patna, *India* 117 B4
Patos, *Braz.* 71 B6

Patos, Lagoa dos, *Braz.*
72 B5

Patos Lagoon, *Braz.* 59 D4

Pátra (Patrae), *Gr.* 92 D3

Patrae *see* Pátra, *Gr.*
92 D3

Paulis *see* Isiro, *Dem. Rep. of the Congo* 143 A4

Pavlodar, *Kaz.* 115 A5

Payer Mountains, *Antarctica* 167 A4

Paysandú, *Uru.* 72 B4

Peace, *river, Can.* 40 C2

Peace River, *Alberta, Can.*
40 C2

Pearl City, *Hawai'i, U.S.*
45 D3

Pearl Harbor, *Hawai'i, U.S.*
45 E3

Peary Channel, *Can.*
164 D3

Peary Land, *Greenland, Den.* 165 C4

Pebane, *Mozambique*
145 B5

Pechenga, *Russ.* 90 A4

Pechora, *Russ.* 94 C2

Pedder, Lake, *Tas., Austral.*
150 E4

Pedernales, *Venez.* 53 F3

Pedro Afonso, *Braz.* 71 B5

Pedro Cays, *Jam.* 50 E3

Pehuajó, *Arg.* 72 C3

Peixe, *Braz.* 71 C5

Pekalongan, *Indonesia*
122 E2

Pekanbaru, *Indonesia*
122 D1

Pelée, Montagne, *Martinique, Fr.* 52 C4

Peleng, *island, Indonesia*
123 D4

Pelican Point, *Namibia*
129 E3

Peloponnesus, *peninsula, Gr.* 92 E3

Pelotas, *Braz.* 72 B5

Pematangsiantar, *Indonesia*
122 C1

Pemba, *Mozambique*
145 A5

Pemba Island, *Tanzania*
143 C6

Penas, Golfo de, *Chile*
73 E1

Peñas, Punta, *Venez.*
53 F4

Penedo, *Braz.* 71 C6

Pennsylvania, *state, U.S.*
43 B5

Penonomé, *Pan.* 49 E6

Pensacola, *Fla., U.S.* 43 D5

Pensacola Mountains, *Antarctica* 166 B3

Penza, *Russ.* 77 C5

Perigoso, Canal, *Braz.*
71 A4

Perm', *Russ.* 94 C2

Peron, Cape, *W. Austral., Austral.* 150 D1

Perpignan, *Fr.* 89 E4

Persian Gulf, *Asia* 113 B4

Perth, *W. Austral., Austral.*
148 D1

Peru, *S. Amer.* 56 B1

Perugia, *It.* 92 C2

Pesaro, *It.* 92 B2

Pescara, *It.* 92 C2

Peshawar, *Pak.* 116 A3

Petacalco Bay, *Mex.* 31 E2

Peter I Island, *Antarctica*
166 C1

Peter the Great Bay *see* Petra Velikogo, Zaliv, *Russ.* 121 B4

Petra Velikogo, Zaliv (Peter the Great Bay), *Russ.* 121 B4

Petrified Forest National Park, *U.S.* 46 C2

Petrolina, *Braz.* 71 B6

Petropavlovsk, *Kaz.*
115 A4

Petropavlovsk Kamchatskiy, *Russ.*
95 B6

Petrozavodsk, *Russ.* 90 C5

Pevek, *Russ.* 95 A5

Phalaborwa, *S. Af.* 144 C3

Philadelphia *see* 'Ammān, *Jordan* 112 A1

Philadelphia, *Pa., U.S.*
43 B6

Philippeville *see* Skikda, *Alg.* 139 A4

Philippine Islands, *Philippines* 101 D5

Philippines, *Asia* 99 D5

Philippine Sea, *Pacific Oc.*
101 D5

Philippopolis *see* Plovdiv, *Bulg.* 93 C4

Philipsburg, *St. Maarten, Neth.* 52 A3

Philip Smith Mountains, *Alas., U.S.* 44 A3

Phitsanulok, *Thai.* 122 A1

Phnom Aural, *peak, Cambodia* 122 B2

Phnom Penh, *Cambodia*
122 B1

Phoenix, *Ariz., U.S.* 42 D2

Phoenix Islands, *Kiribati*
161 C4

Phu Bia, *peak, Laos*
122 A2

Phuket, *Thai.* 122 C1

Phuket, Ko, *Thai.* 122 C1

Piacenza, *It.* 92 B1

Piedras Negras, *Mex.*
48 B3

Pierre, *S. Dak., U.S.* 42 B3

Pietermaritzburg, *S. Af.*
144 D3

Pietersburg *see* Polokwane, *S. Af.* 144 C3

Pilar, Cabo, *Chile* 73 F1

Pilcomayo, *river, Arg., Bol., Parag.* 70 D3

Pillar, Cape, *Austral.*
160 E2

Pinar del Río, *Cuba* 50 C1

Pinatubo, Mount, *Philippines* 123 B4

Pine Creek, *N. Terr., Austral.* 148 A3

Pingxiang, *China* 119 D5

Pinsk, *Belarus* 91 E4

Pinsk Marshes, *Belarus*
91 E4

Piraeus *see* Pireás, *Gr.*
93 D4

Pireás (Piraeus), *Gr.*
93 D4

Pírgos, *Gr.* 92 D3

Pisagua, *Chile* 70 D2

Pisco, *Peru* 70 C1

Písek, *Czech Rep.* 92 A2

Posadowsky Bay, *Antarctica* **167** C6

Possession Islands, *Antarctica* **167** E4

Postmasburg, *S. Af.* **144** D2

Potiskum, *Nigeria* **139** D4

Potosí, *Bol.* **70** D2

Poza Rica, *Mex.* **48** C3

Poznań, *Pol.* **91** E2

Prague *see* Praha, *Czech Rep.* **92** A2

Praha (Prague), *Czech Rep.* **92** A2

Prainha, *Braz.* **69** E4

Pratas Island *see* Dongsha, *China* **119** E5

Preparis Island, *Myanmar* **117** D5

Pressburg *see* Bratislava, *Slovakia* **92** A3

Pretoria (Tshwane), *S. Af.* **144** D3

Pribilof Islands, *U.S.* **31** F2

Prieska, *S. Af.* **144** D2

Prilep, *Maced.* **92** C3

Prince Albert, *Sask., Can.* **40** D2

Prince Albert Mountains, *Antarctica* **167** D4

Prince Charles Mountains, *Antarctica* **167** B5

Prince Edward Island, *province, Can.* **41** D6

Prince of Wales Island, *Nunavut, Can.* **40** A3

Prince of Wales Island, *Alas., U.S.* **44** C5

Prince Patrick Island, *Can.* **30** A2

Prince Rupert, *B.C., Can.* **40** C1

Princess Charlotte Bay, *Qnsld., Austral.* **151** A5

Prince William Sound, *Alas., U.S.* **44** B3

Príncipe da Beira, *Braz.* **70** C2

Prishtina *see* Priština, *Kos.* **92** C3

Priština (Prishtina), *Kos.* **92** C3

Prizren, *Kos.* **92** C3

Progress 2, *research station, Antarctica* **167** B5

Propriá, *Braz.* **71** C6

Prorva, *Kaz.* **114** C2

Providence, *R.I., U.S.* **43** B6

Provideniya, *Russ.* **164** C1

Provo, *Utah, U.S.* **42** C2

Prudhoe Bay, *Alas., U.S.* **44** A3

Prudhoe Bay, *Alas., U.S.* **44** A3

Prut, *river, Mold., Rom.* **93** B5

Prydz Bay, *Antarctica* **167** B5

Prypyats', *river, Belarus* **91** E4

Pskov, *Russ.* **91** D4

Pucallpa, *Peru* **68** E2

Puducherry (Pondicherry), *India* **117** D4

Puebla, *Mex.* **29** E2

Pueblo Nuevo, *Venez.* **53** D1

Puerto Aisén, *Chile* **73** D1

Puerto Ángel, *Mex.* **48** D3

Puerto Ayacucho, *Venez.* **68** B3

Puerto Cabello, *Venez.* **68** A3

Puerto Cabezas, *Nicar.* **49** D5

Puerto Coig, *Arg.* **73** E2

Puerto de Hierro, *Venez.* **53** F3

Puerto Deseado, *Arg.* **73** E3

Puerto La Cruz, *Venez.* **53** F1

Puerto Madryn, *Arg.* **73** D3

Puerto Maldonado, *Peru* **70** C2

Puerto Montt, *Chile* **73** D1

Puerto Natales, *Chile* **73** F2

Puerto Píritu, *Venez.* **53** F1

Puerto Plata, *Dom. Rep.* **51** D5

Puerto Princesa, *Philippines* **123** C4

Puerto Rico, *possession, U.S.* **29** E5

Puerto San Julián, *Arg.* **73** E2

Puerto Santa Cruz, *Arg.* **73** E2

Puerto Vallarta, *Mex.* **48** C2

Puerto Williams, *Chile* **73** F2

Pukch'ŏng, *N. Kor.* **120** B2

Pulo Anna, *island, Palau* **123** C5

Pulog, Mount, *Philippines* **123** A4

Puncak Jaya, *peak, Indonesia* **123** D6

Pune, *India* **116** C3

Punta Arenas, *Chile* **73** F2

Punta Prieta, *Mex.* **48** A1

Puntarenas, *Costa Rica* **49** E5

Punto Fijo, *Venez.* **68** A3

Purus, *river, Braz.* **69** D4

Pusan *see* Busan, *S. Kor.* **120** D3

Put'Lenina, *Russ.* **95** C4

Putumayo, *river, Col., Peru* **68** D2

Pu'uwai, *Hawai'i, U.S.* **45** D1

Pweto, *Dem. Rep. of the Congo* **143** C4

Pyay (Pyè), *Myanmar* **122** A1

Pyè *see* Pyay, *Myanmar* **122** A1

Pyinmaana, *Myanmar* **122** A1

P'yŏnggang, *N. Kor.* **120** C2

P'yŏng-sŏng, *N. Kor.* **120** B1

P'yŏngyang, *N. Kor.* **120** C1

Pyrenees, *mountains, Eur.* **89** E3

Pyu, *Myanmar* **122** A1

Q

Qaanaaq (Thule), *Greenland, Den.* **165** D4

Qaarsut, *Greenland, Den.* **165** E5

Qā'emābād, *Iran* **113** A6

Qā'en, *Iran* **III** C6

Qagcaka, *China* **118** C2

Qaidam Pendi, *China* **118** C3

Qairouan, *Tun.* **92** E1

Qalat (Kalat), *Afghan.* **116** A2

Qal'at Bīshah, *Saudi Arabia* **112** D3

Qallabat, *Sudan* **112** E1

Qamar, Ghubbat al, *Yemen* **113** D4

Qapshaghay, *Kaz.* **115** C5

Qapshaghay Bögeni, *lake, Kaz.* **115** C5

Qaqortoq (Julianehåb), *Greenland, Den.* **165** E6

Qarabutaq, *Kaz.* **114** B3

Qaraghandy, *Kaz.* **115** B4

Qarataū Zhotasy, *Kaz.* **115** C4

Qardho, *Somalia* **141** D5

Qarkilik *see* Ruoqiang, *China* **118** C2

Qarokül, *lake, Taj.* **115** E5

Qarqan, *river, China* **118** C2

Qarqan *see* Qiemo, *China* **118** C2

Qarqaraly, *Kaz.* **115** B5

Qarshi, *Uzb.* **114** E3

Qatar, *Asia* **98** C2

Qattâra, Munkhafad el (Qattara Depression), *Egypt* **140** A2

Qattara Depression *see* Qattâra, Munkhafad el, *Egypt* **140** A2

Qazaly, *Kaz.* **114** C3

Qazaq Shyghanaghy, *bay, Kaz.* **III** A5

Qazvīn, *Iran* **III** B5

Qena, *Egypt* **112** B1

Qerqertarsuaq (Disko), *island, Greenland, Den.* **30** B4

Qeshm, *island, Iran* **113** B5

Qiemo (Qarqan), *China* **118** C2

Qikiqtarjuaq (Broughton Island), *Nunavut, Can.* **41** B5

Qilian Shan, *China* **118** C3

Qingdao, *China* **119** C5

Qinghai Hu, *China* **118** C3

Qing Zang Gaoyuan (Plateau of Tibet), *China* **118** C2

Qiongzhou Haixia, *China* **119** E4

Qiqihar, *China* **119** A5

Qishn, *Yemen* **113** E4

Qitaihe, *China* **119** A6

Qizilqum, *desert, Uzb.* **114** D3

Qogir Feng *see* K2, *peak, China, Pak.* **115** E5

Qom (Qum), *Iran* **III** C5

Qoqek *see* Tacheng, *China* **115** B6

Qo'qon, *Uzb.* **115** D4

Qostanay, *Kaz.* **114** A3

Quanzhou, *China* **119** D5

Qūchān, *Iran* **III** B6

Quebec, *province, Can.* **41** D5

Québec, *Que., Can.* **41** E5

Queen Adelaida Archipelago, *Chile* **59** F2

Queen Charlotte Islands *see* Haida Gwaii, *B.C., Can.* **40** C1

Queen Charlotte Sound, *B.C., Can.* **40** C1

Queen Elizabeth Islands, *Can.* **41** A6

Queen Fabiola Mountains (Yamato Mountains), *Antarctica* **167** A5

Queen Maud Gulf, *Nunavut, Can.* **40** B3

Queen Maud Land, *Antarctica* **166** A4

Queen Maud Mountains, *Antarctica* **166** C3

Queensland, *state, Austral.* **149** C5

Queenstown, *S. Af.* **144** E3

Queenstown, *Tas., Austral.* **148** E3

Quelimane, *Mozambique* **145** B4

Querétaro, *Mex.* **48** C3

Quetta, *Pak.* **116** B2

Quetzaltenango, *Guatemala* **49** D4

Quezon City, *Philippines* **123** B4

Quibala, *Angola* **144** A1

Quilpie, *Qnsld., Austral.* **149** C5

Qui Nhon, *Vietnam* **122** B2

Quipungo, *Angola* **144** B1

Quiriquire, *Venez.* **53** F3

Quito, *Ecua.* **68** C1

Qullai Ismoili Somoni (Communism Peak), *Taj.* **115** D4

Qulsary, *Kaz.* **114** B2

Qum *see* Qom, *Iran* **III** C5

Qŭnghirot, *Uzb.* **114** C2

Quseir, *Egypt* **110** E2

Qusmuryn, *Kaz.* **114** A3

Qusmuryn Köli, *Kaz.* **114** A3

Qyzylorda, *Kaz.* **114** C3

R

Raba, *Indonesia* **123** E4

Rabak, *Sudan* **141** D2

Rabat, *Mor.* **138** A2

Rābigh, *Saudi Arabia* **112** C2

Rach Gia, *Vietnam* **122** B2

Radama, Port *see* Sahamalaza, Baie de, *Madagascar* **145** B6

Radom, *S. Sudan* **141** D1

Rafḥā', *Saudi Arabia* **112** A3

Rafsanjān, *Iran* **III** D6

Raga, *S. Sudan* 141 DI

Ragged, Mount, *W. Austral.,
Austral.* 150 D2

Rainier, Mount, *U.S.*
30 CI

Raipur, *India* 117 C4

Rajin (Najin), *N. Kor.*
120 A3

Rajkot, *India* 116 C3

Rajshahi, *Bangladesh*
117 C5

Raleigh, *N.C., U.S.* 43 C5

Ralik Chain, *Marshall Is.*
160 B3

Ramadi *see* Ar Ramādī, *Iraq*
111 C4

Rancagua, *Chile* 72 B2

Ranchi, *India* 117 C4

Ranco, Lago, *Chile* 72 CI

Rangoon *see* Yangon,
Myanmar 117 D6

Rankin Inlet, *Nunavut, Can.*
40 C3

Rann of Kutch, *dry lake,
India, Pak.* 116 C2

Rapid City, *S. Dak., U.S.*
42 B3

Rasa, Punta, *Arg.* 72 C3

Rasht, *Iran* 111 B5

Rason Lake, *W. Austral.,
Austral.* 150 D2

Ratak Chain, *Marshall Is.*
160 B3

Rat Islands, *Alas., U.S.*
44 C3

Rattray Head, *U.K.* 88 A3

Rawalpindi, *Pak.* 116 A3

Rawlinna, *W. Austral.,
Austral.* 148 D3

Rawson, *Arg.* 73 D3

Razelm, Lacul, *Rom.*
93 B5

Rebecca, Lake, *W. Austral.,
Austral.* 150 D2

Rebun Tō, *Japan* 121 A6

Recife, *Braz.* 71 B6

Recife, Cape, *S. Af.*
129 F4

Red, *river, U.S.* 43 D4

Red Deer, *Alberta, Can.*
40 D2

Redmond, *Oreg., U.S.*
42 BI

Redonda, *island, Antigua &
Barbuda* 52 B3

Red Sea, *Af., Asia* 112 CI

Redwood National and
State Parks, *U.S.* 46 BI

Reggane, *Alg.* 138 B3

Reggio di Calabria, *It.*
92 D2

Regina, *Sask., Can.* 40 D2

Rehoboth, *Namibia*
144 C2

Reims, *Fr.* 88 C4

Reina Adelaida,
Archipiélago, *Chile*
73 FI

Reindeer Lake, *Can.*
40 C3

Reliance, *N.W.T., Can.*
40 C3

Rennes, *Fr.* 88 C3

Reno, *Nev., U.S.* 42 BI

Repulse Bay, *Nunavut, Can.*
41 B4

Repulse Bay, *Qnsld.,
Austral.* 151 B6

Resistencia, *Arg.* 72 A4

Resolute, *Nunavut, Can.*
40 A3

Resolution Island, *Nunavut,
Can.* 41 B5

Reval *see* Tallinn, *Est.*
91 D4

Revillagigedo, Islas, *Mex.*
48 CI

Revillagigedo Islands, *Mex.*
31 EI

Reykjavík, *Ice.* 76 A2

Reynosa, *Mex.* 48 B3

Rēzekne, *Latv.* 91 D4

Rhine, *river, Eur.* 88 C5

Rhir, Cap, *Mor.* 138 A2

Rhir, Cap, *Mor.* 128 BI

Rhode Island, *state, U.S.*
43 B6

Rhodes *see* Ródos, *island,
Gr.* 93 E5

Rhône, *river, Fr.* 89 D4

Ribeirão Preto, *Braz.*
71 D5

Riberalta, *Bol.* 70 C2

Richardson Mountains,
Yukon, Can. 44 A4

Richmond, *Va., U.S.* 43 C6

Riddell Nunataks,
Antarctica 167 B5

Ridder (Lenīnogorsk), *Kaz.*
115 A6

Rīga, *Latv.* 91 D4

Riga, Gulf of, *Latv.* 91 D4

Rigestan, *region, Afghan.*
116 B2

Riiser-Larsen Ice Shelf,
Antarctica 166 A3

Rijeka, *Croatia* 92 B2

Rincón del Bonete, Lago,
Uru. 72 B4

Ringvassøy, *island, Nor.*
90 A3

Riobamba, *Ecua.* 68 DI

Rio Branco, *Braz.* 68 E3

Río Caribe, *Venez.* 53 F3

Río Colorado, *Arg.* 72 C3

Río Cuarto, *Arg.* 72 B3

Rio de Janeiro, *Braz.*
71 D5

Río Gallegos, *Arg.* 73 F2

Rio Grande, *Braz.* 72 B5

Río Grande, *Arg.* 73 F2

Río Muni, *region, Eq.
Guinea* 142 AI

Rio Verde, *Braz.* 71 D4

Rishiri Tō, *Japan* 121 A6

Ritscher Upland, *Antarctica*
166 A3

Riverina, *region, N.S.W.,
Austral.* 151 E5

Riverside, *Calif., U.S.*
42 CI

Riyadh *see* Ar Riyāḍ, *Saudi
Arabia* 112 B3

Road Town, *British Virgin
Is., U.K.* 52 AI

Robertsport, *Liberia*
138 E2

Robinson Range, *W.
Austral., Austral.* 150 C2

Robson, Mount, *Can.*
40 C2

Rocha, *Uru.* 72 B5

Rochester, *N.Y., U.S.*
43 B5

Rockefeller Plateau,
Antarctica 166 D3

Roc-Sah

Rockhampton, *Qnsld., Austral.* **149** C6

Rockingham, *W. Austral., Austral.* **148** D1

Rockingham Bay, *Qnsld., Austral.* **151** B5

Rock Sound, *Bahamas* **50** B3

Rocky Mountain National Park, *U.S.* **46** B3

Rocky Mountains, *Can., U.S.* **30** C2

Ródos, *Gr.* **93** E5

Ródos (Rhodes), *island, Gr.* **93** E5

Roebourne, *W. Austral., Austral.* **148** B1

Roebuck Bay, *W. Austral., Austral.* **150** B2

Rojo, Cabo, *P.R., U.S.* **51** D6

Rojo, Cape, *Mex.* **31** E3

Roma, *Qnsld., Austral.* **149** C5

Roma (Rome), *It.* **92** C2

Romang, *island, Indonesia* **123** E5

Romania, *Eur.* **77** D4

Romano, Cape, *U.S.* **50** A2

Rome see Roma, *It.* **92** C2

Ronne Ice Shelf, *Antarctica* **166** B2

Roosevelt Island, *Antarctica* **166** D3

Roraima, Mount, *Braz., Guyana, Venez.* **69** B4

Rosario, *Arg.* **72** B3

Roseau, *Dominica* **52** C4

Roşiori de Vede, *Rom.* **93** B4

Roslavl', *Russ.* **91** E5

Ross Ice Shelf, *Antarctica* **166** D3

Ross Island, *Antarctica* **167** D4

Rosso, *Mauritania* **138** C1

Ross Sea, *Antarctica* **166** E3

Rostock, *Ger.* **91** E2

Rostov na Donu, *Russ.* **94** D1

Roswell, *N. Mex., U.S.* **48** A2

Rothera, *research station, Antarctica* **166** B1

Rothschild Island, *Antarctica* **166** B2

Roti, *island, Indonesia* **123** E4

Round Mountain, *N.S.W., Austral.* **151** D6

Rouyn-Noranda, *Que., Can.* **41** E4

Rovaniemi, *Fin.* **90** B4

Rovuma, *river, Mozambique, Tanzania* **145** A5

Roxas, *Philippines* **123** B4

Rub al Khali, *desert, Saudi Arabia, Oman, Yemen* **100** D2

Rubtsovsk, *Russ.* **115** A5

Rudbar, *Afghan.* **116** B2

Rūdnyy, *Kaz.* **114** A3

Rudolf, Lake see Turkana, Lake, *Eth., Kenya* **143** A5

Rufiji, *river, Tanzania* **143** C6

Rügen, *island, Ger.* **91** E2

Ruhengeri, *Rwanda* **143** B4

Ruiru, *Kenya* **143** B5

Rukwa, Lake, *Tanzania* **143** C5

Rumbek, *S. Sudan* **141** E2

Rum Cay, *Bahamas* **51** B4

Rundu, *Angola* **144** B2

Rungwa, *river, Tanzania* **143** C5

Ruoqiang (Qarkilik), *China* **118** C2

Ruse, *Bulg.* **93** C4

Russia, *Asia, Eur.* **98** B3

Ruteng, *Indonesia* **123** E4

Rutog, *China* **118** C1

Ruvuma, *river, Mozambique, Tanzania* **143** D6

Ruwenzori, *mountains, Dem. Rep. of the Congo* **143** B4

Rwanda, *Af.* **127** D4

Ryazan', *Russ.* **94** C1

Rybachiy, Poluostrov, *Russ.* **90** A4

Rybinskoye Vodokhranilishche, *Russ.* **77** B5

Rybinsk Reservoir, *Russ.* **79** B5

Ryukyu Islands see Nansei Shotō, *Japan* **119** D6

Rzeszów, *Pol.* **91** F3

S

Saaremaa (Ösel), *island, Est.* **91** D3

Saba, *possession, Neth.* **52** A2

Sabana, Archipiélago de, *Cuba* **50** B2

Sabhā, *Lib.* **139** B5

Sable, Cape, *Fla., U.S.* **50** B2

Sable, Cape, *N.S., Can.* **41** E6

Sable Island, *N.S., Can.* **41** E6

Şabyā, *Saudi Arabia* **112** D2

Sabzevār, *Iran* **111** B6

Sachs Harbour, *N.W.T., Can.* **40** A2

Sacramento, *Calif., U.S.* **42** C1

Şaʻdah, *Yemen* **112** D3

Sado, *island, Japan* **121** C5

Şafājah, *mountains, Saudi Arabia* **110** E3

Şafājah, *Saudi Arabia* **112** B2

Safi, *Mor.* **138** A2

Saga, *Japan* **120** E3

Sagami Nada, *Japan* **121** D6

Saghyz, *Kaz.* **114** B2

Saguaro National Park, *U.S.* **46** D2

Saguenay, *Que., Can.* **41** D5

Sahamalaza, Baie de (Port Radama), *Madagascar* **145** B6

Sahara, *desert, Af.* **128** B2

Sahel, *region, Af.* **128** C2

Samana Cay, *Bahamas*
51 C4

Samar, *island, Philippines*
123 B4

Samara, *Russ.* **94** D2

Samarinda, *Indonesia*
122 D3

Samarqand, *Uzb.* **115** D4

Sambava, *Madagascar*
145 B6

Samborombón, Bahía, *Arg.*
72 C4

Samcheok, *S. Kor.* **120** C3

Samoa, *Oceania* **161** C4

Samoa Islands, *Amer.
Samoa, Samoa* **161** C4

Samsun (Amisus), *Turk.*
110 A3

Samui, Ko, *Thai.* **122** CI

Samut Prakan, *Thai.*
122 BI

Şan'ā' (Sanaa), *Yemen*
112 E3

Sanaa *see* Şan'ā', *Yemen*
112 E3

SANAE IV, *research station,
Antarctica* **166** A3

Sanaga, *river, Cameroon*
142 AI

San Ambrosio, Isla, *Chile*
70 EI

Sanandaj, *Iran* **111** C4

San Antonio, *Tex., U.S.*
42 D3

San Antonio, Cabo de,
Cuba **50** CI

San Antonio, Cape, *Arg.*
59 E3

San Bernardino Strait,
Philippines **123** B4

San Carlos de Bariloche,
Arg. **73** D2

San Carlos de Río Negro,
Venez. **68** C3

San Cristóbal de Las
Casas, *Mex.* **49** D4

Sancti Spíritus, *Cuba*
50 C2

Sandakan, *Malaysia*
122 C3

Sandercock Nunataks,
Antarctica **167** A5

San Diego, *Calif., U.S.*
42 DI

Sandoa, *Dem. Rep. of the
Congo* **142** D3

San Félix, Isla, *Chile*
70 EI

San Fernando, *Philippines*
122 B4

San Fernando, *Trin. &
Tobago* **53** F4

San Francique, *Trin. &
Tobago* **53** F4

San Francisco, *Calif., U.S.*
42 CI

San Francisco de Macorís,
Dom. Rep. **51** D5

Sangha, *river, Cameroon,
Cen. Af. Rep., Congo*
142 A2

Sangihe, Kepulauan,
Indonesia **123** D4

Sangmélima, *Cameroon*
142 AI

Sangre Grande, *Trin. &
Tobago* **53** F4

Sanikiluaq, *Nunavut, Can.*
41 C4

San Jorge, Golfo, *Arg.*
73 D2

San Jorge, Gulf of, *Arg.*
59 E2

San Jose, *Calif., U.S.*
42 CI

San José, *Costa Rica*
49 E5

San José de Chiquitos, *Bol.*
70 D3

San Juan, *Arg.* **72** B2

San Juan, *P.R., U.S.* **51** D6

San Juan del Norte, *Nicar.*
49 E5

San Juan Mountains, *Colo.,
U.S.* **42** C2

Sankt-Peterburg (Saint
Petersburg), *Russ.*
94 BI

Sankuru, *river, Dem. Rep. of
the Congo* **142** B3

San Lázaro, Cabo, *Mex.*
48 D3

San Lorenzo, *Ecua.* **68** CI

San Lorenzo, Cabo, *Ecua.*
68 CI

San Luis, *Arg.* **72** B2

San Luis Potosí, *Mex.*
48 C3

San Luis Río Colorado,
Mex. **48** AI

San Marino, *Eur.* **76** D3

San Martín, *research
station, Antarctica*
166 B2

San Matías Gulf, *Arg.*
59 E3

San Matías, Golfo, *Arg.*
73 D3

San Miguel, *river, Bol.*
70 C2

San Miguel, *El Salv.*
49 D5

San Miguel de Tucumán,
Arg. **72** A3

San Pedro, *river, Cuba*
50 C3

San Pedro de Macorís,
Dom. Rep. **51** D5

San Pedro Sula, *Hond.*
49 D5

San Rafael, *Arg.* **72** B2

San Román, Cabo, *Venez.*
53 DI

San Salvador, *El Salv.*
49 D5

San Salvador (Watling),
island, Bahamas **51** B4

San Salvador de Jujuy, *Arg.*
70 E2

Santa Ana, *El Salv.* **49** D5

Santa Barbara, *Calif., U.S.*
42 CI

Santa Clara, *Cuba* **50** C2

Santa Cruz, *river, Arg.*
73 E2

Santa Cruz, *Bol.* **70** D3

Santa Cruz de Tenerife, *Sp.*
138 BI

Santa Cruz Islands,
Solomon Is. **160** C3

Santa Fe, *Arg.* **72** B4

Santa Fe, *N. Mex., U.S.*
42 C2

Santa Inés, Isla, *Chile*
73 F2

Santa Maria, *Braz.* **72** A5

Santa Maria, Cabo de,
Angola **142** DI

Santa Maria, Cape, *Bahamas* **50** B3
Santa Marta, *Col.* **68** A2
Santa Marta Grande, Cabo de, *Braz.* **57** D4
Santa Marta Grande, Cape, *Braz.* **59** D4
Santander, *Sp.* **89** D3
Santanilla, Islas (Swan Islands), *Hond.* **50** EI
Santarém, *Braz.* **56** B3
Santa Rosa, *Arg.* **57** E3
Santa Rosa, *Arg.* **72** C3
Santiago, *Chile* **72** B2
Santiago, *Dom. Rep.* **51** D5
Santiago de Compostela, *Sp.* **89** E2
Santiago de Cuba, *Cuba* **50** D3
Santiago del Estero, *Arg.* **72** A3
Santo Domingo, *Dom. Rep.* **51** D5
Santos, *Braz.* **71** E5
San Valentín, Monte, *Chile* **73** EI
San Vito, Capo, *It.* **92** DI
Sanya, *China* **119** E4
São Francisco, *river, Braz.* **71** C5
São José, Baía de, *Braz.* **71** A5
São José do Rio Preto, *Braz.* **71** D4
São Luís, *Braz.* **71** A5
São Manuel *see* Teles Pires, *river, Braz.* **69** E5
São Marcos, Baía de, *Braz.* **71** A5
São Marcos Bay, *Braz.* **58** B4
Saona, Isla, *Dom. Rep.* **51** D5
São Paulo, *Braz.* **71** E5
São Paulo de Olivença, *Braz.* **68** D3
São Sebastião, Ponta, *Mozambique* **145** C4
São Tomé, *island, Sao Tome & Principe* **129** D2
Sao Tome and Principe, *Af.* **127** D2

São Vicente, Cabo de, *Port.* **89** FI
Sapporo, *Japan* **121** B6
Sapri, *It.* **92** B3
Sarajevo, *Bosn. & Herzg.* **92** B2
Sarakhs, *Iran* **114** E3
Saraktash, *Russ.* **114** A2
Saransk, *Russ.* **77** C5
Sarasota, *Fla., U.S.* **50** AI
Saratov, *Russ.* **77** C5
Sarco, *Chile* **72** AI
Sardinia, *island, It.* **92** DI
Sariwŏn, *N. Kor.* **120** C2
Sarmi, *Indonesia* **123** D6
Särna, *Sw.* **90** C2
Sarny, *Ukr.* **92** F3
Sarygamysh Köli, *Turkm., Uzb.* **114** D2
Saryözek, *Kaz.* **115** C5
Saryshaghan, *Kaz.* **115** C4
Sasebo, *Japan* **120** E3
Saskatchewan, *province, Can.* **40** D2
Saskatchewan, *river, Can.* **40** D2
Saskatoon, *Sask., Can.* **40** D2
Sassari, *It.* **92** CI
Sassnitz, *Ger.* **91** E2
Satu Mare, *Rom.* **93** A4
Saudi Arabia, *Asia* **98** C2
Sault Sainte Marie, *Mich., U.S.* **43** B5
Saurimo, *Angola* **142** D3
Sava, *river, Eur.* **92** B3
Savannah, *Ga., U.S.* **43** D5
Savanna-la-Mar, *Jam.* **50** D3
Savissivik, *Greenland, Den.* **165** D3
Savonlinna, *Fin.* **90** C4
Savu Sea, *sea, Indonesia* **148** A2
Sawu, *island, Indonesia* **123** E4
Sayḥūt, *Yemen* **113** E4
Saynshand (Buyant-Uhaa), *Mongolia* **119** B4
Saywūn, *Yemen* **113** E4
Scandinavia, *region, Eur.* **78** B3

Scarborough, *Trin. & Tobago* **53** F4
Schefferville, *Nfld. & Lab., Can.* **41** C5
Scilly, Isles of, *U.K.* **88** C2
Scoresbysund *see* Ittoqqortoormiit, *Greenland, Den.* **165** D5
Scotia Sea, *Atl. Oc.* **166** AI
Scotland, *region, U.K.* **88** A3
Scott Base, *Antarctica* **167** D4
Scott Mountains, *Antarctica* **167** A5
Scott Nunataks, *Antarctica* **166** D3
Seal, Cape, *S. Af.* **144** E3
Seal Bay, *Antarctica* **166** A3
Seattle, *Wash., U.S.* **42** AI
Segezha, *Russ.* **90** B5
Ségou, *Mali* **138** D2
Seine, *river, Fr.* **88** C4
Sekondi-Takoradi, *Ghana* **138** E3
Sekseūil, *Kaz.* **114** C3
Selaru, *island, Indonesia* **123** E5
Selayar, *island, Indonesia* **123** E4
Selebi Phikwe, *Botswana* **144** C3
Selvas, *region, Braz.* **58** B2
Selwyn Mountains, *N.W.T., Can.* **40** B2
Semarang, *Indonesia* **122** E3
Semey (Semipalatinsk), *Kaz.* **115** B5
Semipalatinsk *see* Semey, *Kaz.* **115** B5
Semnān, *Iran* **114** EI
Senanga, *Zambia* **144** B2
Sendai, *Japan* **121** C6
Senegal, *Af.* **126** CI
Sénégal, *river, Af.* **128** CI
Senja, *island, Nor.* **90** A3
Sennar, *Sudan* **141** D2
Seogwipo, *S. Kor.* **120** E2
Seongnam, *S. Kor.* **120** C2
Seosan, *S. Kor.* **120** D2

239

Seo-Sil

Simeulue, *island, Indonesia*
122 C1

Simferopol', *Ukr.* 93 B6

Simpson Desert, *N. Terr.,
Austral.* 151 C4

Sinai, *peninsula, Egypt*
140 B3

Sinai, Mount *see* Mûsa,
Gebel, *Egypt* 140 B3

Singapore, *Asia* 99 E4

Singapore, *Singapore*
122 D2

Singida, *Tanzania* 143 C5

Singkawang, *Indonesia*
122 D2

Sinkat, *Sudan* 140 C3

Sinop, *Braz.* 71 C4

Sinop (Sinope), *Turk.*
110 A2

Sinop Burnu, *Turk.* 93 C6

Sinope *see* Sinop, *Turk.*
110 A2

Sint Nicolaas, *Aruba, Neth.*
53 D1

Sinŭiju, *N. Kor.* 120 B1

Sionaiin *see* Shannon, *Ire.*
88 B2

Sioux City, *Iowa, U.S.*
42 B3

Sioux Falls, *S. Dak., U.S.*
42 B3

Siping, *China* 120 A1

Siple Island, *Antarctica*
166 D2

Sipura, *island, Indonesia*
122 D1

Siracusa, *It.* 92 E2

Sirḥān, Wādī as, *Jordan,
Saudi Arabia* 110 D2

Sīrjān (Sa'īdābād), *Iran*
113 A3

Sisimiut (Holsteinsborg),
Greenland, Den. 165 E5

Sítio do Mato, *Braz.* 71 C5

Sitka, *Alas., U.S.* 44 C5

Sittwe (Akyab), *Myanmar*
117 C5

Sivas, *Turk.* 110 A3

Siv. Donets', *river, Ukr.*
93 A6

Sîwa, *Egypt* 140 A1

Siyal Islands, *Egypt*
140 B3

Sjælland, *island, Den.*
91 E2

Skadarsko Jezero, *Alban.,
Montenegro* 92 C3

Skagerrak, *strait, Eur.*
88 A5

Skagway, *Alas., U.S.* 44 B5

Skeleton Coast, *Namibia*
144 C1

Skien, *Nor.* 76 B3

Skien, *Nor.* 91 D1

Skikda (Philippeville), *Alg.*
139 A4

Skopje, *Maced.* 92 C3

Slave Coast, *Benin, Nigeria,
Togo* 138 E3

Slavgorod, *Russ.* 115 A5

Slovakia, *Eur.* 76 D3

Slovenia, *Eur.* 76 D3

Smallwood Reservoir, *Nfld.
& Lab., Can.* 41 C5

Smara, *W. Sahara, Mor.*
138 B2

Smeïda *see* Taoudenni, *Mali*
138 C3

Smila, *Ukr.* 93 A5

Smith *see* Sumisu Jima,
island, Japan 121 E6

Smith Bay, *Alas., U.S.*
44 A3

Smith Bay, *Can.* 30 A3

Smith Island, *Nunavut, Can.*
41 C4

Smolensk, *Russ.* 94 C1

Smyley Island, *Antarctica*
166 C2

Smyrna *see* İzmir, *Turk.*
110 B1

Snake, *river, U.S.* 42 B1

Sobaek Sanmaek, *S. Kor.*
120 D2

Sobradinho, Represa de,
Braz. 71 B5

Sobradinho Reservoir, *Braz.*
58 C5

Sobral, *Braz.* 71 A6

Sochi, *Russ.* 77 D5

Society Islands, *Fr.
Polynesia, Fr.* 161 C5

Socorro Island, *Mex.*
31 E1

Socotra (Suquṭrá), *island,
Yemen* 113 E5

Söderhamn, *Sw.* 90 C3

Sofia *see* Sofiya, *Bulg.*
93 C4

Sofiya (Sofia), *Bulg.*
93 C4

Sōfu Gan (Lot's Wife),
island, Japan 121 E6

Sognefjorden, *bay, Nor.*
90 C1

Soheuksando, *island, S. Kor.*
120 E1

Sŏjosŏn-man, *N. Kor.*
120 B1

Sokcho, *S. Kor.* 120 C2

Sokhum *see* Sokhumi, *Rep.
of Ga.* 110 A3

Sokhumi (Sokhum), *Rep. of
Ga.* 110 A3

Sokoto, *Nigeria* 139 D4

Solimões *see* Amazon, *river,
Braz.* 68 D3

Solomon Islands, *Oceania*
160 C2

Solomon Sea, *P.N.G.,
Solomon Is.* 160 C2

Solovetskiye Ostrova, *Russ.*
90 B5

Solwezi, *Zambia* 144 A3

Somalia, *Af.* 126 C5

Somaliland, *region, Somalia*
141 D4

Somali Peninsula, *Eth.,
Somalia* 128 C5

Sombrero, *island, Anguilla,
U.K.* 52 A2

Somerset Island, *Nunavut,
Can.* 40 A3

Sŏnch'ŏn, *N. Kor.* 120 B1

Songea, *Tanzania* 143 D5

Songhua Hu, *China*
119 B5

Songjianghe, *China*
120 A2

Songnim, *N. Kor.* 120 C2

Songo, *Angola* 142 C2

Sonmiani Bay, *Pak.*
116 B2

Sonoran Desert, *U.S.*
31 D2

Sonsorol Islands, *Palau*
123 C5

Sorocaba, *Braz.* 71 E5

Sorol Atoll, *F.S.M.* 123 C6

Trombetas, *river, Braz.*
69 C5
Tromsø, *Nor.* **90** A3
Trondheim, *Nor.* **90** C2
Trujillo, *Peru* **68** E1
Truk Islands *see* Chuuk,
F.S.M. **160** B2
Tshikapa, *Dem. Rep. of the
Congo* **142** C3
Tshwane *see* Pretoria, *S.
Af.* **144** D3
Ts'khinvali, *Rep. of Ga.*
111 A4
Tsugaru Kaikyō, *Japan*
121 B6
Tsumeb, *Namibia* **144** B2
Tsushima, *islands, Japan*
120 E3
Tsushima Strait, *Japan*
120 E3
Tual, *Indonesia* **123** E5
Tubarão, *Braz.* **71** E4
Ţubruq (Tobruk), *Lib.*
139 A6
Tubuai Islands *see* Austral
Islands, *Fr. Polynesia, Fr.*
161 D5
Tucson, *Ariz., U.S.* **42** D2
Tucuruí, *Braz.* **71** A4
Tucuruí, Represa de, *Braz.*
71 A4
Tuguegarao, *Philippines*
123 A4
Tukchi, *Russ.* **95** C5
Tuktoyaktuk, *N.W.T., Can.*
40 A2
Tula, *Russ.* **94** C1
Tulsa, *Okla., U.S.* **43** C4
Tumaco, *Col.* **68** C1
Tumaco, Ensenada de, *Col.*
68 C1
Tumbes, *Peru* **68** D1
Tumen, *China* **120** A3
Tumen, *river, China, N. Kor.*
120 A3
Tumucumaque, Serra de,
Braz., Fr. Guiana, Suriname
69 C5
Tunduru, *Tanzania*
143 D6
Tunis, *Tun.* **139** A4
Tunis, Gulf of, *Tun.* **92** D1
Tunisia, *Af.* **126** B3

Tununak, *Alas., U.S.* **44** B2
Tura, *Russ.* **95** C4
Turan Lowland, *Kaz.,
Turkm., Uzb.* **100** C2
Ţurayf, *Saudi Arabia*
110 D3
Turbat, *Pak.* **116** B2
Turiaçu, Baía de, *Braz.*
71 A5
Turkana, Lake (Lake
Rudolf), *Eth., Kenya*
143 A5
Turkey, *Asia, Eur.* **98** B2
Türkistan, *Kaz.* **115** D4
Türkmenabat (Chärjew),
Turkm. **114** D2
Türkmenbaşy, *Turkm.*
114 D2
Turkmenistan, *Asia* **98** C2
Turks and Caicos Islands,
possession, U.K. **51** C4
Turks Island Passage,
Turks & Caicos Is., U.K.
51 C5
Turks Islands, *Turks &
Caicos Is., U.K.* **51** C5
Turku (Åbo), *Fin.* **90** C3
Turpan Pendi, *China*
118 B2
Turquino, Pico, *Cuba*
50 D3
Tuvalu, *Oceania* **160** C3
Ţuwayq, Jabal, *Saudi
Arabia* **112** C3
Tuxpan, *Mex.* **48** C2
Tuxtla Gutiérrez, *Mex.*
49 D4
Tuz Gölü, *Turk.* **110** B2
Tuzla, *Bosn. & Herzg.*
92 B3
Tver', *Russ.* **77** B4
Tweed Heads, *Qnsld.,
Austral.* **149** D6
Tynda, *Russ.* **95** D5
Tyrrhenian Sea, *Eur.*
92 C1
Tyumen', *Russ.* **94** D2

U

Uaupés, *river, Braz.* **68** C3

Ubangi, *river, Cen. Af. Rep.,
Congo, Dem. Rep. of the
Congo* **128** C3
Uberaba, *Braz.* **71** D5
Uberlândia, *Braz.* **71** D5
Ucayali, *river, Peru* **70** B1
Uchiura Wan, *Japan*
121 B6
Udachnyy, *Russ.* **95** C4
Udaipur, *India* **116** C3
Udine, *It.* **92** B2
Uele, *river, Dem. Rep. of the
Congo* **142** B3
Ufa, *Russ.* **94** D2
Uganda, *Af.* **127** D4
Uíge, *Angola* **142** C2
Uiseong, *S. Kor.* **120** D2
Uitenhage, *S. Af.* **144** E3
Ujjain, *India* **116** C3
Ujungpandang *see*
Makassar, *Indonesia*
123 E4
Ukraine, *Eur.* **77** D4
Ulaanbaatar (Ulan Bator),
Mongolia **119** A4
Ulaangom, *Mongolia*
118 A3
Ulan Bator *see*
Ulaanbaatar, *Mongolia*
119 A4
Ulanhot, *China* **95** E5
Ulan Ude, *Russ.* **95** D4
Uleåborg *see* Oulu, *Fin.*
90 B4
Uliastay, *Mongolia*
118 A3
Ulithi Atoll, *F.S.M.* **123** B6
Ülken Borsyq Qumy, *Kaz.*
114 C2
Ulleungdo (Dagelet),
island, S. Kor. **120** C3
Ulsan, *S. Kor.* **120** D3
Ulukhaktok, *N.W.T., Can.*
40 A3
Uluṟu (Ayers Rock), *N.
Terr., Austral.* **150** C3
Ul'yanovsk, *Russ.* **77** B5
Umeå, *Sw.* **90** C3
Umeälven, *river, Sw.*
90 B3
Umm Lajj, *Saudi Arabia*
112 B2

247

Vaygach, Ostrov, *Russ.*
    165 A5
Velikiye Luki, *Russ.* 91 D5
Velikiy Novgorod, *Russ.*
    94 Cl
Venable Ice Shelf,
    Antarctica 166 C2
Venezia (Venice), *It.*
    92 B2
Venezuela, *S. Amer.* 56 A2
Venezuela, Golfo de, *Venez.*
    68 A2
Venezuela, Gulf of, *Venez.*
    58 A2
Venice *see* Venezia, *It.*
    92 B2
Venice, Gulf of, *Eur.*
    92 B2
Ventspils, *Latv.* 91 D3
Vera, Bahía, *Arg.* 73 D3
Veracruz, *Mex.* 48 C3
Verde, *river, Braz.* 71 D4
Verde, Cape, *Senegal*
    128 Cl
Verde, Península, *Arg.*
    72 C3
Véria, *Gr.* 92 D3
Verkhoyansk, *Russ.* 95 C5
Verkhoyanskiy Khrebet,
    Russ. 95 C5
Vermont, *state, U.S.* 43 B6
Vernadsky, *research station,*
    Antarctica 166 Bl
Verona, *It.* 92 Bl
Vesterälen, *island, Nor.*
    90 A3
Vestfjorden, *bay, Nor.*
    90 A2
Vesuvio, *peak, It.* 92 C2
Vesuvius, *peak, It.* 78 E3
Viangchan (Vientiane),
    Laos 122 A2
Viborg, *Den.* 91 Dl
Vichy, *Fr.* 89 D4
Victoria, *state, Austral.*
    149 E5
Victoria, *B.C., Can.* 40 Dl
Victoria, *river, N. Terr.,*
    Austral. 150 B3
Victoria, *Seychelles* 98 E2
Victoria, Lake, *Kenya,*
    Tanzania, Uganda
    143 B5

Victoria Falls, *Zambia,*
    Zimb. 144 B3
Victoria Falls, *Zimb.*
    144 B3
Victoria Island, *Can.*
    40 A3
Victoria Land, *Antarctica*
    167 E4
Victory Peak *see* Jengish
    Chokusu, *China, Kyrg.*
    115 D6
Viedma, *Arg.* 72 C3
Vienna *see* Wien, *Aust.*
    92 A2
Vientiane *see* Viangchan,
    Laos 122 A2
Vieques, *island, P.R., U.S.*
    52 Al
Vietnam, *Asia* 99 D4
Vieux Fort, *St. Lucia*
    53 D4
Vigan, *Philippines* 123 A4
Vigo, *Sp.* 89 E2
Vijayawada, *India* 117 D4
Vila Bela da Santíssima
    Trindade (Mato Grosso),
    Braz. 70 C3
Vilhelmina, *Sw.* 90 B3
Vilhena, *Braz.* 70 C3
Vil'kitskogo, Proliv, *Russ.*
    164 B3
Villa Bens *see* Tarfaya,
    Mor. 138 B2
Villahermosa, *Mex.* 49 D4
Villarrica, *Parag.* 71 E4
Villavicencio, *Col.* 68 B2
Vilnius, *Lith.* 91 E4
Vindelälven, *river, Sw.*
    90 B3
Vinh, *Vietnam* 122 A2
Vinnytsya, *Ukr.* 93 A5
Vinson Massif, *Antarctica*
    166 C2
Virgin Gorda, *British Virgin*
    Is., U.K. 52 A2
Virginia, *state, U.S.* 43 C5
Virgin Islands, *Caribbean*
    Sea 31 E5
Visby, *Sw.* 91 D3
Viscount Melville Sound,
    Nunavut, Can. 40 A3
Vishakhapatnam, *India*
    117 D4

Vistula, *river, Pol.* 79 C4
Viterbo, *It.* 92 Cl
Viti Levu, *island, Fiji*
    160 C3
Vitim, *Russ.* 95 D4
Vitória, *Braz.* 71 D6
Vitória da Conquista, *Braz.*
    71 C6
Vitsyebsk, *Belarus* 91 E5
Vizianagaram, *India*
    117 D4
Vladimir, *Russ.* 77 B5
Vladivostok, *Russ.* 95 D6
Volcano Islands, *Japan*
    101 C6
Volga, *river, Russ.* 79 C5
Volga River Delta, *Russ.*
    114 Cl
Volgograd (Stalingrad),
    Russ. 94 Dl
Volgograd Reservoir, *Russ.*
    79 C5
Volgogradskoye
    Vodokhranilishche, *Russ.*
    77 C5
Volonga, *Russ.* 77 A5
Vólos, *Gr.* 93 D4
Vol'sk, *Russ.* 114 Al
Volta, Lake, *Ghana*
    138 E3
Voltaire, Cape, *W. Austral.,*
    Austral. 150 A2
Vopnafjördur, *Ice.* 76 A2
Vorkuta, *Russ.* 94 C3
Voronezh, *Russ.* 94 Cl
Vostok, *research station,*
    Antarctica 167 C5
Vostok, Lake, *Antarctica*
    167 C5
Voyageurs National Park,
    U.S. 47 A4
Voznesens'k, *Ukr.* 93 A5
Vrangelya, Ostrov
    (Wrangel Island), *Russ.*
    95 A5
Vryburg, *S. Af.* 144 D3
Vryheid, *S. Af.* 144 D3
Vyazemskiy, *Russ.* 95 D6
Vyaz'ma, *Russ.* 91 E5
Vyborg, *Russ.* 90 C4
Vyshniy Volochek, *Russ.*
    91 D5

W